D1531438

THE DEFINITIVE GUIDE TO CRIMINAL JUSTICE AND CRIMINOLOGY ON THE WORLD WIDE WEB

The Criminal Justice Distance
Learning Consortium

PRENTICE HALL
UPPER SADDLE RIVER, NEW JERSEY 07458

Library of Congress Cataloging-in-Publication Data

The definitive guide to criminal justice and criminology on the World
    Wide Web / the Criminal Justice Distance Learning Consortium.
        p.   cm.
    Includes bibliographical reference and index.
    ISBN 0-13-096251-1
        1. Criminal justice, Administration of—United States—Computer
    network resources.   2. Criminal justice, Administration of—United
    States—Computer network resources—Directories.   3. Criminology—
    United States—Computer network resources.   4. Criminology—United
    States—Computer network resources—Directories.   I. Criminal
    Justice Distance Learning Consortium.
    KF242.C72D44   1999
    025.06'364—dc21   98-8359
                                                                            CIP

Acquisitions Editor: *Neil Marquardt*
Editorial Assistant: *Jean Auman*
Production Management and Composition: *North Market Street*
        Graphics, Lancaster, PA
Managing Editor: *Mary Carnis*
Creative Director: *Marianne Frasco*
Director of Manufacturing & Production: *Bruce Johnson*
Manufacturing Buyer: *Ed O'Dougherty*
Marketing Manager: *Frank Mortimer, Jr.*
Cover Designer: *Liz Nemeth*

©1999 by Prentice-Hall, Inc.
Simon & Schuster/A Viacom Company
Upper Saddle River, New Jersey 07458

Printed in the United States of America

10   9   8   7   6   5   4   3   2

ISBN 0-13-096251-1

Prentice-Hall International (UK) Limited, *London*
Prentice-Hall of Australia Pty. Limited, *Sydney*
Prentice-Hall Canada Inc., *Toronto*
Prentice-Hall Hispanoamericana, S.A., *Mexico*
Prentice-Hall of India Private Limited, *New Delhi*
Prentice-Hall of Japan, Inc., *Tokyo*
Simon & Schuster Asia Pte. Ltd., *Singapore*
Editora Prentice-Hall do Brasil, Ltda., *Rio de Janeiro*

The best aspect of the Internet has nothing to do with technology. It's us. Getting in touch with each other is more exciting than the coolest computer game or the hottest information.

—Newsweek *Magazine*
(via America Online's Talking E-Mail service, January 5, 1998)

I do not fear computers. I fear the lack of them.

—*Isaac Asimov*

CONTENTS

CHAPTER 3

CRIMINOLOGY AND CRIMINAL JUSTICE SITES ON THE WEB 29

CHAPTER 4

E-MAIL AND E-MAIL SOFTWARE 53

CHAPTER 5

E-MAIL DISCUSSION LISTS, NEWSGROUPS, 'ZINES, AND E-JOURNALS   67

CHAPTER 6

SEARCH ENGINES AND WEB MAPS   77

CHAPTER 7

NETIQUETTE AND WEB MANNERS   89

FOREWORD

Those who use the Internet on a daily basis can probably remember the moment they first discovered its truly universal value. For me it was a day in 1994, when a copy of Mosaic was placed on my newly networked office computer. Discovering that one could find materials easily and design one's own multimedia-filled Web pages was life-changing for me.

Like many others who have found the Internet an indispensable tool in their everyday lives, it's swiftly becoming more and more difficult to remember what things were like before it. If, for example, I had to revert to teaching my criminology courses without Web pages, discussion forums, and e-mail, I'd probably look for another endeavor.

Discussions of the Internet and the World Wide Web now take place everywhere: in classrooms, on campus, in newspapers, and on television. While the criminal justice community was a little late in catching the wave, it's now quickly making up for lost time. At the 1998 Academy of Justice Sciences meetings in Albuquerque, New Mexico, there were over 100 papers on various topics related to the Internet and distance learning. It is to these discussions, and how they are impacting criminology and the criminal justice field, that this book contributes. While many have become expert users of the Internet, new faculty, students, and practitioners get on-line for the first time every day. Others find that once the initial euphoria wears off, it's difficult to locate the right information quickly—particularly high-quality criminal justice–related information.

This text serves as a major road map for criminal justice Net users. Designed specifically to look at the Internet from a criminal justice–centered perspective, the book offers something for beginners and for intermediate and advanced users. For example, the material on e-mail starts with the basics, moves on to discussions of Net e-mail etiquette (netiquette) and ethics, and ends with examples of the growing number of e-mail–based discussion lists available to the criminal justice community. If you're looking for technical assistance, such as how to unsubscribe from a mailing list, it's here. However, the focus remains on the value of mailing lists for those in criminal justice.

There are many useful indices in the book, each presenting a number of Web sites to which the reader can refer for additional information on criminal justice on the Net. Particularly useful is the chapter on criminal justice careers on-line (Chapter 8). It might even slow the e-mail flow to folks like myself from students asking, "What can I do with a degree in criminology?" or "Where can I find criminal justice jobs?"

Another hot topic—and one with which this book deals—is security. Those working in criminal justice need to pay special attention to Net security issues. From making sure that e-mail is not inadvertently captured by the wrong person(s) to protecting the network infrastructure on which our business, governmental, and military institutions now are built, security is a major concern. As dramatic as is the current need for information technology experts, those trained in computer crime prevention, computer forensics, and network security already are much in demand.

It appears that the Web is now poised to become a major vehicle for criminal justice distance learning, virtual collaboration, and intrasystem communication. A brief note on each follows.

By combining the software talents of those producing on-line gaming worlds, 3D virtual spaces, and avatars with text and voice chat environments, we predict that interactive simulations will become a major form of criminal justice distance learning. Students as avatars will participate not only in simulated 3D classrooms, but will work through scenarios as varied as crime scene investigations, courtroom procedures, and jail and prison management. In such a learning environment, Web pages, on-line databases, newsgroups, and clip art galleries can be employed to prepare students to be better role players and, ultimately perhaps, more effective police officers, attorneys, and citizens.

Virtual collaboration will blossom as the Web provides inexpensive real-time access for group endeavors. Collaboration software (e.g., Microsoft NetMeeting™) already permits shared text and audio chat, embedded Web cams, exchange of files, a shared white board, group demos through sharing programs over a network, and group work on a single copy of a software program (e.g., a desktop publishing program). As the ability to translate text into the readers' languages on the fly becomes more efficient, global communication will increase dramatically. Virtual collaboration will allow distant researchers to carry out their projects, law enforcement agencies to securely exchange sensitive case information, and students to work with faculty and experts of their choosing.

Communication between the various branches of the criminal justice system is now much easier. An example comes from the police department of Largo, Florida, and their efforts to provide instant information on domestic violence cases to the courts and victims' shelters. Officers take photographs and record audio at the crime scene. By 10 A.M. the next morning, a digital case file is created in the form of a Web page with photos, 911 tapes, and scanned reports. The judge handling the initial appearance to set bail has access to the Web pages, and, for the first time, can make truly informed decisions. Local victims' shelters are given password access to the Web sites as well, and are thus able to determine the seriousness of the woman's injuries and possible need for intervention.

These measures, combined with other domestic violence model policies, have led to a nearly 100 percent guilty plea rate for Largo arrestees. Efforts such as these will continue to sprout up. In the not too distant future, we envision officers in squad cars equipped with laptops and wireless modems browsing to secure Web forms to fill out their reports and sending the reports instantly into a database server, resulting in immediately available case information for those who need access.

The first step in making use of these hybrid networked technologies is a good understanding of the Internet's basic protocols, such as e-mail, the Web, newsgroups, FTP, and chat. It is our hope that this text will unleash for you the potential that the Internet has for criminology and criminal justice.

Cecil E. Greek
Associate Professor of Criminology
Florida State University
and
Co-Director
The Criminal Justice Distance
Learning Consortium

PREFACE

As we enter the twenty-first century, the future of criminal justice education stands before us. It has become clear to many of us in the justice field that education within our discipline will soon embrace the distance learning model. Look around, and you will see that the call for quality distance education is being taken up by an ever-growing cadre of students, educators, and professionals.

Much of what is possible in the field of distance learning builds substantially on the World Wide Web. The Web, which is barely a decade old, holds the potential to extensively alter the way in which the educational enterprise is conducted.

With this trend in mind, I am proud to welcome you to *The Definitive Guide to Criminal Justice and Criminology on the World Wide Web*. This guide is supported by a dedicated Web site that you can reach at http://talkjustice.com. Both the guide and the Web site are sponsored by my agency, the Justice Research Association (JRA), the Criminal Justice Distance Learning Consortium (CJDLC), and Prentice Hall Publishing Company.

In assembling this guide, we here at JRA and CJDLC wanted to make available, for the first time ever, a comprehensive *print* volume that students in the disciplines of criminal justice and criminology could use to learn about the fantastic resources offered by the World Wide Web. We also wanted to develop a justice-specific guide—not merely a book built around a general framework with criminal justice and criminology content added as an afterthought (as some guides do). I hope you will agree that we have succeeded on both counts.

As you read through this guide you will learn about the historical development of the Internet and the Web. If you don't already know how to surf the Web, you will be introduced to the software, hardware, and types of connections needed to enter today's world of Internet technology. E-mail, Web search engines, security issues, netiquette (Web etiquette), and careers in criminal justice and criminology are all discussed.

Among the most useful features of this guide, however, are the up-to-date and comprehensive lists of Web resources that it contains. Chapter 3, for example, lists dozens of useful criminology and criminal justice sites on the Web. Chapter 8 provides a catalog of career resources available via the Internet and includes links to many government and private job sites. An Internet glossary, provided by SquareOne Technology, follows the chapters and rounds out this volume.

The *Talk Justice* site is discussed in the final chapter. It supports this guide in a number of ways. First, the site is built around a discussion group feature, making it possible for visitors to leave messages for other site participants, to thread those messages, and to reenter the ongoing discussion at any time. A chat facility makes it possible for our guests to participate in real-time discussions with others about any criminal justice–related issue. The *Talk Justice* Cybrary, one of the site's central features, contains all of the links listed in this guide—and more. Constant updating of the Cybrary ensures that links are as current as possible. Should you come across a link in this guide that is dated or no longer functions, please visit the Cybrary for updated link information.

We also invite you to visit the Justice Research Association. Point your Web browser at http://cjcentral.com/jra and you will reach the JRA home page. There you will find a description of our activities, including a discussion of our role in creating and maintaining this guide and a description of ongoing efforts to build our most comprehensive project to date—the Criminal Justice Distance Learning Consortium (CJDLC). You can visit the CJDLC at http://cjcentral.com/cjdlc.

Enjoy the guide. Should you have any comments or suggestions for improvement, please send them to me at admin@talkjustice.com.

Frank Schmalleger, Ph.D.
Director
The Justice Research Association
and
Founder and Co-Director
The Criminal Justice Distance
Learning Consortium

THE
DEFINITIVE GUIDE TO
CRIMINAL JUSTICE AND
CRIMINOLOGY ON THE
WORLD WIDE WEB

CHAPTER I

A BRIEF HISTORY OF THE INTERNET

What hath God wrought?
—*Samuel F. B. Morse, in the first telegraph message ever sent (1844)*

If you want to stay current...into the [twenty-first] century, you need to learn about the Internet. Futurists predict that information and access to it will be the basis for personal, business, and political advancement in the [twenty-first] century.... The Internet can shrink the world and bring knowledge, experience, and information on nearly every subject imaginable straight to your computer.
—The Electronic Frontier Foundation's Guide to the Internet[1]

CHAPTER OUTLINE

- What Is the Internet?
- The Web Is Born
- What Is the World Wide Web?
- Who Runs the Web?
- Recommended Readings

WHAT IS THE INTERNET?

The Internet is a vast collection of computers tied together by an electronic network that spans the globe. The Internet, which is a late-twentieth-century creation, has already had a significant impact on the way in which people communicate. It's influence is growing exponentially and will be felt well into the twenty-first century.

The Internet holds the potential to bring about a qualitative change in the way people live, work, and learn (indeed, for many people it has already done so). As a consequence, it ranks among the greatest inventions of all time.

Some people compare the development of the Internet to the invention of the printing press—which in its early days as a hand-powered machine dramatically changed the way people communicated. The widespread and relatively easy distribution of thoughts and ideas through the medium of print (such as books, newspapers, and magazines) shaped a number of vitally important events over the course of centuries, including wars, political campaigns, revolutions, and the growth of scientific knowledge.

INTERNET: a vast collection of computers tied together by an electronic network that spans the globe.

As Michael Hanrahan explains, "Much like the Gutenberg Press radically changed the way people communicated in 16th Century Europe, the Internet is in the process of revolutionizing our communication, information distribution, and the very structure of our lives."[2] Some contemporary social commentators put it this way:

> The information age has been ushered in by new and powerful methods of communication. Gutenberg's invention of the printing press took books out of the ecclesiastical libraries and put them into the hands of the people. Then, the telephone system emerged to allow people instantaneous communication with one another. Now the Internet merges both these technologies, bringing people and information together without the middleman (publisher) necessitated by books or the primarily one-to-one synchronous limitations of the telephone system. This is a new dimension—an electronic, virtual world where time and space have almost no meaning. People in geographically distant lands communicate across time zones without ever seeing each other, and information is available 24 hours a day from thousands of places. The implications of this new global communication and information system are staggering.[3]

The Internet is a child of the information age—an era characterized by rapid communication and the electronic dissemination of information. The information age has a relatively long history, going back at least 140 years. Some people[4] trace the beginning of the modern age of information to 1858—the year in which the first transatlantic telegraph cable was laid. That cable attempted to provide instantaneous communication between Europe and the North American continent. Although the cable remained in service for only a few days before succumbing to the turbulent waters of the North Atlantic, the technology it represented provided a quantum leap beyond the slow physical transmission of information required by the printing press. In 1866 a new and successful transatlantic cable was laid, and it remained in use for almost a century.

The historical event that was to have the most immediate impact on the development of the Internet, however, was the October 1957 launching of the world's first artificial satellite. Named *Sputnik 1*, the 10-pound device was sent into orbit by the former Soviet Union and became a focus of cold-war fears about technological supremacy. *Sputnik* set off a race into space between the world's two superpowers—the former Soviet Union and the United States. As a result of the space race, American President Dwight David Eisenhower created a new agency within the Department of Defense, named the Advanced Research Projects Agency, or ARPA. Shortly after its creation, administrators at ARPA began planning to exploit the potential held by developing computer technology. The result was the Advanced Research Projects Agency Network (**ARPANET**). The first node to be integrated into ARPANET was established at UCLA in 1969. Stanford Research Institute, the University of California at Santa Barbara, and the University of Utah all entered ARPANET later that year. By 1971, there were 15 nodes established, including university, Department of Defense, and commercial computers serving the defense industry. The project became international in 1973 with the establishment of nodes at the University College of London and the Royal Radar Establishment in Norway. The Internet was demonstrated publicly for the first time in October 1972 at the International Computer Communication Conference.

About the same time, the International Network Working Group (INWG)—which grew out of a conference at Sussex University in England in 1973—established standards for developing the Transmission Control Protocol (TCP) and Internet Protocol (IP), commonly known as **TCP/IP**. TCP/IP standards were intended to permit ARPANET computers to communicate efficiently with one another.

> **TCP/IP**: Transmission Control Protocol/Internet Protocol. This protocol, an agreed-upon set of rules directing computers on how to exchange information with each other, is the foundation of the Internet. Other Internet protocols, such as FTP, Gopher, and HTTP, depend on TCP/IP to function.

In 1981, another network that was to play an important role in the development of the Internet was founded. Known as BITNET (Because It's Time Network), this new system was designed specifically to facilitate the use of e-mail and mailing lists. Also in 1981, a network designed to allow computer science departments to communicate with one another was formed. Known as CSNET, it was a creation of the National Science Foundation and also facilitated the exchange of e-mail. In 1987, BITNET and CSNET combined to form CREN, the Corporation for Research and Education Networking.

THE WEB IS BORN

Emerging standards led to quick growth in both CREN and the ARPANET. By the mid-1980s the Internet was born. True to its ARPANET roots, in its early days the Internet linked scientists, university professors, researchers, and software and hardware developers. By 1987, the number of host computers connected to the Internet had reached 10,000. Two years later the number had grown beyond the 100,000 mark, and by 1992 more than 1 million host machines were connected to the Internet. In 1990, ARPANET officially ceased operation. Around the same time, the taboo against commercial use of the Internet began to be replaced with an entrepreneurial spirit as commercial businesses began to establish presences on the Internet as a way of reaching customers. The growth of the Internet is shown in Figure 1-1.

The data in Figure 1-1 are mostly estimates. They are also a bit dated. Nobody can say exactly how many people are using the Internet today. There are, however, estimated to be more than 30 million host computers now in operation, with as many as 300 million users around the world. Every 30 minutes, a new network becomes part of the Internet, and that entry time is dropping. Statistics show that the number of Internet users is growing by 15 percent per month. However you look at it, the rate of growth in Internet use continues to be phenomenal!

The year 1990 is very important for another reason. It is the year the Web was born! A lot of people trace the birth of the Web to activities that were under way at the European Laboratory for Particle Physics (**CERN**) in the 1980s. Located near Geneva, Switzerland, CERN is credited with being the official birthplace of the World Wide Web. In 1984, CERN effectively applied the TCP/IP standards that had been developed nearly a decade earlier by the International Network Working Group. Using object-oriented technology developed by NeXT Software, CERN scientists created the world's first Web server and client machines and introduced their own browser software. CERN's WWW project was tasked with developing a distributed hypermedia system that would allow access in an easy-to-use graphical format from any desktop computer to information from across the world.

Tim Berners-Lee, who worked at CERN, brought together the ideas that made the World Wide Web a reality. Berners-Lee wrote the software that made possible the first WWW browser, running under NeXTStep software. He also developed the first WWW server, along with most of the communications software it required. You can read Berners-Lee's original proposal to CERN for development of the WWW at http://www.w3.org/pub/WWW/Proposal. Authored in November of 1990, it is entitled "WorldWideWeb: Proposal for a HyperText Project."

Internet growth[6]

Date	Hosts	Date	Hosts	Networks	Domains
1969	4	07/89	130,000	650	3,900
04/71	23	10/89	159,000	837	
06/74	62	10/90	313,000	2,063	9,300
03/77	111	01/91	376,000	2,338	
08/81	213	07/91	535,000	3,086	16,000
05/82	235	10/91	617,000	3,556	18,000
08/83	562	01/92	727,000	4,526	
10/84	1,024	04/92	890,000	5,291	20,000
10/85	1,961	07/92	992,000	6,569	16,300
02/86	2,308	10/92	1,136,000	7,505	18,100
11/86	5,089	01/93	1,313,000	8,258	21,000
12/87	28,174	04/93	1,486,000	9,722	22,000
07/88	33,000	07/93	1,776,000	13,767	26,000
10/88	56,000	10/93	2,056,000	16,533	28,000
01/89	80,000	01/94	2,217,000	20,539	30,000
		07/94	3,212,000	25,210	46,000
		10/94	3,864,000	37,022	56,000
		01/95	4,852,000	39,410	71,000
		07/95	6,642,000	61,538	120,000
		01/96	9,472,000	93,671	240,000
		07/96	12,881,000	134,365	488,000
		01/97	16,146,000		828,000
		07/97	19,540,000		1,301,000

FIGURE 1-1

The growth of the Internet. Source: Zakon, Robert Hobbes. "Hobbes' Internet Timeline v2.4a." February 22, 1996, p. 2. Web posted at http://info.isoc.org/guest/zakon/Internet/History/HIT.html. Reprinted with permission.

A Web prototype developed by Berners-Lee was first demonstrated in December 1990. The official birth date of the Web, however, is May 17, 1991, for it was on that day that Web-based access to CERN computers was made freely available to all Internet users. The creation of browser software for common operating systems, such as Microsoft Windows and the Apple Operating System, ensured the rapid expansion of the Web.

When President Clinton took office in 1992, his administration placed a high priority on developing what was being called the "information super-highway." The information superhighway was envisioned as a vast network of interconnected computers that would make it possible for everyone to carry out research, send e-mail, shop, and perform a wide variety of daily functions on-line. Vice President Al Gore focused many of his efforts on developing the information superhighway, and he was successful in gaining passage of the U.S. National Information Infrastructure Act (NIIA) of 1993. The NIIA grew out of the Clinton administration's call to establish a national technology policy for America designed to "invest in a 21st century infrastructure, establish education and training programs for a high skills workforce, empower America's small businesses with technology, enhance industrial performance through critical technology research and development, and create a world class business environment for private sector investment and innovation."[7] Also in 1993, the National Science Foundation created the InterNIC. The InterNIC is a cooperative activity between the National Science Foundation, AT&T, and Network Solutions, Inc. The InterNIC facilitates domain name registration through the **Domain Name System** (DNS).

Domain names are used to identify a location on the Internet. The domain name for the Web site that supports this guide, for example, is talkjustice.com. You can reach *Talk Justice* on the Web by entering its address into your Web browser. For *Talk Justice,* the address is simply http://talkjustice.com, although you can also use http://www.talkjustice .com if you wish. You can reach the InterNIC itself at the following address: http://www.internic.net. The InterNIC provides services that go beyond domain name registration. (We will have much more to say about using Internet addresses in the next chapter.)

One of the most useful InterNIC services for beginners is *Roadmap.* Developed by Patrick Crispen, *Roadmap* is an on-line workshop available via a series of 27 e-mail messages. The messages, sent about four times per week, explain in some detail how to navigate the Internet. They are automatically sent to workshop registrants free of charge. The workshop takes about six weeks to complete. Registration instructions for the *Roadmap* workshop are included at the end of this chapter.

UNIFORM RESOURCE LOCATOR (URL): the address for any location on the Internet or the World Wide Web; expressed in this fashion: http://talkjustice.com or http://www.talkjustice.com.

A domain name functions as a **Uniform Resource Locator,** or **URL** (although there are also other types of URLs). A URL specifies a location on the Internet such as the address of a **Web page.** Underlying any URL is a numerical address based on the Internet Protocol. Such numerical addresses are called IP addresses for short. The IP address for *Talk Justice,* for example, is 209.37.81.17, and you can reach *Talk Justice* by using that number in place of its URL (but don't type "www" in front of it). A few sites, including some that are used primarily for the dissemination of information within corporations or other organizations, have not registered domain names with the InterNIC and are reachable (if at all) only via their IP address.[8] In case you're wondering, multiple domain names can reside on a single IP address, although that rarely happens.

WEB PAGE: a World Wide Web document, usually in HTML format, capable of being displayed by a Web browser.

InterNIC-assigned domain names follow a logical structure. The first part of a domain name, such as "talkjustice," can be almost anything of the site administrator's choosing (if the name has not already been registered by someone else). Name extensions, however, indicate the category into which the site falls. When domain name extensions were first developed, sites were categorized into five basic groups, as follows:

.gov	government
.edu	education
.com	commercial
.mil	military
.org	organization

The explosive growth in the number of domain names filed with the Inter-NIC has led to expansion of the naming system. New extensions are being created to more accurately categorize individuals and organizations. A movement toward the use of a two-country extension is also under consideration (and is already in use in a number of countries). A country extension looks something like this: http://talkjustice.com.us. It indicates that the site called "talkjustice.com" runs from a computer located in the United States. Unfortunately, however, not all country codes have been fully implemented.

WHAT IS THE WORLD WIDE WEB?

As you may have gathered by now, the Internet forms the backbone of the **World Wide Web** (WWW), but the Web is not the Internet. Nor, for that matter, is the Internet the Web. The **Internet,** simply put, consists of a huge number of linked computers that are capable of communicating with one another through certain agreed-upon standards for the transmission of information. These, standards, called *protocols,* consist primarily of the Transmission Control Protocol and the Internet Protocol (TCP/IP). TCP/IP protocols allow computers to talk with each other regardless of the software operating system they are running (e.g., Windows 98, Unix, Mac OS, OS2, VMS) or the hardware they use. Hence, by using a shared suite of protocols, desktop computers powered by processors manufactured by companies such as Intel Corporation and running (for example) Windows 98, can efficiently communicate with VAX machines (e.g., older mainframe computers) running VMS software or with machines powered by Alpha processors running Unix software.

WORLD WIDE WEB (WEB, WWW, W3): a worldwide collection of text and multimedia files and other network services interconnected via a system of hypertext documents residing on computers around the world.

The Internet can also be viewed in terms of the content it is capable of providing to users. Seen this way, the Internet is an information-rich environment supported by a wide variety of functional applications such as e-mail, news, Telnet, FTP, and Gopher (some of which are discussed later in this guide). The World Wide Web is merely another application supported by the Internet, although it has quickly become the most popular application on the Internet. From a technical standpoint, the Web is simply another set of protocols that support rich graphical capabilities. The real significance of the Web lies in the fact that it provided the first graphical user interface (GUI) to the Internet. Whereas the Internet was once a text-only medium, Web protocols have enabled it to support rich graphics, animation, audio, and video.

The communications protocol underlying the Web is termed **HyperText Transfer Protocol** (**HTTP**). On the Web, hypertext is a navigational tool linking data objects (like text, graphics, video, and sound) together by association. The links (from one page to another or within pages) form what is essentially a web of pages—hence the use of the term "World Wide Web." Berners-Lee and Cailliau described the process in their original CERN proposal as follows: "A hypertext page has pieces of text which refer to other texts. Such references are highlighted and can be selected with a mouse. . . . When you select a reference, the browser [the software used to access the WWW] presents you with the text which is referenced: you have made the browser follow a hypertext link."[9]

HTTP (HYPERTEXT TRANSFER PROTOCOL): the communications protocol underlying the Web.

HTML (HYPERTEXT MARKUP LANGUAGE): a programming language used to create Web sites.

The HTTP protocol is supported by a programming language called **HyperText Markup Language** (**HTML**). HTML programmers create Web sites consisting of a series of Web pages linked to one another on the same site through hypertext. Hence, clicking on a linked word, phrase, or image will transport you to another Web page. Linked objects appear as high-lighted or underlined text or as images on a Web page.

In the old days (just a few years ago, actually), HTML programmers had to work with raw code and had to add every instruction to their Web pages by typing it in on the keyboard. Today, however, page-creation software (e.g., Microsoft's FrontPage®, Adobe's PageMaker®, Claris Corporation's Home Page®, and Symantec Corporation's Visual Page®) automates the process of Web site creation.

The development of the Web also depended on the emergence of **browsers**—software capable of interpreting HTML and presenting it to Web surfers in the form of visually rich, or graphical, information. Because browsers are built around hypertext links, using a browser is a lot like flip-ping through pages in a book—except that browsers make it possible to go directly to the page you want without having to skim through page after page of hard-copy text!

> **BROWSER:** a program run on a computer for viewing World Wide Web pages. Examples include Netscape Navigator®, Microsoft Inter-net Explorer®, and Mosaic.

One of the first Web browsers to receive widespread acceptance was **Mosaic.** Mosaic was developed by the National Center for Supercomput-ing Applications (NCSA). It was easy to use, was available on Unix, PC, and Macintosh platforms, and was freely distributed. In April 1994 Netscape Communications Corporation was formed. The company built its popular browser, Netscape Navigator, using Mosaic software as a base. Other browsers, including the popular Microsoft Internet Explorer (MIE), soon followed.

With the creation of HTML and the invention of Web browsers, the Internet left the era of "naked text" and became capable of communicat-ing to its users rich images, graphics, sound, and even video. Today's Java-based applets, VRML (which supports three-dimensional graphics), and ActiveX technology, are making Web-based motion, sound, and even video commonplace. Other innovative technologies, such as RealAudio® and RealVideo® (now combined in one software product called RealPlayer®) and Macromedia Corporation's Shockwave® plug-ins, are extending the capabilities of browsers into previously unimagined areas. A new form of HTML, known as Dynamic HTML, has enhanced possibilities for Web content. Dynamic HTML can be used to create content that can be changed on the fly, adding greater interactivity to the Web and adding more multimedia capabilities to Web pages. Dynamic HTML is leading to the merging of computers and television, while simultaneously creating a truly interactive environment for the user. Dynamic HTML is supported only by versions 4.0 (and later) of Navigator and Explorer.

WHO RUNS THE WEB?

Any huge, rapidly growing global entity requires careful coordination. Web administration today rests primarily in the hands of the World Wide Web Consortium (W3C), also known as the World Wide Web Initiative. The W3C was founded in 1994 to develop common protocols for the evolution of the World Wide Web. It is an international industry consortium, jointly hosted by the Massachusetts Institute of Technology Laboratory for Computer Science (MIT/LCS) in the United States, the Institut National de Recherche en Informatique et en Automatique (INRIA) in Europe, and the Keio University Shonan Fujisawa Campus in Asia. Initially, the W3C was established in collaboration with CERN.

The consortium is led by Tim Berners-Lee, director of the W3C, and Jean-François Abramatic, chairman of the W3C. It is funded by member organizations and continues to work with the global community to produce specifications and reference software that are made freely available throughout the world. You can reach the World Wide Web Consortium at http://www.w3.org/Consortium.

RECOMMENDED READINGS

Web-Based Histories of the Internet

✔ Michael Hauben and Ronda Hauben, *Netizens: On the History and Impact of Usenet and the Internet* (a work in progress): http://www.columbia.edu/~rh120. The most comprehensive work on Internet history on the Web.

✔ Barry Leiner, Vinton Cerf, Jon Postel, and others, *A Brief History of the Internet:* http://www.isoc.org/internet-history.

✔ Henry Edward Hardy, Master's thesis on *Internet History* (1993): http://info.isoc.org/guest/zakon/Internet/History/History_of_the_Net.html.

✔ Jack Richard, *Internet History:* http://www.boardwatch.com/mag/95/jun/bwm1.htm.

- Public Broadcasting System, *Net History:* http://www.pbs.org/internet/history.

- Gregory R. Gromov, *The Roads and Crossroads of Internet History:* http://www.internetvalley.com/intval.html.

- Vinton Cerf, *How the Internet Came to Be:* http://info.isoc.org/guest/zakon/Internet/History/How_the_Internet_came_to_Be

- Robert Hobbes Zakon, *Hobbes' Internet Timeline:* http://info.isoc.org/guest/zakon/Internet/History/HIT.html.

- Stan Kulikowski II, *A Timeline of Network History:* http://info.isoc.org/guest/zakon/Timeline_of_Network_History.

Multimedia-Based Internet Histories

- With the Shockwave plug-in installed, visit Vint Cerf's http://www.mci.com/aboutyou/interests/technology/clicker/index.html. A must see!

- MCI's Shockwave-based animations of how the Web works: http://www.mci.com/aboutyou/interests/technology/internet/guide.shtml.

- The American Discovery television channel, *A History of the Internet—How Did We Get Here Anyway?:* http://www.discovery.com/DCO/doc/1012/world/technology/internetbest/opener.html.

Web-Based Guides to the Internet

Patrick Crispen, *Internet Roadmap*—a free, 27-lesson, self-paced workshop on the World Wide Web. Crispen's Workshop is written mostly for beginners and is delivered in an easy-to-follow, entertaining series of e-mail messages. Sign up for *Roadmap* by visiting http://rs.internic.net/nic-support/roadmap96.

Books

- Katie Hafner and Matthew Lyon, *Where Wizards Stay Up Late: The Origins of the Internet* (New York: Simon and Schuster, 1996).

- Peter Salus, *Casting the Net: From ARPANET to Internet and Beyond* (New York: Addison Wesley, 1995).

CHAPTER II

SURFING THE WEB

The Web reminds me of early days of the PC industry. No one really knows anything. All experts have been wrong.

—Steve Jobs, Wired[10]

He who travels much knows much.

—Thomas Fuller, Gnomologia

CHAPTER OUTLINE

- Making the Connection
- Choosing Your Browser
- Once You're Connected: Using Your Browser
    URLs
    Navigational Buttons
    Internal and External Hyperlinks
    Bookmarks
    Plug-Ins
- Using the Web

MAKING THE CONNECTION

Before you can begin to browse the Web you will need to have certain kinds of hardware and software. Almost any computer is capable of receiving information from the Internet, although not all can run the latest software that makes surfing the Web a pleasurable experience. For a fast connection and for a machine that supports the most capable browsers, you will probably want to use a newer computer. If you are using a PC, you can install capable Web browsers on a 486-type machine running Windows 3.1. For better performance, however, you will want a Pentium-based machine. Pentium II's, Pentium Pros, and Pentiums that are MMX enabled (or later-generation processors) will give you better satisfaction than earlier models.

Before you can connect to the Web you will need to have an Internet connection. Internet connections take a variety of forms, from those provided by **on-line services** to **dial-up connections** to **direct connections.** On-line services, such as America Online, require registered users to pay a monthly fee. They have established telephone numbers in most areas that allow users to connect to the service. Once logged on to the on-line service, users are able to browse a wide variety of information sources, message forums, and software libraries provided by the service. America Online and other on-line services have incorporated e-mail programs, newsreaders, and Web browsers into their proprietary software so that registered users can send and receive e-mail, transfer files between computers on the Internet, browse the Web, participate in newsgroup discussions, and even create their own Web pages. On-line services provide Internet access without requiring users to have a direct connection to the Internet or to sign up for service through an Internet service provider.

An on-line service, however, may not be your first choice. If you are working through a university's computer system (most likely a local area network, or LAN) the system may have a direct connection to the Internet. If so, accessing the Web will be a simple matter of starting the browser installed on the machine you are using (assuming one is available) and typing in the URL of the site you want to visit.

If you do not have a direct connection and you have not joined an on-line service you will probably need to establish a dial-up connection to the Internet. A dial-up connection requires a modem and an **Internet service provider** (ISP). ISPs are companies that complete the dial-up connection between your computer's modem and the Internet, allowing you to browse the Web, read newsgroups, and send and receive e-mail. Depending on where you live, a large number of ISPs may be available in your area. If you live in a relatively remote area, however, your choices of ISPs may be limited—or you may need to make a long-distance telephone call in order to connect with an ISP of your choice.

Pricing, features, and dependability of ISPs vary widely. One easy way to select an ISP is to use a service provided by Netscape Communications Corporation called ISP Select. ISP Select can help you find the ISP that's best for you. The service allows you to compare the prices and services of a variety of ISPs, create new ISP accounts, and get and configure the software you need to connect to the ISP of your choice. ISP Select is available via Netscape Communications Corporation at the following:

http://home.netscape.com/assist/isp_select

You may also choose to connect to the Internet through a cable modem (if such service is available in your area), a satellite connection (which requires you to install a small dish for sending and receiving signals from a satellite), or ISDN or ASDL lines. Because these are rather specialized connections and are often quite expensive, we will not discuss them here. However, even people who connect to the Internet through such cutting-edge technology will still need to sign up with an ISP as an intermediary.

Once you are connected to the Internet, your machine becomes a **client computer.** The machine to which you are connected is called a host machine, a server, or a **Web server.** At this point you are ready to begin surfing (usually pronounced "surfin' "), or browsing, the Web!

CHOOSING YOUR BROWSER

Today's browser software comes down to what is essentially a choice between two major competitors: Netscape Navigator and Microsoft Internet Explorer (MSIE). Although it is possible to get satisfactory results with earlier versions of both browsers (or other browsers, for that matter), this guide will assume that you are running Netscape Navigator version 4.04 or later (which we will refer to simply as "Navigator") or Microsoft Internet Explorer 4.0 or later (which we will refer to as "Explorer"). Both programs are freely available for download via the Internet and are relatively easy to install on your computer. If you already have an Internet connection, but are not running the latest browser, we recommend that you download and install a copy now.

TO DOWNLOAD INTERNET EXPLORER, GO TO:
http://www.microsoft.com/ie

TO DOWNLOAD NAVIGATOR, GO TO: **http://www.netscape.com**

Many sites on the Internet display Navigator and Explorer icons, and most such images will be linked to download sites for the software (meaning that if you click on the icons with your mouse you will be taken to a download site and asked if you want to receive the free software). *Talk Justice,* the site that supports this guide, has similar links allowing you to download both products. The images you will see may look like this:

If you are working on a PC, both programs run best under Windows 95, Windows 98, or Windows NT. Explorer can be run tightly integrated with the Windows operating system and can make your desktop into a kind of "Web space," or a virtual extension of the World Wide Web. It can also be run as a stand-alone program.

ONCE YOU'RE CONNECTED: USING YOUR BROWSER

Once you are connected to the Internet, the first thing you are likely to do is use your browser to navigate the Web. Four major navigational features are available on most browsers:

- URLs
- Navigational buttons
- Internal and external hyperlinks (e.g., images, text, video, and sound)
- Bookmarks

Figure 2-1 shows these features as they appear in Netscape Navigator (version 4.04). Figure 2-2 illustrates the same features in Microsoft's Internet Explorer (version 4.0). Each navigational feature will be discussed in the pages that follow.

URLs

As mentioned earlier, URL is an acronym for Uniform Resource Locator. URLs specify addresses/locations on the Internet and help you get where you want to go. Most URLs take the form http://www.prenhall.com/cjtoday. In this example, the URL has three parts, each of which is separated by slashes.

1. The first part of a URL (before the two slashes) tells your browser the type of resource at the address you are about to specify and the method to use to access that resource. In this case, "http" (which stands for HyperText Transfer Protocol) tells your browser that it is being instructed to load and display a hypertext document. When you type in a URL, most contemporary browsers assume that you intend to enter the "http" prefix, thus making it unnecessary to do so. In place of "http" you could enter "ftp," "mailto," "gopher," "telnet," "news," and other commands. You could even enter a "file" command, telling your browser to open a file located on a local hard drive (that is, one that resides on your machine or on your local network).

2. The second part of any URL that begins with "http" specifies the Internet name of the computer where the data you want to access is lo-

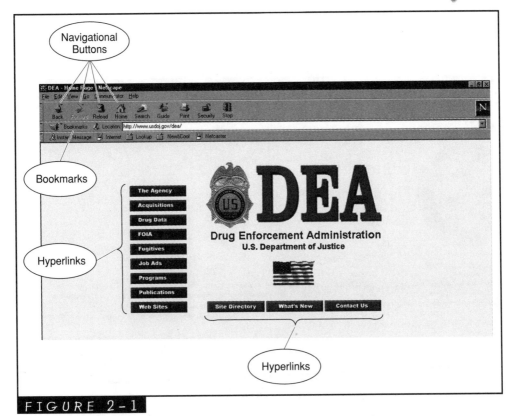

FIGURE 2-1

Navigational features available in Netscape Navigator. Reprinted with permission of Netscape Communications, Inc., and the Drug Enforcement Administration.

cated. In this case, the second part is www.prenhall.com, which refers your browser to the World Wide Web, where it is to find a domain named "prenhall.com." "Prenhall.com" is the domain name of Prentice Hall Publishing Company's World Wide Web server. (Prentice Hall is the company that publishes this guide, and the products it produces are often available electronically as well as in hard copy.) As you become more familiar with URLs you will notice that *some* sites do not require you to enter "www" in the address you specify.

3. URLs that begin with "http" usually have additional information following the domain name. In this example, "cjtoday" refers to the directory on the Prentice Hall server in which information about the popular introductory textbook *Criminal Justice Today* is located.

It is worthwhile noting that we have chosen to work with a URL that is generic. That is, we have not specified any particular file for your browser

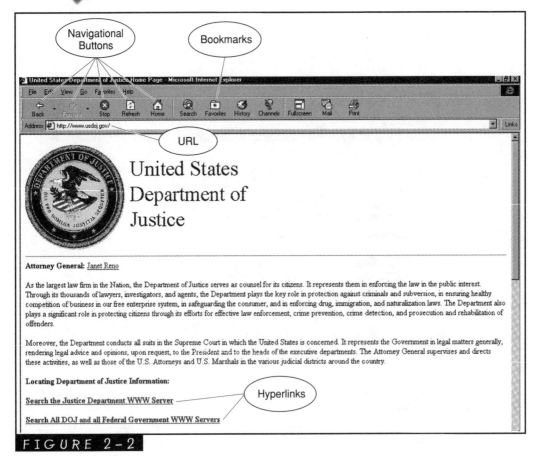

FIGURE 2-2

Navigational features available in Microsoft Internet Explorer. Reprinted with permission of Microsoft Corporation.

to open. Once it reaches the indicated location on the Web, your browser will open whichever file the site creators (or Webmasters) at that site have defined as their starting page.

It is possible for us to be more specific, telling our browser to open a particular file. You could, for example, enter the following URL in your browser:

http://www.prenhall.com/crim2day/html/start.html

This URL will cause your browser to load a file named "start.html" ("html" or "htm" is an extension indicating a file written in HyperText Markup Language) in a subdirectory named "html" (which probably means that it holds mostly HTML and not other kinds of files), which in turn is part of a directory named "crim2day" within the Prentice Hall domain on the World Wide Web. In this example, "crim2day" is the directory of *Criminology Today*, a popular introductory criminology textbook (or http://www .prenhall.com/cjcentral.com). Keep in mind, however, that we often may not know what files exist at a given site and that file names may change far more quickly than site names. Hence, the best choice may be to begin with the default file that loads at a location we are interested in.

To summarize what we have said, we can think of a URL as specifying a *protocol*, followed by (1) a *domain* address to which you wish to connect, (2) the *directory* within that domain that you wish to access, and (3) the *file* that you wish to view or locate. Hence, a generic way of thinking about URLs would be as follows:

protocol://domain name/directory name/file name

Some useful tips to remember about URLs include the following:

- A URL contains no spaces.

- A URL always uses right-leaning (forward) slashes—that is, slashes that slant to the right.

- The first slash in any URL is always a double slash, preceded by a colon.

- Do not capitalize the protocol. For example, "http" should always be lowercase. Keep in mind, however, that some URLs contain capital letters. Depending on the kind of server you are trying to contact, it may be necessary to type those letters as capitals (in other cases, either lowercase or capital letters will do, since they will all be interpreted as lowercase).

- If you can't reach the site you are trying to connect with, check the URL carefully to be sure that you have typed it correctly. One wrong character, one out-of-place period or slash, can make or break a successful connection.

- Although you will often see URLs with *ending* forward slashes, you do not need to type them.

- Once you have reached a site and have loaded a page, you can find the URL to any link on that page simply by passing your mouse pointer over the link. You will see the pointer turn into a hand, and the URL will appear in the browser's status bar (usually located at the bottom left of your screen).

One way to enter a URL in your browser is to type it into the **location window** just under the **toolbar.** Placement of the location window is shown in Figures 2-1 and 2-2. Most popular browsers keep track of sites you've visited and allow you to easily return. To do so in Explorer, just click on the history icon in the toolbar. You will see a list of places you've recently visited. Click on the one to which you wish to return, and Explorer will take you there without having to retype the URL for that location. You can do the same thing in Navigator by clicking on the "Go" command above the toolbar icons. The history feature, however, applies only to your current session. Once you close your browser, such history information about the sites you've visited is lost.

Today's browsers are smart, however, in the sense that they remember the URLs of sites you've visited—even from previous sessions. If you begin to type a URL into the location window for a site that you visited a couple of days ago, for example, your browser will fill out the rest of the URL for you. If the browser's "guess" as to where you want to go is wrong, simply continue typing until you have entered the correct URL.

Browsers are smart in another way. Generally, when you view a page containing a link that you've already visited, the hypertext words will appear in a different color—usually red or pink. You can revisit the site by clicking on the link whose color has changed.

Navigational Buttons

Common navigational buttons in most browsers include "forward," "back," "reload" (or "refresh"), and "stop." Navigational buttons are primarily used to help you retrace your steps. If, for example, you viewed a page that you liked, but then went on to visit other sites, you could use the "back" button to return to previously visited pages. After locating those pages, you could then use the "forward" button to get back to where you were. The "forward" and "back" buttons can move you speedily through sites you have already visited because much of the information your browser needs to display a page is stored in the browser's **cache.** It stays there long after you have viewed that page. Cache contents are periodically deleted, so you can't count on navigational buttons to take you back to sites visited long ago. Nonetheless, the "forward" and "back" buttons provide a convenient way of quickly navigating sites you've already visited during the current session.

Other navigational buttons include "stop" and "reload." Clicking the "stop" button tells your browser to abort the loading process. You may want to use the stop button if you change your mind about visiting a site or if a site seems to be taking too long to load. Delays in loading a Web page can have a number of causes, including a slow modem, a bad telephone connection, a busy Web, a slow site, or a stalled connection. If you are experiencing a stalled connection, you may have no way of knowing it—except that the page you are trying to load never arrives at your computer. In that case, clicking "stop" and then "reload" (or "refresh" in Explorer) may be your best choice. A word of caution: The Web can be notoriously slow when filled with users (they don't call it the "World Wide Wait" for nothing). Don't get into the habit of clicking the "stop" and "reload" buttons frequently because doing so starts the process of loading a page all over again. *That* can take far more time than waiting for a page from a busy site.

You can also use the reload button to update a page. If you viewed a page a few minutes ago and then return to it using your "back" button, the contents of the page may have changed. This is especially true for pages like those found in the *Talk Justice* message forums (discussed later in this guide) where people are constantly posting new messages. Since your browser loads a previously viewed page from your cache, it may be necessary to hit the "reload" button when visiting some pages in order to see updated content. With pages that change only infrequently, this process is rarely necessary.

Internal and External Hyperlinks

You can think of Web pages as electronic files stored on computers located all over the world. Web pages, as mentioned earlier, are really HTML documents. As such they generally contain a number of hyperlinks. Hyperlinks provide a way of jumping between pages and between sites. Clicking on a hyperlink will take you to the spot designated by the Web designer who created the page you are using.

> **HYPERLINK:** a connection between two anchors, or locations, on the Web. Clicking on one anchor will take you to the linked anchor. Hyperlinks can refer to anchors within the same document, page, or site, or to totally different documents in widely varying locations.

You can tell which text on a page is linked to another page (or which text is "hot") by looking at its color. Links generally appear in a different color than the rest of the text (usually blue) and they are normally underlined. Keep in mind, however, that graphic images can also be links to other content. When you move your cursor over a text link or over a graphic link, your cursor will change from an arrow to a hand.

Bookmarks

You can keep track of URLs that are of special interest to you by using **bookmarks.** Bookmarks are available in Explorer by clicking on the icon marked "Favorites." In Navigator the bookmark feature is plainly labeled "Bookmarks." You can instruct your browser to add sites to your bookmarks. Doing so will create a personalized menu of listed URLs that you can use as shortcuts. To add a site to bookmarks in Navigator, click on the Bookmarks selection and then click "Add Bookmark." This procedure will add the site you are visiting to the bookmark menu.

> **BOOKMARK:** a pointer to a particular Web site. Within browsers, you can bookmark interesting pages so that you can return to them easily.

You can also create categories to contain your bookmarks, and you can organize your bookmarks by category. Once you have created categories (or folders) for your bookmarks, you can click on "Bookmarks" and then "File Bookmark" in order to place the URL of the site you are visiting into a selected category. In Explorer, the process for adding bookmarks is similar. Just click on "Favorites" and then "Add to Favorites." Explorer also gives you the choice "Organize Favorites," which you can use to create new categories and to move URLs between categories. In Navigator, you can organize your bookmarks by clicking "Bookmarks," then "Edit Bookmarks." Like Explorer, Navigator allows you to drag and drop URLs in order to move them between categories.

As you learn more about bookmarks, you will see that they can be used to create a personalized Web page that you can store on your computer and open with your browser. Doing so is easiest with Navigator, which stores bookmarks in a file called "bookmark.htm" in your Navigator subdirectory. You can tell any Web browser to open a "bookmark.htm" file created by Navigator and in doing so you will find a handy listing of all sites that you have bookmarked. Figure 2-3 shows a screen capture of a bookmark .htm file used at the Justice Research Association (JRA is the sponsor of this manual) for easy access to frequently visited criminal justice sites. Once opened in any browser, clicking on a selection within this file will take the user directly to the site chosen.

Preferences on browsers at JRA are set to load personalized bookmark files at startup directly from the user's machine. You can set preferences in your browser to either open a file on your machine at startup or to open any file you specify—even one on the Web. You might, for example, set your browser to open the file containing the *Talk Justice* Cybrary links (which are listed in detail in the next chapter) when it starts. To do so in Navigator, you would click on "Edit" in the toolbar, then select "Options," click on "Navigator," "**home page**," and then enter the URL of the home page you wish to use in the "location" field. If you want to use the *Talk Justice* Cybrary as your browser's default opening page, you would enter http://talkjustice.com/cybrary.htm. (You must, of course, be logged on to the Internet in order to reach this page.) Doing the same thing in Explorer requires you to click on "View," "Internet Options," "General," and then to

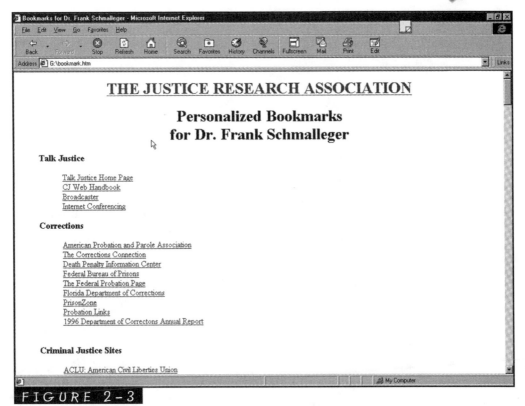

FIGURE 2-3

The start of a personalized bookmark file in HTML format. This one belongs to Dr. Frank Schmalleger, Director of the Justice Research Association.

fill in the selection labeled "home page" with the URL or name of the file you wish to load at startup. Keep in mind that if the file is on your computer you must specify a complete path to the file, not just the name of the file. You can easily do so by using the "browse" button next to the "home page" selection on most browsers.

HOME PAGE: the first page of a Web site. Also, the Web site that automatically loads each time you launch your browser.

Here's a more detailed description of how to set home pages in Navigator and Explorer, using the *Talk Justice* Cybrary as an example:

Netscape 4.x

1. At the top of your browser, click on "Edit."

2. Then click on "Preferences."

3. See where it says "Home page"? Fill in the "location" box with http://talkjustice.com/cybrary.htm.

4. Click OK.

5. You're done!

Netscape 3.x

1. At the top of your browser, click on "Options."

2. Then click on "General Preferences."

3. Under the "Appearances" folder, find the "Startup" heading.

4. Under that heading, enter http://talkjustice.com/cybrary.htm into the field that says "Home Page Location."

5. Click "OK."

6. You're done!

Internet Explorer 4.0

1. At the top of your browser, click on "View."

2. Then click on "Options."

3. Then click on the folder heading that says "General."

4. Enter http://talkjustice.com/cybrary.htm in the box that says "Address."

5. Click "OK."

6. You're done!

Internet Explorer 3.x

1. At the top of your browser, click on "View."

2. Then click on "options."

3. Then click on the folder heading that says "Navigation."

4. Under "Customize," enter http://talkjustice.com/cybrary.htm in the box that says "Address."

5. In the same area, make sure that you've selected "Start Page."

6. Click "OK."

7. You're done!

If you don't set a home page preference, then most browsers, on starting up, will immediately take you to their own predefined home page. Netscape Navigator, for example, will first take you to the Netscape home page. Internet Explorer (MSIE) is automatically set to take you to Microsoft's Web site. If you decide to disable these default features and specify your own home page, you can still click on the large "N" on the right side of Navigator's toolbar to reach the Netscape home page at any time. Similarly, from within Explorer you can click on the large blue "E" or spinning globe (depending on which version of the browser you are running) in the upper right corner to reach the Microsoft home page.

A final note: If you have specified a home page of your own, you can return to it at any time by clicking on "home" in the toolbar of either Navigator or Explorer.

Plug-Ins

Web browsers, amazing as they are, are actually capable of displaying only a few types of data. Prior to the release of Netscape Navigator 2.0, browsers could recognize only limited forms of information, including (1) plain text (2) HTML data, and (3) certain image types such as Graphics Interchange Format (GIF) and Joint Photographic Experts Group (JPEG) files.

Helper applications (small programs that extend the capabilities of Web browsers[11]) were needed to use other types of information, such as video or audio files. Prior to the availability of modern browsers, it was necessary for anyone surfing the Web to download an audio or video file to his or her computer, and then run a helper application that could read it. Helper applications are software programs that are external to browsers and that are used to play or view files locally. A common helper application today is Adobe Acrobat Reader®, a software program that allows you to view pages of text as graphics—permitting publication on the Web of page images that are essentially snapshots of the original printed document.

A number of previously popular helper applications have recently been replaced with plug-ins. **Plug-ins** are software applications that are seamlessly integrated into your browser and that allow you to open a wide variety of file types, such as video and audio. Because plug-ins act as though they are a part of your browser, they allow Web page designers to embed sounds, video, and multimedia effects into their Web sites, permitting you to view or hear such special effects in what appears to be a seamless fashion.

PLUG-INS: add-on programs designed to work seamlessly with your browser and to enhance its capabilities.

Although hundreds of plug-ins exist for most popular browsers, the data formats most of them support are rarely used. A few plug-ins, however, are virtually essential for avid Web surfers. Important and widely used plug-ins include RealAudio (to listen to real-time audio), RealVideo (or RealPlayer, which incorporates both audio and video players), Shockwave or Shockwave Flash® (to view animations), QuickTime® (to watch video), Microsoft's ActiveMovie Player® (for MSIE), Cosmo Player® and Netscape's Live3D® (for three-dimensional graphics). A special form of plug-in technology has been created by Microsoft Corporation. Called ActiveX®, this proprietary technology is designed to work primarily with Microsoft's Internet Explorer browser.

One of the most essential plug-ins for browsing the Web is RealPlayer. The latest version plays both audio and video files found on many Web sites. You can download a free version of RealPlayer from *Talk Justice* or directly from the RealPlayer home page at the following:

http://www5.real.com

You can also download RealPlayer software from many sites that use Real Networks technology. Most such sites display a RealPlayer icon on which you can click to go to the download site. The icon looks something like this:

Many people consider Macromedia's Shockwave plug-in an essential addition to your Web browser. Download Shockwave, or the newer Shockwave Flash, from Macromedia at the following:

http://www.macromedia.com

They can also be downloaded from any site displaying the Shockwave icon (below). If you download RealPlayer version 5.0 or higher from the Real-Audio site, you will find that Shockwave Flash comes with it.

Some of today's most popular plug-ins are bundled with browsers and are seamlessly integrated from the user's point of view. Almost all of today's plug-ins are available at one central Web location called Plug-In Plaza. Plug-in Plaza makes plug-ins available by category, including the following:

- MultiMedia
- Graphics
- Sound
- Document Viewers
- Productivity Plug-Ins (such as map viewers and spell checkers)
- VRML/3-D Plug-Ins

Plug-in Plaza can be reached on the Web at http://browserwatch.internet .com/plug-in.html.

USING THE WEB

Visit the Microsoft and Netscape sites on the Web at the following addresses:

- Microsoft: http://www.microsoft.com
- Netscape: http://www.netscape.com

Then do the following:

1. Write a page about each of these sites, describing what features are available at both. Compare the sites. Which site do you like better? Why?

2. Find the page that allows you to download a free copy of Navigator. Find the page that allows you to download a free copy of Explorer. Read about the features of both programs. Which sounds better to you? Why?

CHAPTER III

CRIMINOLOGY AND CRIMINAL JUSTICE SITES ON THE WEB

While a number of my colleagues remain skeptical about the role the Internet will play in the future of criminal justice and criminal justice education, it is obvious that the Net is the most significant communication tool ever devised, one with world changing potential.
—*Cecil Greek, Webmaster, Florida State University, School of Criminology*[12]

CHAPTER OUTLINE

- Surf's Up
  - *Using the Justice Information Center*
  - *The JRA Image Map of the CJ System*
- Site Listings
  - *General Criminal Justice and Criminology Sites*
  - *Justice Statistics*
  - *Law Enforcement Resources*
  - *Courts and Law-Related Sites*
  - *Corrections Sites*
  - *Victims of Crime*
  - *Violence Against Women*
  - *Crime Prevention*
  - *Terrorism*
  - *Unsolved Crimes*
  - *Forensics*
  - *Gangs*
  - *Juvenile Justice Sites*

Missing and Abused Children
Live Feeds from Police Scanners
International Resources
Associations
Criminal Justice Guides on the Web
- Using the Web

SURF'S UP

Once you have established an Internet connection and have your Web browser up and running, it is time to begin the journey through **cyberspace.**

CYBERSPACE: the computer-created matrix of virtual possibilities, including Web sites, on-line services, e-mail, discussion groups, and newsgroups, wherein human beings interact with each other and with technology itself.

A fantastic place to begin any Web-based excursion in criminology or criminal justice is the home page of the Justice Information Center (JIC). JIC is a service of the National Criminal Justice Reference Service (NCJRS). NCJRS is one of the most extensive sources of information on crime statistics, crime prevention, and research and evaluation in the area of crime control. The site also provides links to many other sites with information on victimology, juvenile justice, and international criminology. JIC serves an international community of policymakers and professionals, and you can be among them by pointing your browser at the JIC home page, which is located at http://www.ncjrs.org.

Using the Justice Information Center

JIC makes an excellent criminal justice Web starting point because it is essentially a collection of clearinghouses supporting all bureaus of the U.S. Department of Justice (DOJ), Office of Justice Programs (OJP), the National Institute of Justice (NIJ), the Office of Juvenile Justice and Delinquency Prevention (OJJDP), the Bureau of Justice Statistics (BJS), the Bureau of Justice Assistance (BJA), the Office for Victims of Crime (OVC), and the OJP Program Offices. It also supports the Office of National Drug Control Policy (ONDCP), home of our nation's cabinet-level "drug czar," and provides a list of extensive links to other criminal justice and criminology-related information on the Web.

When you arrive at the JIC home page, you will find that it is arranged by topical areas, each of which is clickable. The Justice Information Center home page can be seen in Figure 3-1.

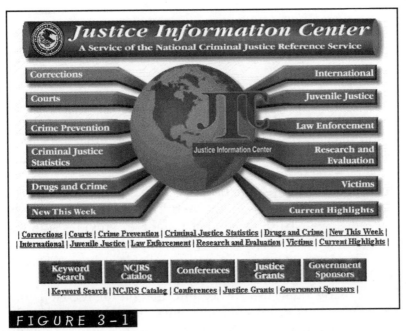

FIGURE 3-1

The Justice Information Center's home page on the Web. You can reach it at http://www.ncjrs.org.

The JIC home page provides an **image map** with clickable selections. Major selections are (1) corrections, (2) courts, (3) crime prevention, (4) criminal justice statistics, (5) drugs and crime, (6) international, (7) juvenile justice, (8) law enforcement, (9) research and evaluation, (10) victims, (11) new this week, and (12) current highlights.

Each selection leads to a number of hypertext links. Clicking on "Law Enforcement," for example, brings up a number of other choices, including "Documents," "World Wide Web Sites," and "Listservs." Choosing "Documents" takes you to a list of more than 100 NCJRS-sponsored documents that can be immediately downloaded in either text or Adobe Acrobat® format. Selecting "World Wide Web Servers" displays a list of approximately 35 law enforcement–related servers—each of which can be accessed by clicking on its title.

Arrayed along the bottom of the JIC page, in a separate listing, are these selections:

☛ Keyword Search

☛ NCJRS Catalog

↙   Conferences

↙   Justice Grants

↙   Government Sponsors

Of these, "Keyword Search" is especially useful, as it allows you to search the entire JIC site for topics or articles of interest. Clicking on "Keyword Search" and then entering "jails" in the search form that appears, for example, will provide you with numerous articles that are available through NCJRS in which the word *jails* appears.

Another highly useful feature of the JIC site is the access it provides to the NCJRS Abstracts Database on the Web. The NCJRS Abstracts Database (formerly called the NCJRS Document Database) provides summaries of criminal justice literature—government reports, journal articles, books, and more. The database was previously available only on CD-ROM and via DIALOG (a fee-based information retrieval service).

NCJRS regularly publishes Justice Information (or JUSTINFO), which details current events, upcoming meetings, ongoing and recently published research, and new developments in the justice field. As discussed in Chapter 5, you can subscribe to JUSTINFO electronically by sending an e-mail message to listproc@ncjrs.org. In the body of the message, type "subscribe justinfo yourfirstname yourlastname" (without the quotes). If you have any problems using JIC or the NCJRS database, you can send e-mail to "Ask NCJRS!" at the following address: askncjrs@ncjrs.org. You should receive an answer within 48 hours. For general information about NCJRS, send a blank e-mail message to look@ncjrs.org. More information on sending and receiving e-mail can be found in Chapter 4.

The JRA Image Map of the CJ System

Another excellent starting point for Web-based criminal justice explorations is an image map created by the Justice Research Association at its *Talk Justice* site. The map, which is reproduced in black and white in Figure 3-2, can be viewed on-line at http://talkjustice.com/cjmap.htm. The diagram used in designing the map has been turned into a hot-linked image. Clicking on areas within the image will take you to resources related to those areas. Clicking on "arrest" within the map, for example, leads you to a number of police and civil liberties links. A note of caution is in order

FIGURE 3-2

The Talk Justice *Image Map. Adapted from the Bureau of Justice Statistics, 1997. Modified image courtesy of Cecil Greek. http://talkjustice.com/cjmap.htm.*

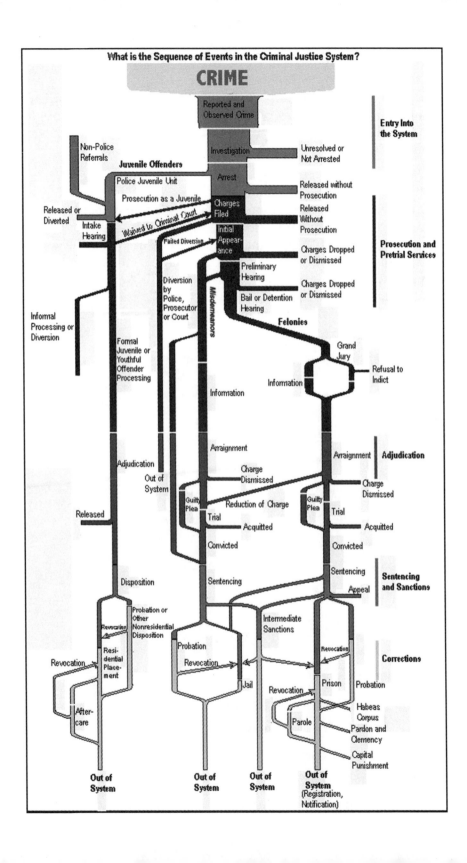

What is the Sequence of Events in the Criminal Justice System?

when working with image maps: Not all browsers support them. The *Talk Justice* image map is best viewed with Explorer 4.0 or later, although any version later than 3.0 should work. Navigator can also properly display the map, but you should use the most current version available.

SITE LISTINGS

The JIC and *Talk Justice* sites, comprehensive as they may be, are only two of many interesting criminal justice sites on the Web. The Web is literally awash in sites that should be of interest to anyone in the field of criminology or criminal justice. The remaining pages in this chapter provide a list of such sites. Although space won't permit including all criminology and criminal justice sites, a representative collection of some of the most popular sites is provided here. Links in this chapter are organized under the following headings:

- General Criminal Justice and Criminology Sites
- Justice Statistics
- Law Enforcement Resources
- Courts and Law-Related Sites
- Corrections Sites
- Victims of Crime
- Violence Against Women
- Crime Prevention
- Terrorism
- Unsolved Crimes
- Forensics
- Gangs
- Juvenile Justice Sites
- Missing and Abused Children
- Live Feeds from Police Scanners
- International Resources
- Associations
- Criminal Justice Guides on the Web

As you work through the links listed in this guide, you should keep in mind that the Web is a dynamic medium. URLs change constantly. Some may have changed since this guide was printed. If you find a URL in this list that is no longer current, you should check the *Talk Justice* Cybrary for the latest listings and updates. You can reach the Cybrary at http://talkjustice.com/cybrary.htm. If you wish to tell us about a URL that has changed but has not been updated in the Cybrary, send e-mail to admin@ talkjustice.com.

General Criminal Justice and Criminology Sites

BUREAU OF JUSTICE ASSISTANCE: http://www.ojp.usdoj.gov/BJA The Bureau of Justice Assistance (BJA) is a division of the U.S. Department of Justice, Office of Justice Programs. Its mission is to provide leadership and a wide range of assistance to local criminal justice strategies that make America's communities safer.

CONTACT CENTER CRIME RESOURCES: http://www.contact.org/uscrime.htm

CRIME RESEARCH CENTRE (AUSTRALIA): http://www.ecel.uwa.edu.au/crc

CRIMINAL JUSTICE NET: http://www.criminal-justice.net A source for news and information of relevance to the criminal justice area. Criminal Justice Net is constantly expanding. Check back often.

CRIMINOLOGY AND CRIMINAL JUSTICE: http://www.soc.umn.edu/ ~overall/crime.htm

CRIMINOLOGY AT THE UNIVERSITY OF HAMBURG (GERMANY): http://www.uni-hamburg.de/~kriminol

CRIMINOLOGY RESOURCES ON THE NET: http://adhocalypse.arts.unimelb.edu.au/Dept/Crim

DEATH PENALTY INFORMATION CENTER: http://www.essential.org/dpic Founded in 1990, the Death Penalty Information Center is a non-profit organization serving the media and the public with analysis and information on issues concerning capital punishment. The center prepares in-depth reports, issues press releases, conducts briefings for journalists, and serves as a resource to those working on this issue. Many reports, along with a wealth of statistics, are available at this site.

FLORIDA STATE UNIVERSITY'S CRIMINAL JUSTICE RESOURCE SITE:
http://www.criminology/fsu.edu/cj.html One of the oldest criminal
justice resources on the Web, this site consists mostly of links to
other sites.

FINANCIAL CRIMES ENFORCEMENT NETWORK:
http://www.ustreas.gov/fincen

JUSTICE TECHNOLOGY INFORMATION NETWORK: http://www.nlectc.org

LAW AND SOCIETY ASSOCIATION HOME PAGE: http://128.119.199.27/lsa

NATIONAL CENTER ON INSTITUTIONS AND ALTERNATIVES:
http://www.ncianet.org/ncia/index.html NCIA provides research information about criminal justice reform, including NCIA research
results and publications.

MAX PLANCK INSTITUTE FOR THE STUDY OF SOCIETIES (GERMANY):
http://www.mpi-fg-koeln.mpg.de

MICROSOFT'S JUSTICE PAGE:
http://www.microsoft.com/industry/justice

**THE NATIONAL CRIMINAL JUSTICE REFERENCE SERVICE'S JUSTICE INFORMA-
TION CENTER (JIC): http://www.ncjrs.org** Described in detail at the
start of this chapter, JIC provides links to many other criminal justice
sites on the Web. JIC site groups information under a number of
major headings, including corrections, courts, crime prevention,
criminal justice statistics, drugs and crime, international (criminal
justice), juvenile justice, law enforcement, research and evaluation,
and victims of crime. The site is also searchable by keyword or key
phrase.

THE NATIONAL INSTITUTE OF JUSTICE: http://www.ojp.usdoj.gov/nij
Sponsoring agency of the National Criminal Justice Reference Ser-
vice. The National Institute of Justice is a component of the Office of
Justice Programs, which also includes the Bureau of Justice Assis-
tance, Bureau of Justice Statistics, Office of Juvenile Justice and
Delinquency Prevention, and the Office for Victims of Crime.

NORDIC CRIMINOLOGY LINKS:
http://rvik.ismennt.is/~tho/NK/NK_2.2a.html

PREVENTING CRIME: WHAT WORKS, WHAT DOESN'T, WHAT'S PROMISING (THE SHERMAN REPORT): http://cjcentral.com/sherman/sherman.htm An insightful report about emerging issues in criminology and criminal justice.

Preventing Crime:
WHAT WORKS, WHAT DOESN'T, WHAT'S PROMISING

SCARMAN CENTRE FOR THE STUDY OF PUBLIC ORDER: http://www.le.ac.uk/scarman

UNITED NATIONS CRIME AND JUSTICE INFORMATION NETWORK: http://www.ifs.univie.ac.at/~uncjin/uncjin.html

U.S. DEPARTMENT OF JUSTICE: http://www.usdoj.gov Provides links to all DOJ agencies.

WEB OF JUSTICE: http://www.co.pineallas.fl.us/bcc/juscoord/explore.htm

WESTERN (U.S.) SOCIETY OF CRIMINOLOGY: http://www.sonoma.edu/cja/wsc/wscmain.html

WESTERN SOCIETY OF CRIMINOLOGY STUDENT PAPER COMPETITION: http://www.sonoma.edu/cja/WSC/WSC97STU.html

Justice Statistics

BUREAU OF JUSTICE STATISTICS: http://www.ojp.usdoj.gov/bjs The Bureau of Justice Statistics (BJS), a component of the Office of Justice Programs in the U.S. Department of Justice, is the primary source within the United States for criminal justice statistics.

NATIONAL ARCHIVE OF CRIMINAL JUSTICE DATA: http://www.icpsr.umich.edu/NACJD/index.html NACJD provides mostly data sets for secondary analysis for researchers interested in almost any aspect of American criminal justice.

SEARCH: http://www.search.org Search, located in Sacramento, California, was formally known as the National Consortium for Justice Information and Statistics.

SOURCEBOOK OF CRIMINAL JUSTICE STATISTICS:
http://www.albany.edu/sourcebook Home of the on-line version of the *Sourcebook of Criminal Justice Statistics*—the largest compilation of criminal justice statistics available anywhere. The *Sourcebook* site is run by the State University of New York at Albany and is updated continuously as new statistics become available.

U.S. GOVERNMENT STATISTICS:
http://www.whitehouse.gov/WH/html/briefroom.html

Law Enforcement Resources

COPNET: http://police.sas.ab.ca

DIRECTORY OF LAW ENFORCEMENT AGENCIES: http://www.officer.com

THE FBI'S HOME PAGE ON THE WEB: http://www.fbi.gov Lots of interesting links, including information on the latest statistics from the Uniform Crime Reporting Program. See Figure 3-3. Selections on the FBI's home page include the following:

CRIME ALERT: A list of fugitives wanted by the FBI, complete with photos and descriptions of their alleged crimes.

FBI ACADEMY: Descriptive material about the FBI Academy, located on the United States Marine Corps Base at Quantico, Virginia. Information about the FBI's Behavioral Science Unit, popularized by TV shows like the *X-Files*, is available through this link.

CONGRESSIONAL AFFAIRS: Various statements and reports on the crime problem by the Attorney General and the U.S. Congress.

INFORMATION TECHNOLOGY SUPPORT PROCUREMENT (ITSP): This section of the FBI's Web site relates to the acquisition of law enforcement technology.

DIRECTOR'S SPEECHES: The text of more than a dozen speeches given by FBI Director, Louis J. Freeh. The speeches are available in html format.

FIGURE 3-3

The FBI's home page on the Web: http://www.fbi.gov.

EMPLOYMENT: General FBI employment guidelines, along with information on jobs available in field offices across the country and specific FBI employment vacancies.

FAQ: Answers to frequently asked questions about the FBI.

FBI LAB: An overview of the FBI Laboratory—one of the largest and most comprehensive forensic labs in the world.

FBI'S MOST WANTED: An overview of the FBI's 10 most wanted fugitives—with crime descriptions and photos. Includes a missing children's directory.

FIELD OFFICES: A list of FBI field offices across the country, including contact information.

FOIA FILES: Documents made available to the public under the federal Freedom of Information Act. The information available on this page includes FBI files on Amelia Earhart, Elvis Presley, Jackie Robinson, Klaus Barbie, and Project Blue Book. These files can be viewed only if you have the Adobe Acrobat Reader plug-in.

HISTORY: An overview of FBI history.

INFRASTRUCTURE PROTECTION: Provides a wealth of information about the Infrastructure Protection Task Force (IPTF), a multi-agency task force created on July 15, 1996. The IPTF is tasked with identifying and coordinating existing expertise and capabilities in the government and private sector as they relate to critical infrastructure protection from both physical threats and cyberthreats. According to the FBI, major infrastructure categories include (1) banking and finance, (2) the continuity of government services, (3) electrical power generation and transmission, (4) emergency services, (5) gas and oil distribution and storage, (6) telecommunications, (7) transportation, and (8) water supply systems.

KIDS AND YOUTH: A page designed to help educate young people about DNA testing, polygraph testing, fingerprinting, child abduction, gangs, and crime detection. The page also provides children with Internet safety tips.

MAJOR INVESTIGATIONS: An overview of major investigations now in progress.

OVERVIEW: A somewhat detailed overview of the FBI, including an FBI fact sheet.

PRESS RELEASES: Recent FBI presses releases, available for viewing from within your browser.

PROGRAMS: This page provides an overview of FBI programs and cooperative law enforcement services. Included are data from the Explosives Unit–Bomb Data Center as well as descriptions of the Violent Criminal Apprehension Program (VICAP), the Integrated Automated Fingerprint Identification System (IAFIS) System, the National Computer Crime Squad (NCCS), and the FBI Community Outreach Program (COP).

PUBLICATIONS: FBI publications available for downloading, including the Uniform Crime Reports.

TOUR: Information about touring FBI offices in Washington, D.C.

UNIFORM CRIME REPORTS: Detailed statistical information on crime in the United States via the FBI's Uniform Crime Reporting Program.

WHAT'S NEW: A quick reference service for frequent Web site visitors who want to keep up-to-date on the latest additions to the site.

FBI LAW ENFORCEMENT BULLETINS: http://www.fbi.gov/leb/leb.htm

IRA WILSKER'S LAW ENFORCEMENT SITES: http://www.ih2000.net/ira An information-rich site maintained by a dedicated professional in the law enforcement field. Well worth a visit.

LAW ENFORCEMENT LINKS: http://www.leolinks.com A law enforcement guide to the WWW. In the words of the Webmaster: "We lay claim to having some of the best law enforcement and related links to be found anywhere on the World Wide Web."

N.C. STATE BUREAU OF INVESTIGATION: http://www.jus.state.nc.us/ Justice A site maintained by an exemplary state investigative agency.

THE POLICE GUIDE: http://policeguide.com One of the largest police sites on the Internet. The site consists of 238 separate Web pages— and is growing.

Courts and Law-Related Sites

CALIFORNIA STATE LAW AND OTHER LEGAL INFORMATION: http://www.leginfo.ca.gov

CORNELL'S LEGAL INFORMATION INSTITUTE: http://www.law.cornell.edu A starting point for Cornell University's Legal Information Institute.

COURT-TV: http://www.courttv.com The latest on current trials nationwide.

THE 'LECTRIC LAW LIBRARY: http://www.lectlaw.com An excellent collection of on-line legal materials and resources.

THE LEGAL INFORMATION INSTITUTE (LLI) AT CORNELL UNIVERSITY: http://www.law.cornell.edu/index.html Another starting point for the Legal Information Institute. LLI provides both archived and contemporary Supreme Court opinions under the auspices of Project Hermes, the court's electronic-dissemination project. The opinions are searchable.

THE LEGAL LIST: http://www.lcp.com/The-Legal-List/TLL-home.html

LEGAL ONLINE: http://www.legalonline.com

NATIONAL DISTRICT ATTORNEY'S ASSOCIATION:
http://www.ndaa.org/ndaa.htm

OHIO NORTHERN UNIVERSITY LAW LIBRARY:
http://www.law.onu.edu

THE UNITED STATES CODE: http://law.house.gov/usc.htm

U.S. COURT OF APPEALS FEDERAL CIRCUIT:
http://www.law.emory.edu/fedcircuit

U.S. HOUSE OF REPRESENTATIVES INTERNET LAW LIBRARY:
http://law.house.gov

UNIVERSITY OF CHICAGO LAW SCHOOL LIBRARY:
http://www.law.uchicago.edu/Library

VIRTUAL LAW LIBRARY:
http://www.law.indiana.edu/law/v-lib/lawindex.html

WASHBURN UNIVERSITY SCHOOL OF LAW—VIRTUAL LAW LIBRARY:
http://lawlib.wuacc.edu/washlaw/reflaw/reflaw.html A great law
school site, with lots of links!

Corrections Sites

THE CORRECTIONS CONNECTION: http://www.corrections.com Voted a
Microsoft "Outstanding Criminal Justice Site," the Corrections Connections provides links to almost any correctional organization in
the country and to all kinds of corrections information.

FEDERAL BUREAU OF PRISONS: http://www.bop.gov/bopmain.html The
BOP site provides various selections, including Quick Facts and Sta-
tistics, Weekly Population Reports, Program Statements (Policies),
Inmate Information, and Employment Information.

THE NATIONAL INSTITUTE OF CORRECTIONS:
http://www.bop.gov/nicpg/nicmain.html NIC is an agency under
the U.S. Department of Justice. It provides assistance to federal,
state, and local corrections agencies working with adult offenders.

Victims of Crime

VICTIM-OFFENDER MEDIATION ASSOCIATION: http://www.igc.org/voma

FBI HATE CRIME STATISTICS: http://www.fbi.gov/ucr/hatecm.htm

GENERAL VICTIMS ASSISTANCE INFORMATION: http://www.ncjrs.org/victhome.htm

NATIONAL ORGANIZATION FOR VICTIM ASSISTANCE: http://www.access.digex.net/~nova

VIOLENCE, PUBLIC HEALTH, AND THE MEDIA: http://www.annenberg.nwu.edu/pubs/violence

Violence Against Women

DATE RAPE INFORMATION: http://www.cs.utk.edu/~bartley/acquaint/acquaintRape.html

DOMESTIC VIOLENCE: http://www.feminist.org/other/dv/dvhome.html

FALSE MEMORY SYNDROME FOUNDATION: http://advicom.net/~fitz/fmsf

FRATERNITIES AND RAPE—BIBLIOGRAPHY: http://www.vix.com/pub/men/rape/frat.html

MANAVI SOUTH ASIAN WOMEN'S ORGANIZATION AGAINST VIOLENCE: http://www.research.att.com/~bala/manavi

MEN AGAINST DOMESTIC VIOLENCE: http://www.silcom.com/~paladin/madv

RECLAIM THE NIGHT: http://www.vicnet.net.au/vicnet/reclaim/rtnight.htm

SAFETYNET DOMESTIC VIOLENCE—THE ORGANIZATION: http://www.cybergrrl.com/planet/dv/orgs.html

SAFETYNET DOMESTIC VIOLENCE—THE RESOURCES: http://www.cybergrrl.com/planet/dv.html

SEXUAL HARASSMENT: WHAT EVERY WORKING WOMAN NEEDS TO KNOW: http://www.cs.utk.edu/~bartley/other/9to5.html

SEXUAL ABUSE SURVIVORS:
http://copper.ucs.indiana.edu/~ljray/survs.html

SEXUAL ASSAULT INFORMATION: http://www.cs.utk.edu/~bartley/saInfoPage.html

VIOLENCE AT ABORTION CLINICS:
http://www.matisse.net/politics/caral/violencepage.html

Crime Prevention

ARMED ROBBERY PAGE: http://www.ior.com/~jdmoore

ASSAULT PREVENTION INFORMATION: http://galaxy.tradewave.com/editors/weiss/APINintro.html

NATIONAL CRIME PREVENTION COUNCIL: http://www.ncpc.org

NATIONAL FRAUD INFORMATION CENTER: http://www.fraud.org

NATIONAL GRAFFITI INFORMATION NETWORK:
http://www.infowest.com/business/n/ngin

PARTNERSHIPS AGAINST VIOLENCE (PAVNET): http://www.pavnet.org
NCJRS says that PAVNET is "a model of Internet use." The PAVNET home page is reproduced in Figure 3-4.

Here's a description of PAVNET, taken from a recent government publication.[13]

> The Internet can help convey information about how to respond to violence. At the federal, state, and local levels there is no lack of programs that deal with violence, addressing it from several perspectives, among them criminal justice, health, and education. Until recently, however, there was no easy way to find out what these programs are and where they operate. The NIJ-initiated Partnerships Against Violence Network (PAVNET) changed all that by centralizing this information and making it available on-line.
>
> PAVNET Online, as the resource is called, is a compendium of information about hundreds of programs under way all over the country and includes information about technical assistance and funding. The information has also been published in traditional print format (and on computer diskettes), but Internet availability makes it possible for users to search, view, download, and copy the information whenever they want so that they need not buy and store hard copies or diskettes.

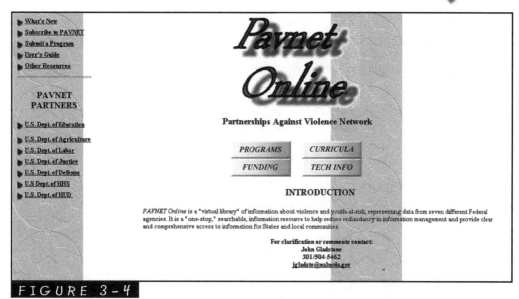

What's New
Subscribe to PAVNET
Submit a Program
User's Guide
Other Resources

PAVNET PARTNERS

U.S. Dept. of Education
U.S. Dept. of Agriculture
U.S. Dept. of Labor
U.S. Dept. of Justice
U.S. Dept. of Defense
U.S Dept. of HHS
U.S. Dept. of HUD

Pavnet Online

Partnerships Against Violence Network

PROGRAMS   CURRICULA
FUNDING   TECH INFO

INTRODUCTION

PAVNET Online is a "virtual library" of information about violence and youth-at-risk, representing data from seven different Federal agencies. It is a "one-stop," searchable, information resource to help reduce redundancy in information management and provide clear and comprehensive access to information for States and local communities.

For clarification or comments contact:
John Gladstone
301/504-5462
jgladsto@nalusda.gov

FIGURE 3-4

The PAVNET homepage. http://www.pavenet.org.

PAVNET represents the combined efforts of several federal agencies, each of which has contributed information from its own clearinghouse. A distributed database structure is being constructed to enable each agency to upload and manage its own information and to link the agencies' systems. Although data will be entered from many sources, there is a single point of entry for the user, who will continue to perceive PAVNET as a centralized and seamless information resource.

THE STOLEN BIKE REGISTRY: http://www.telalink.net/~cycling/stolen.html

Terrorism

THE COUNTER-TERRORISM PAGE: http://www.terrorism.com

Unsolved Crimes

AMERICA'S MOST WANTED: http://www.amw.com

ANOTHER AMERICA'S MOST WANTED SITE: http://www.foxnetwork.com

CRIME SCENE EVIDENCE FILES: http://www.crimescene.com Cases in which law enforcement agencies are asking for help.

UNSOLVED CRIMES: http://www.emeraldcity.com/crimefiles/crimefiles.htm Solve unsolved crimes from around the country (rewards offered).

Forensics

FORENSIC MEDIA: http://www.netexpress.net/~forensic

FORENSICS SCIENCE RESOURCES: http://www.tncrimlaw.com/forensic

FORENSICS SCIENCE SOCIETY: http://www.demon.co.uk/forensic/index.html

FORENSICS WEB: http://www.eskimo.com/~spban/forensic.html

Gangs

THE FEDERAL GANG VIOLENCE ACT: http://www.senate.gov/member/ca/feinstein/general/gangs.html

GANGS: A BIBLIOGRAPHY: http://www-lib.usc.edu/~anthonya/gang.htm

GANGS IN THE SCHOOLS: http://eric-web.tc.columbia.edu/alerts/ia46.html

THE NATIONAL YOUTH GANG CENTER: http://www.iir.com/nygc

YOUTH GANGS—OUT OF CONTROL: http://www.townhall.com/frc

Juvenile Justice Sites

THE AMERICAN BAR ASSOCIATION'S JUVENILE JUSTICE CENTER: http://www.abanet.org/crimjust/juvjus/home.html

THE ACADEMY FOR EDUCATIONAL DEVELOPMENT: http://www.aed.org

CHILD QUEST INTERNATIONAL: http://www.childquest.org

CHILDREN'S DEFENSE FUND: http://www.childrensdefense.org

HANDSNET: http://www.handsnet.org/handsnet

JOIN TOGETHER ONLINE: http://www.jointogether.org

THE JUVENILE JUSTICE CLEARINGHOUSE:
http://www.fsu.edu/~crimdo/jjclearinghouse

NATIONAL COUNCIL ON CRIME AND DELINQUENCY (NCCD):
http://www.nccd.com NCCD conducts research and initiates programs and policies to reduce crime and delinquency. NCCD seeks to
influence public policies that affect the nature of crime and delinquency and the future of the justice system.

NATIONAL COUNCIL OF JUVENILE AND FAMILY COURT JUDGES:
http://www.ncjfcj.unr.edu

NORTH CAROLINA CENTER FOR THE PREVENTION OF SCHOOL VIOLENCE:
http://www2.ncsu.edu/ncsu/cep/PreViolence/CtrPreSchVio.html

SAMHSA'S TREATMENT IMPROVEMENT PROTOCOLS:
http://text.nlm.nih.gov/ftrs/dbaccess/tip

TEXAS YOUTH COMMISSION—CATALOG OF PROGRAMS:
http://www.tyc.state.tx.us/catalog.html

U.S. DEPARTMENT OF HEALTH AND HUMAN SERVICES, DIVISION OF CHILDREN
AND YOUTH POLICY: http://aspe.os.dhhs.gov/hsp/cyphome.htm

Missing and Abused Children

NATIONAL CENTER FOR MISSING CHILDREN:
http://www.scubed.com/public_service/index.html

NATIONAL CLEARINGHOUSE ON CHILD ABUSE:
http://www.calib.com/nccanch

Live Feeds from Police Scanners
To access these sites you'll need RealAudio Player.

POLICESCANNER.COM: http://www.policescanner.com Here you'll find
the latest live audio-enabled police sites.

THE PLANO, TEXAS, POLICE DEPARTMENT'S LIVE AUDIO FEED:
http://www.audionet.com/radio/scanners/plano_pd.ram

NYPD LIVE FEED:
http://www.audionet.com/radio/scanners/new_york.pd.ram

LAPD LIVE FEED:
http://www.audionet.com/radio/scanners/los_angelos_pd.ram

YOU CAN DOWNLOAD REALAUDIO PLAYER FROM:
http://www.real.com/products/player

International Resources

THE EUROPEAN INSTITUTE FOR CRIME PREVENTION AND CONTROL (HEUNI):
http://heuni.unojust.org Affiliated with the United Nations, HEUNI
is the European link in the network of institutes operating within the
framework of the United Nations Crime Prevention and Criminal
Justice Program.

INFOLAW: http://www.infolaw.co.uk An extensive directory of legal
resources in the United Kingdom, including government agencies,
law schools, legal associations, and law publishers.

INTERNATIONAL LAW RESOURCES: http://www.un.org/law Includes
sections on the International Court of Justice; the law of the sea;
codification, development, and promotion of international law;
international treaties; international trade law; and the International
Criminal Tribunal for the Former Yugoslavia (ICTY).

OFFICE OF INTERNATIONAL CRIMINAL JUSTICE:
http://www.acsp.uic.edu/index.shtm

ROYAL CANADIAN MOUNTED POLICE (RCMP):
www.rcmp-grc.gc.ca/html/rcmp2.htm

THE RULE OF LAW ONLINE: http://www.rol.org The Rule of Law project
(ROL) was established to create a multilingual, World Wide Web–
based information resource that would facilitate transfer of the U.S.
democratic experience to those in the former Soviet Union who
were involved in reforming the legislative process, restructuring
government institutions, and building civil society. Later, the Rule
of Law Online became a model for the UN Online Crime and Justice Clearinghouse (UNOJUST)—an information-sharing and

-dissemination vehicle for the 14 regional and interregional institutes associated with the UN Crime Prevention and Criminal Justice Program.

SCOTLAND YARD (UNITED KINGDOM): **www.met.police.uk** Like a visit to England!

UNITED NATIONS ONLINE CRIME AND JUSTICE CLEARINGHOUSE (UNOJUST): **http://www.unojust.org** Provides links to services of the United Nations Crime Prevention and Criminal Justice Program and associated UN institutes.

UNITED KINGDOM CJ LINKS: **http://www.leeds.ac.uk/law/ccjs/ukweb.htm**

UNITED NATIONS CRIME AND JUSTICE INFORMATION NETWORK: **http://www.ifs.univie.ac.at/~uncjin/uncjin.html** Includes links to the UN Institutes of the crime program; UNOJUST; UN documents; the UN itself; statistical sources; country-specific information; and international laws, treaties, and member-country constitutions.

WORLD FACTBOOK OF CRIMINAL JUSTICE SYSTEMS: **http://www.ojp.usdoj.gov/bjs/abstract/wfcj.htm** Maintained by the Bureau of Justice Statistics, the *Factbook* provides narrative descriptions of the criminal justice systems of 42 countries around the world.

Associations

THE ACADEMY OF CRIMINAL JUSTICE SCIENCES (ACJS): **http://www.nku.edu/~acjs** The Academy of Criminal Justice Sciences is an international organization established in 1963 to foster professional and scholarly activities in the field of criminal justice. ACJS currently has over 3,800 active members.

THE AMERICAN BAR ASSOCIATION, CRIMINAL JUSTICE SECTION: **http://www.abanet.org/crimjust**

AMERICAN BOARD OF CRIMINALISTS: **HTTP://www.criminalistics.com/ABC**

AMERICAN SOCIETY OF CRIMINOLOGY (ASC): **http://www.bsos.umd.edu/asc**

AMERICAN SOCIETY OF INDUSTRIAL SECURITY:
http://www.securitymanagement.com/home.html

ASSOCIATION OF PUBLIC SAFETY OFFICERS:
http://www.henge.com/~gtraylor/apco.html

AUXILIARY AND RESERVE POLICE: http://www.apolice.com

CALIFORNIA ASSOCIATION OF CRIMINALISTS:
http://www.criminalistics.com/CAC

HIGH TECHNOLOGY CRIME INVESTIGATION ASSOCIATION: http://htcia.org/

INTERNATIONAL NARCOTICS CONTROL BOARD:
http://undcp.or.at/en_incbhome.html

INTERNATIONAL ASSOCIATION OF CHIEFS OF POLICE:
http://www.amdahl.com/ext/iacp

INTERNATIONAL ASSOCIATION OF CORRECTIONAL OFFICERS:
http://www.acsp.uic.edu/iaco/kv1603tc.htm

INTERNATIONAL ASSOCIATION OF CRIME ANALYSTS: http://www.iaca.net

INTERNATIONAL ASSOCIATION OF LAW ENFORCEMENT PLANNERS:
http://www.dps.state.ak.us/ialep/index.html

INTERNATIONAL CENTER FOR THE PREVENTION OF CRIME:
http://www.crime-prevention-intl.org

NATIONAL COMPUTER SECURITY ASSOCIATION: http://www.ncsa.com

NATIONAL DRUG ENFORCEMENT OFFICERS ASSOCIATION:
http://www.ndeoa.org

NATIONAL SHERIFFS ASSOCIATION: http://www.sheriffs.org

SOCIETY OF POLICE FUTURISTS INTERNATIONAL:
http://www.policefuturists.org

Criminal Justice Guides on the Web

THE CRIMINAL JUSTICE WORLD WIDE WEB HANDBOOK (AKA, "THE CJ WEB HANDBOOK"): **http://www.acsp.uic.edu/handbook** *The CJ Web Handbook* is published electronically through the joint efforts of the Illinois Criminal Justice Information Authority's Research and Analysis Unit and the University of Illinois at Chicago's Office of International Criminal Justice. The *Handbook,* which is available to anyone, is an HTML document intended to help criminal justice officials take advantage of the benefits of electronic, on-line digital communications using the Web. It is intended primarily for those wishing to build their own Web sites.

THE DEFINITIVE GUIDE TO CRIMINAL JUSTICE AND CRIMINOLOGY ON THE WORLD WIDE WEB: **http://www.cjcentral.com/cjdlc/TOC.htm** Sample chapters only.

 USING THE WEB

Visit the following Justice Information Center and *Talk Justice* sites on the Web:

- Justice Information Center: http://www.ncjrs.org
- *Talk Justice:* http://talkjustice.com

Then do the following:

1. Write a page describing the features available at each of these sites. Compare the sites. What does JIC offer that *Talk Justice* doesn't? What are the major differences between the two?

2. Use the JIC site to research community policing. How many references can you find to community policing? How many full text documents on the topic are available through the site? What other sites does JIC refer you to for additional community policing information?

CHAPTER IV

E-MAIL AND E-MAIL SOFTWARE

In 1994, 31 million people in the United States—at home and at work—were using e-mail. This year [1997], the number is expected to more than double to 66 million, and by 2000, e-mail users will number 107 million. These users generated more than 812 billion messages in 1994, and this year they'll hit the Send button 2.7 trillion times. By 2000, that figure will explode to 6.9 trillion messages a year.

—Windows Magazine[14]

I have received no more than one or two letters in my life that were worth the postage.

—*Henry David Thoreau*

I have made this letter longer than usual, only because I have not had the time to make it shorter.

—*Blaise Pascal, Provincial Letters*

CHAPTER OUTLINE

- Introduction
- Sending Messages
- Receiving Messages
- Emoticons and Abbreviations
- Free E-Mail
- Locator and Directory Services
- E-Mail Security
- Using the Web

INTRODUCTION

One of the most useful tools available to anyone on the Internet is electronic mail. Electronic mail is called **e-mail** for short. E-mail allows you to exchange messages with other Internet users. Almost all on-line services and Internet service providers assign you at least one e-mail address. Some, like America Online, provide as many as five. Almost every Internet service provides free e-mail. That is, e-mail usually costs no more than what you would normally pay to use your Internet service. You can send and receive any number of messages (although the size of messages is sometimes limited by your Internet provider's hardware and software) at any time of the day. Once you begin using e-mail for distant communication you will find that it is far cheaper than telephone calls![15]

In order to send and receive e-mail messages you must either be a member of an on-line service (in which case your e-mail capabilities are integrated with the software you received) or have e-mail software loaded on your computer. You will need e-mail software if you are connecting to the Internet via an Internet service provider. Today's most popular e-mail programs are Netscape's Messenger®, which is prepackaged as a component of Netscape Communicator®; Microsoft's Internet Mail®, which is bundled with Microsoft Internet Explorer; and Eudora® by Qualcomm Corporation. As of this writing, all three of these e-mail programs are free. The most powerful, in terms of the number of features it supports, is probably Eudora—but only in its nonfree professional version, Eudora Pro®. A freeware version of Eudora, called Eudora Light® (see Figure 4-1), is available from Qualcomm Corporation at http://www.eudora.com/eudoralight.

E-MAIL: electronic mail. A modern form of communication utilizing computers and the Internet.

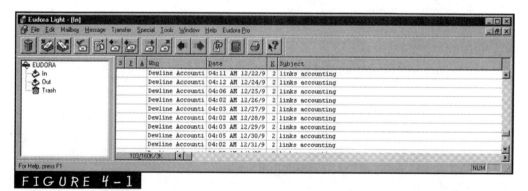

FIGURE 4-1

The Eudora Light® (freeware) e-mail program. This in-box message list shows accounting reports automatically generated by one of the Justice Research Association's servers. Download free Eudora software at http://www.eudora.com/eudoralight.

E-mail software not only allows you to send messages across the Internet, but most of today's e-mail programs make it possible for you to incorporate color images, audio, and even motion and video into your e-mail messages. You can send talking e-mail by recording your voice and embedding it in your e-mail message before sending. You can also include a photo or video of yourself as you speak—making for a true multimedia experience for your message recipients! Keep in mind, however, that these features are recent innovations and have not always been a part of e-mail. Many advanced e-mail features require that your e-mail recipients have the technology (both hardware and software) to electronically decipher the messages you send and to display all of the enhancements you have included. Remember that if you get too far out on the leading edge of e-mail technology, only a relatively few people may possess the technology to read your messages.

SENDING MESSAGES

Perhaps the best way to begin working with any e-mail software (short of reading the manual) is to create an outgoing message. An outgoing message is one that you send to someone else. Each mail program is a bit different. In order to compose a new message in Internet Mail, you need to click on the open envelop icon found on the upper left side of the toolbar. The icon is labeled "new message." Clicking on this icon will open a composition window, allowing you to type in the message you want to send.

After typing your message in the **composition field,** you will need to address the message. Do this by entering the name of the recipient in the TO field. E-mail addresses take the form of username@domainname. If you wanted to write to the Webmaster at the *Talk Justice* site, for example, you would address your message to admin@talkjustice.com. You can also send e-mail to a member of an on-line service. If you wanted to write to one of the many addresses used by the Justice Research Association, for example, you might send mail to usjustice@aol.com. In this case, the "aol.com" portion of the address refers to an e-mail box residing on America Online. If you are using an on-line service and want to send mail to someone on the same service (AOL, for example), you could merely type the name of the intended recipient in the "TO" box. Hence, for the example just given, if you were an AOL member and were to use the built-in mail service, you would simply type the username "usjustice" without specifying the domain (aol.com). If you inadvertently typed in the complete address, including the domain name, your on-line service should still properly interpret the address and send your mail to the correct recipient.

Keep in mind that you can always send the same message to more than one recipient. You can have a number of "TOs," or you can designate "cc" (carbon copy) recipients, and you can use "bcc" to send mail to someone other than the main recipient without showing the recipient who else your message was sent to.

All e-mail programs contain an **address book.** It is a good idea to keep addresses of frequent mail recipients in your address book. When you want to send mail, you can simply open the address book and click on the name of your intended recipient. The "TO" field will be automatically filled in with that person's e-mail address. Similarly, when you begin to type a person's name (or nickname, which you can also assign) into the "TO" field, your e-mail software will check your address book in order to determine if an entry exists for that person. If so, it will automatically fill in the "TO" field for you. (You can, of course, overwrite the "TO" entry manually if the address book selects the wrong recipient.)

It is always a good idea to fill in the **subject** field of the message you are sending. You might enter some brief text indicating what the message is about. If you are writing about the death penalty, for example, you might enter "Death penalty comments," or something similar.

Today's e-mail programs also allow you to use **file attachments.** A file attachment is simply a file attached to your e-mail message. When the message arrives in the recipient's e-mail box, he or she will see that the message contains an attachment. Attachments can be saved on a computer for later use or viewing, or you can double-click on most attachments (which may appear as a folder or file icon within the e-mail message) and open or run the file immediately. If you are sending proprietary forms of information such as recorded sound or video, make sure that the recipient has the necessary software on his or her computer to interpret or play such attachments.

Most programs also allow you to set a priority that will be associated with your message when it appears in the recipient's e-mail box. In order to do so from within the "New Message" window of Internet Mail you will first need to click on "mail," then "set priority." Eudora allows you to set message priority by clicking on the down arrow next to the small blank box that appears in the upper left-hand corner of your composition window.

You can also include a predefined **signature** in your e-mail messages. Internet Mail allows you to create a signature card and attach it to all of your messages. Recipients can conveniently drag the card into Windows Notepad® or Cardfile® and save it on their computer. Messenger allows you to predefine a signature block to be attached to all messages—or to specify a file to be used as your signature. You can, for example, create a simple plain text (ASCII) file for Messenger to insert at the end of any messages you send. Eudora gives you the choice of whether to include a signature with a message you are about to send and then allows you to specify a choice from among a number of predefined signature blocks (or files).

After you have finished typing your message, you can send it. The button you need to click on varies slightly from program to program. If you are using Internet Mail you will need to click on the little envelope icon on the left of the icon bar. Anyone using Messenger will need to click on the envelope icon above the word "send." Eudora users should click the "send" button as well (although there is no icon associated with it).

If you decide not to send a message right away, you can save it for later editing. In order to open the message later, it will be necessary for you to locate the message in your "unsent messages," "drafts," or "saved messages" folder (depending on the software you are using) and click on it.

RECEIVING MESSAGES

When someone sends you a message, it is stored on the mail server of your on-line service or Internet service provider. In order to retrieve messages addressed to you, you must tell your mail program to check the mail server for your messages. Internet Mail requires you to click on "send and receive." Messenger (see Figure 4-2) wants you to click on "get messages." And Eudora provides you with a small envelope topped by a checkmark, which stands for "check mail." Most mail programs will also automatically check to see if you have mail. In order to enable this feature, however, you may have to click on "preferences" or "options" from within one of the pull-down menus on the menu bar.

You can set your e-mail program to store messages for you on the mail server even after you've read them. Alternatively, you can store mail that you have received on your own machine. If you are working in a network environment, all messages might be stored on a central server (which is not necessarily the same thing as a mail server) under your username. Generally, it is a good idea not to store messages on the mail server. Use your own machine for storage. Doing so will save a considerable amount of disk space on the mail server (especially if all users do the same thing). Moreover, most mail servers will delete mail you have read after a set period of time (30 or 90 days, for example).

When you receive a message you have a number of options. You can read the message and close it, allowing it to remain stored on the hard disk of your machine. You can decide not to read the message, and it will be saved automatically for your later use. You can file the message in a mail folder that you designate, you can print it (in which case it will remain visible on your screen until you take some other action), or you can delete it.

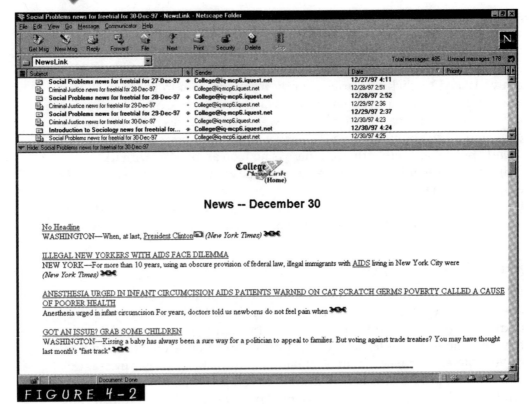

FIGURE 4-2

Netscape Messenger.

You can delete a message or a series of messages that you have selected with your mouse simply by clicking "delete" in most mail programs. Eudora, being a bit different, requires you to click on the trash can icon in order to delete the message. It is important to know that deleted messages are still saved by most e-mail programs in a special "trash" folder. You generally have to click on a menu option titled "empty trash" (or something similar) in order to permanently delete a message. Eudora, however, treats deleted messages a bit differently. All messages stored in Eudora's Trash mailbox are automatically deleted when you quit Eudora (although you can turn off this option).

You can, of course, choose to reply to mail that you receive. If you click on "reply" in Internet Mail (see Figure 4-3) and Messenger or click the little envelope in Eudora's icon toolbar that has the blue arrow pointing to the left by it, you will be asked whether you want to reply to the sender or the author or to all of the people to whom the original message was addressed. Often you can reply only to the sender because you may have

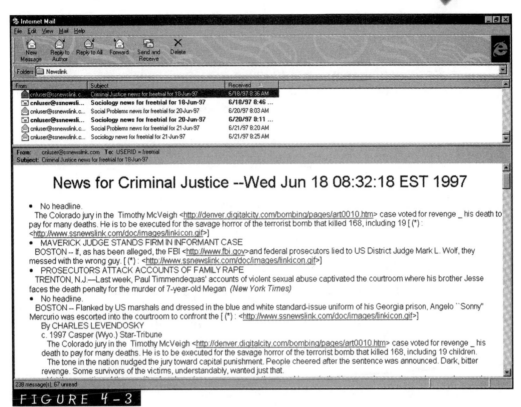

FIGURE 4-3

Microsoft's Internet Mail. The user is viewing filed criminal justice news stories received from Prentice Hall's NewsLink service. Messages that appear in bold in the message list have not yet been read.

been the only recipient. Once you click "reply," you will see the same window that is used to originate a message you want to send. In this case, however, the recipient's "TO" address will already be filled in, and the subject line will change to something like [RE: Death penalty comments]. Although you can change the subject line, your e-mail program is trying to be helpful by indicating which message you are replying to.

You can also forward e-mail by clicking on the "forward" icon or menu selection. If you choose to forward mail, you will need to fill in the address of the person(s) to whom you wish to forward the message. You need not type anything in the composition field that appears unless you wish to do so. If you type a message into the composition field of a message addressed to a forwarded address, the person to whom you are sending mail will receive your comments, followed by the message you are forwarding. Don't worry if the message you are about to forward doesn't appear in the composition field. Your e-mail program will still forward the message correctly.

Most e-mail programs save copies of messages that you have sent, enabling you to search or reread those messages at a later date. Your "sent" message folder usually contains such messages. The search feature built into most e-mail programs can prove to be a handy feature after you have sent a lot of messages and wish to find a particular one!

EMOTICONS AND ABBREVIATIONS

Today's e-mail programs have advanced far beyond early software that could deliver only text messages. Even so, the use of emoticons is still widespread. Emoticons are icons that express emotion. They are formed by a combination of keystroke characters that form a facial (or other) expression. Since people who read your e-mail messages cannot hear your voice, they can't tell whether you are trying to be funny, sarcastic, or serious. When you are kidding around, it is a good idea to include emoticons in your mail so that people don't take you too seriously. Emoticons are also called *smileys*, since the most common form of emoticon used on the Web is a smiling (or laughing) face. Common smileys, along with their translations, include the following:

:-) or :^) or :)	"I'm laughing." These are your basic smileys used to inflect a sarcastic or joking tone into the writer's message.
I-)	More laughter (eyes closed).
:-(or :'-(or :(	"I'm crying." "I'm sad." The boo hoo smiley.
:-o	"Oops!" or "Uh-oh!"
;-)	"I just made a flirtatious and/or sarcastic remark." This kind of smiley is called a *winky*.
>:->	"That was kind of devilish."
(-:	Laughter from a left-handed writer.
~~:-(	"I've been flamed."

While smileys add personality to your messages, abbreviations save keystrokes. Some common ones include the following:

BFN	Bye for now
BTW	By the way
G	Grin
GGG	Really big grin
HTH	Hope this helps
IJWTK	I just want to know
IJWTS	I just want to say
IMO	In my opinion

IMHO	In my humble opinion
LOL	Laughing out loud
OTOH	On the other hand
ROTFL	Rolling on the floor laughing
YMMV	Your mileage may vary

Sometimes, but not always, e-mail abbreviations are enclosed in pointed brackets (e.g., <LOL> or <GGG>).

FREE E-MAIL

A number of services on the Internet offer free e-mail addresses. Some provide an e-mail box that you can use, personalized with a username and password of your choosing. Others, like BigFoot.Com, allow you to register a username "for life."

Bigfoot is a unique kind of service. It doesn't provide you with an e-mail box in the traditional sense, but rather forwards your mail to any e-mail address that you specify. Let's say that you set up a Bigfoot e-mail account with the username "bigdaddy." You could give anyone anywhere your Bigfoot e-mail address, which would be bigdaddy@bigfoot.com. Then, if you change service providers or on-line services, all you need to do is to tell Bigfoot where to send your mail. Keep in mind that to use Bigfoot you need to have existing e-mail service. Bigfoot's advantage lies in the fact that you can move, change e-mail addresses as often as you like, and still get all of the mail sent to your Bigfoot address at any time—even if people don't know which on-line service or ISP you are using.

You can get a Bigfoot e-mail address free. (The Justice Research Association's Bigfoot address is usjustice@bigfoot.com.) Bigfoot will then forward all mail sent to your "Bigfoot for life" address to one genuine e-mail account. Bigfoot allows you to have a copy of all your e-mail forwarded to up to five e-mail accounts. Bigfoot also provides filtering services, which allow you to have your incoming e-mail delivered or rejected based on criteria that you specify. If, for example, someone keeps flaming you with personal mail or repeatedly sends junk mail you don't want, you can tell Bigfoot to filter out mail from that individual.

Some of the best Bigfoot features are available as premium services for which you pay a small yearly fee. Bigfoot premium services include the following: (1) consolidation (where Bigfoot will consolidate messages from multiple e-mail accounts to one address of your choosing); (2) an e-mail reminder service whereby you can set up reminders to yourself for holidays, birthdays, and so forth; (3) a security feature, which you can use to have your incoming messages and attachments automatically filtered for viruses and other security threats; (4) an automatic reminder feature, which will automatically respond to incoming e-mail messages while you're away.

Other free e-mail services are available through many of the major search engines (discussed in Chapter 9). Some of them, like Bigfoot, provide "e-mail for life" addresses. As you surf the Web, you are likely to come across many advertisements for these free services. A typical Yahoo ad, for example, looks like this:

The following are the best of these free services.

EUDORA WEB-MAIL: http://www.eudoramail.com Free personalized e-mail.

MAILEXCITE: http://mail.excite.com Advertised as "Free Private E-Mail at the Same Address Forever."

YAHOO'S FREE E-MAIL: http://mail.yahoo.com If you visit the Yahoo home page, click on the tiny "e-mail" word. It's next to "Chat" and under the "Search" button.

LYCOS E-MAIL: http://www.lycosemail.com/member/login.page Visit the Login Page for help with setting up your free account.

NET@DDRESS: http://www.netaddress.com From USA Net, the Internet Post Office.

SWITCHBOARD'S FREE E-MAIL SERVICE: http://webmail.switchboard.com/member/login.page Another "e-mail for life" site.

WHOWHERE? FREE E-MAIL AND DIRECTORY SERVICES: http://www.mailcity.com In the words of WhoWhere: "FREE web-based e-mail, available through any Internet connection—anytime, anywhere."

LOCATOR AND DIRECTORY SERVICES

What's Bill Gates's e-mail address? It's billg@microsoft.com. Are we breaching a confidence by telling you this? No, Bill's address is listed in most white-pages information directories on the Web. In fact, he has many addresses. We got this one by searching Four11.Com. Four11 lists this address under its "Celebrities Directory" and identifies the holder of this address as "Bill Gates: Microsoft Founder." If you want to see a picture of Mr. Gates, try another e-mail address search service at http://www.cs.indiana.edu:800/finger/gateway. Go to the site, enter billg@microsoft.com, and hit the return key. You'll notice that this site works in reverse. That is, if you give it an address, it will tell you who owns it.

If you want to find the e-mail addresses of friends, relatives, or almost anyone, try searching the following directory services:

FOUR11 DIRECTORY SERVICES: http://www.four11.com A free, easy-to-use directory. Includes Web yellow pages, white pages, the AT&T 800 directory, and a celebrity directory.

BIGFOOT: http://www.bigfoot.com Bigfoot provides a mail directory locator service for the many people and businesses it has registered on-line.

THE INTERNET ADDRESS FINDER (IAF): http://www.iaf.net Promotes itself as "the Internet's fastest and most convenient white pages service." Contains almost 7 million listings.

SWITCHBOARD: http://www.switchboard.com A comprehensive people locator.

WHOWHERE?: http://www.whowhere.com Find e-mail addresses, phone numbers, and street addresses of almost anyone on the Web with this comprehensive directory.

THE WORLD E-MAIL DIRECTORY: http://www.worldemail.com Over 18 million e-mail addresses at your fingertips.

THE WORLD WIDE WEB "FINGER" GATEWAY: http://www.cs.indiana.edu:800/finger/gateway "Finger" was an old command used on text-based systems to find someone's identity on the Internet. The new Web-based Finger facility makes searching a breeze. To use this service, you need to know the person's e-mail address. You can then learn who owns that address.

Keep in mind that if you have an e-mail address, you can add it to any of these directories. You will, however, have to visit them to find out how.

MARY HOUTEN-KEMP'S

EVERYTHING E-MAIL™

You should also be aware of the best site on the Web for learning anything you ever wanted to know about e-mail. The site, "Mary Houten-Kemp's EveryThing E-Mail," includes (1) e-mail tips, (2) an e-mail glossary, (3) a list of mailing list discussion groups, (4) information on starting a mailing list, (5) a how-to guide on finding e-mail addresses, (6) a discussion of autoresponder services, (7) information on how to receive news by e-mail, (8) a discussion of unsolicited e-mail issues, and (9) links to free e-mail software. Mary Houten-Kemp's "EveryThing E-Mail" can be reached at http://everythingemail.net. The Houten-Kemp site is in the process of moving and changing its name. You will soon find the new site, "All About E-mail," at http://www.allaboutemail.com.

E-MAIL SECURITY

E-mail conversation is far from private. Other forms of electronic communication, including telephone calls and fax transmissions, are protected under a number of laws such as the Electronic Communications Privacy Act of 1986. Unfortunately for e-mailers, framers of the 1986 statute did not include most computer communications under the law.

E-mail security is difficult to ensure because e-mail messages are usually transferred from one computer to another as they make their way along the Internet to their final destinations. At each stop, almost any message can be intercepted and read by prying eyes. Why would someone want to read your e-mail? Hackers love the challenge of eavesdropping in cyberspace. Business competitors, on the other hand, can use what should be confidential information against you or your company. Remember that information, especially in today's world, is power.

Your company may feel that an employer has a right to read any e-mail you send using its system. Some companies appear to believe that reading an employee's e-mail is more than a right—it is a responsibility. Employers reason that employees should not be using the company's computers to send personal mail and that employees should not be wasting time at work doing so. High-technology companies often assert the right to read any mail sent over their computers as a precaution against industrial sabotage.

Universities are in a position similar to that of industrial corporations. Although most do not read student/faculty e-mail as a matter of policy, the possibility remains that they could do so if they wanted to. It is certainly better for any sender of e-mail to be safe rather than sorry.

A couple of personal protection rules to remember when sending e-mail are as follows: (1) Don't send anything via e-mail that you wouldn't want anyone other than the intended recipient to see. (2) Use e-mail encryption techniques whenever you are sending sensitive information. (Security issues will be discussed at greater length in Chapter 9.)

 USING THE WEB

Visit some of the free e-mail and directory services sites described in this chapter. Then do the following:

1. Compare at least three free e-mail sites. What features does each offer? What are the limitations of each site? Which do you like best? Why?

2. Use a few of the directory sites listed in this chapter to locate some of your friends or family members. Which directory site seems to be the best? Why?

CHAPTER V

E-MAIL DISCUSSION LISTS, NEWSGROUPS, 'ZINES, AND E-JOURNALS

> One thing on the Net is certain: there is always someone willing to argue about anything!
>
> *—Anonymous*

> There is no pleasure to me without communication: there is not so much as a sprightly thought comes into my mind that it does not grieve me to have produced alone, and that I have no one to tell it to.
>
> *—Michel de Montaigne (1533–92), French writer*[16]

CHAPTER OUTLINE

- Introduction
- E-Mail Discussion Lists
  - *Criminology and Criminal Justice Discussion Lists*
  - *Criminology and Criminal Justice Announcement Lists*
  - *Discussion List Resources*
- Newsgroups
- 'Zines and E-Journals
- Using the Web

INTRODUCTION

The quotation from the sixteenth-century French essayist, Michel de Montaigne, which begins this chapter, highlights the importance of interpersonal communication for the human soul. It seems that we, as human beings, have an innate need to share our thoughts and to tell others about the way we feel. The Internet provides a perfect medium for interpersonal communication, as it expands exponentially the number of people we are able to reach.

Communication on the Internet takes many forms. This chapter describes four: (1) e-mail discussion lists, (2) Internet newsgroups, (3) electronic journals, and (4) Internet-based magazines (called 'Zines). Each constitutes a form of communication not available a mere decade or so ago, and each is quite different from the others. We will discuss all four.

E-MAIL DISCUSSION LISTS

An e-mail **discussion list** sends e-mail messages from anyone participating in the list to all members of the list simultaneously. E-mail discussion lists work through a **listserver** (or **listserv**), which accepts e-mail contributions from group members and then redistributes them to all other members. In other words, when someone sends out a message, it goes to everybody on the list. Messages received by the listserver are sent to list members as soon as they arrive. Once a message has been sent, however, it is no longer available on-line.[17] Hence, if a new member joins an e-mail discussion list, he or she cannot access previous messages that were sent to the list.

> **LISTSERV:** a mailing list program that copies and distributes electronic mail to everyone subscribed to a particular e-mail discussion list.

> **LISTSERVER:** a computer on which a listserv program runs.

A discussion list requires nothing other than an Internet connection and e-mail software. You must join the list, however, before you can participate. To **subscribe,** you will have to send a message to the listserver telling it to add you to the list. You will most likely need to send a message that takes the following form:

SUBSCRIBE LISTNAME YOURFIRSTNAME YOURLASTNAME

In this example, the SUBSCRIBE command is followed by the name of the list you want to subscribe to, which is in turn followed by your name. Sometimes (depending on the list you are subscribing to) it is not necessary to type your name. By typing SUBSCRIBE you are giving the listserver a command to add you to the list. No punctuation is needed, and the command can generally be in lowercase or in capital letters.

When you send a command to the listserver, it is a good idea to delete your signature block (if one is automatically inserted into your e-mail messages), since the listserver will attempt to interpret the words it contains as commands. The listserver may respond by filling up your e-mail box with messages telling you that it doesn't understand what you are telling it to do.

The subscription process can vary widely from list to list. Joining some lists is accomplished simply by sending e-mail to the list moderator requesting list membership. The moderator will then issue the necessary commands to the listserver to add you to the list.

Keep in mind that two addresses are associated with any discussion list: (1) the address for the listserver, which is administrative and is used only for commands (such as SUBSCRIBE) and not for any messages that you may want to send to the entire list, and (2) the discussion list address, to which messages intended for list members are sent. The e-mail discussion list for criminal justice Webmasters, for example, has a listserver address of listserv@rol.org, while messages are sent to list members at cjhtml-l@rol.org.

When you join a list, the first message you receive will automatically be generated by the listserver. It will cover administrative details, such as list-serv commands for working with the list, and provide important information, such as the e-mail address that you will need to use to send messages to the discussion group. *Save this message.* If you ever want to leave the list (a process called **unsubscribing**), you will have to refer to it in order to know what command to use to sign off! If you don't know how to properly sign off of a list, you run the danger of receiving loads of unwanted e-mail for a very long time.

There are two types of lists: (1) announcement lists in which you receive messages but cannot post to the list and (2) discussion lists in which everyone on the list can participate in the discussion. Some lists are **closed**, accepting only members with certain credentials. The Police Discussion List, for example, is available only to active or retired law enforcement officers. Other lists are **moderated**, meaning that submitted messages are first read by the list moderator, who then decides whether they should be sent to the list or not. Moderators sometimes delete obscene messages and flames, keeping them from being passed along to list members.

Once you join a discussion group, you do not have to actively participate in it by sending messages or by replying to other **posts.** If you prefer, you can stay in the background, reading messages that are of interest to you and assuming the status of a **lurker** on the list. You may find, however, that the list is sending you 50 or 100 messages a day or more! If you join more than one list, you can be easily overwhelmed by the sheer quantity of mail you receive.

In order to better manage mail received from listservers, you may want to use **mail filter** features built into your e-mail software. Filter options allow you to create special folders for each discussion list to which you belong and then route incoming mail from a list into a folder that you specify. You can also consolidate all messages from each discussion list using the DIGEST command. The DIGEST command tells the listserver to send you only one message each day containing all of the list's postings for that day. If you want to learn more about listserv commands, visit the L-Soft site at http://www.lsoft.com/listserv.stm. L-Soft originated much of the software that runs today's listservers.

The next three sections provide a roster of criminology and criminal justice lists of both the announcement and discussion variety, followed by a catalog of discussion list resources. Included are instructions for joining.

Criminology and Criminal Justice Discussion Lists

AMNESTY INTERNATIONAL: To subscribe send e-mail to
listserv@suvm.syr.edu
In the body of the message type:
subscribe AMNESTY *yourfirstname yourlastname*

THE AUSTRALIAN CRIMINAL JUSTICE AND CRIMINOLOGY MAILING LIST:
To subscribe send e-mail to **listserv@sulaw.law.su.oz.au**
In the body of the message type:
subscribe CRIM-L *yourfirstname yourlastname*

CRIMINAL JUSTICE DISCUSSION LIST: To subscribe send e-mail to
listserv@cunyvm.cuny.edu
In the body of the message type:
subscribe CJUST-L *yourfirstname yourlastname*

CRITICAL DISCUSSION OF CRIME, SOCIETY, AND THE POLITICS OF PUNISH-MENT LIST: To subscribe send e-mail to **listproc@weber.ucsd.edu**
In the body of the message type:
subscribe CSPPLIST-L *yourfirstname yourlastname*

THE FIREARMS-POLITICS LIST: To subscribe send e-mail to **firearms-politics-request@tut.cis.ohio-state.edu**
In the body of the message type:
subscribe FIREARMS-POLITICS *yourfirstname yourlastname*

FORENSICS DISCUSSION LIST: To subscribe send e-mail to **FORENS-REQUEST@ACC.FAU.EDU**
In the body of the message type:
subscribe FORENS-L *yourfirstname yourlastname*

THE NATIONAL CRIME SURVEY (NCS) DISCUSSION LIST: To subscribe e-mail to **listserv@umdd.umd.edu**

In the body of the message type:
subscribe NCS-L *yourfirstname yourlastname*

THE POLICE DISCUSSION LIST (FOR SWORN POLICE OFFICERS): To subscribe
send e-mail to **listserv@cunyvm.cuny.edu**
In the body of the message type:
subscribe POLICE-L *yourfirstname yourlastname*

THE VICTIM ASSISTANCE LIST: To subscribe send e-mail to **listserv@
pdomain.uwindsor.ca**
In the body of the message type:
subscribe VICTIM-ASSISTANCE *yourfirstname yourlastname*

Criminology and Criminal Justice Announcement Lists

Some mailing lists simply send you information. They do not permit discussion among list members. They are called **announcement lists.** A number of criminal justice announcement lists provide very useful information. Primary among them are the following.

FARISLAW BULLETIN (INCLUDES INTERNATIONAL AND U.S. SUPREME COURT DECISIONS): **http://www.farislaw.com/lists.html** You can subscribe at the FARISLAW home page, or you can send e-mail to:

faris3-request@farislaw.com (for the HTML version)
faris5-request@farislaw.com (for the text version)

Include the word SUBSCRIBE in the body of your message.

JUSTINFO: THE NEWSLETTER OF THE NATIONAL CRIMINAL JUSTICE REFERENCE SERVICE: To subscribe send e-mail to **listproc@aspensys.com**
In the body of the message type:
subscribe JUSTINFO *yourfirstname yourlastname*

THE JUVENILE JUSTICE NEWSLETTER: To subscribe send e-mail to
listproc@aspensys.com
In the body of the message type:
subscribe JUVJUST *yourfirstname yourlastname*

LEGAL INFORMATION INSTITUTE E-MAIL BULLETINS:
http://www.law.cornell.edu/focus/bulletins.html

SUPREME COURT OPINIONS FROM THE LEGAL INFORMATION INSTITUTE:
To subscribe send e-mail to **listserv@lii.law.cornell.edu**

In the body of the message type:
subscribe LIIBULLETIN *yourfirstname yourlastname*

Discussion List Resources

A number of on-line resources can help you better understand how e-mail discussion lists work. Some sites are dedicated to helping you find the addresses of discussion groups that might be of interest to you. Still others provide listserver and discussion list catalogs and indexes. A list of such resources follows.

AMERICA ONLINE MAILING LISTS: **http://www.idot.aol.com/mld/ production** More than 2600 lists sorted alphabetically by category.

CATALOG.COM: **http://catalog.com/vivian/interest-group-search.html** A list of lists.

CYBER TEDDY: **http://www.webcom.com/teddy/listserv.html** An on-line guide to mailing list information and newsgroups.

E-MAIL DISCUSSION GROUPS: **http://www.nova.edu/ Inter-Links/listserv.html**

IFLA'S INTERNET MAILING LISTS GUIDES AND RESOURCES: **http://www .nlc-bnc.ca/ifla/I/training/listserv/lists.htm** A discussion of mailing lists and links to related resources.

INFORMUNDI: **http://ourworld.compuserve.com/homepages/ajra/mailingl.htm** A PowerPoint presentation for a quick course on mailing lists. Try it. It's worthwhile!

THE L-SOFT LIST: **http://www.lsoft.com/lists/listref.html** *The* catalog of LISTSERV lists!

LISZT: **http://www.liszt.com** Great for locating e-mail discussion lists and newsgroups. You can search by keyword. Over 50,000 topics are indexed here.

NEOSOFT.COM: **http://www.NeoSoft.com/internet/paml** Publicly accessible mailing lists.

REFERENCE.COM: **http://www.reference.com** A mailing list and newsgroup directory.

TILE.NET: **http://www.tile.net/tile/listserv** A reference source for Internet discussion groups.

NEWSGROUPS

Some people compare **newsgroups** to virtual coffee shops, where friends gather to discuss topics of mutual interest. Like e-mail discussion lists, newsgroups are electronic forums. A newsgroup differs from an e-mail discussion list, however, in that messages contributed to the group remain on the server, available for review by anyone—including those new to the group. Newsgroups cover an enormous array of subjects and provide a way to quickly meet and connect with people from all over the world who share your interests.

> **NEWSGROUPS:** electronic discussion forums consisting of collections of related postings (also called *articles*) on a particular topic that are posted to a news server, which then distributes them to other participating servers.[18]

Because our current system of Internet-based newsgroups grew out of a network called Usenet, newsgroups are often referred to as **Usenet newsgroups.** Newsgroups of today still reflect the original USENET framework.

It is not necessary to join a newsgroup in the same way that you join an e-mail discussion list. It is necessary, however, to have special newsreader software. Newsreader software comes bundled with most popular browser software, such as Navigator and Explorer. You can, if you wish, buy stand-alone newsreaders or download them from the Net.

Although newsgroups come and go, around 20,000 newsgroups exist on the Internet at any one time. The first time you log on to the Internet and start your newsreader software it will poll the news server operated by your Internet service provider in order to find out what newsgroups your ISP supports. Not every ISP supports all newsgroups, and it may be necessary to contact your ISP if you want to join an unsupported newsgroup.

Newsreader software requires you to choose which newsgroups you wish to **subscribe** to before it will display the messages those newsgroups contain. Subscribing consists merely of downloading a list of group-specific messages from your ISP's news server to your newsreader. Once you subscribe to a newsgroup and read some of the messages it contains, your newsreader software will remember what you've read. The *next* time you start up your newsreader it will check the groups to which you are subscribed and download the new messages that have been contributed since your last visit. If you join a lot of newsgroups, be prepared to wait a long time for the messages to be downloaded to your computer.

Before you subscribe to any newsgroup, however, it is a good idea to look for suitable groups by asking your newsreader software to search through all available newsgroups using search terms keyed to your interests. You might, for example, search for groups containing the words *crime* or *justice* in their titles. A search (in the spring of 1998) for newsgroups containing the word *crime* revealed the existence of the following newsgroups (not all of which were active at the time):

    alt.crime
    alt.crime.bail-enforce
    alt.true-crime
    asu.general.crime_stop
    clari.local.california.sfbay.crime
    clari.news.crime
    clari.news.crime.abductions
    clari.news.crime.abuse
    clari.news.crime.assaults
    clari.news.crime.fraud+embezzle
    clari.news.crime.general
    clari.news.crime.hate
    clari.news.crime.issue
    clari.news.crime.juvenile
    clari.news.crime.misc
    clari.news.crime.murders
    clari.news.crime.murders.misc
    clari.news.crime.murders.political
    clari.news.crime.organized
    clari.news.crime.sex
    clari.news.crime.theft
    clari.news.crime.top
    clari.news.crime.war
    clari.news.crime.white_collar
    clari.news.law.crime
    clari.news.law.crime.sex
    clari.news.law.crime.trial
    clari.news.law.crime.violent

You might also want to review the two-part article "List of Active Newsgroups," available at one of the following newsgroups:

    news.lists
    news.groups
    news.answers

You do not have to actively participate in a newsgroup discussion to read newsgroup messages. The messages are there for all to read—like pages in a book. If you want to contribute your own message, you can. Otherwise, as with e-mail discussion lists, you can be a lurker rather than a contributor.

'ZINES AND E-JOURNALS

A number of electronic journals (called **e-journals**) and electronic magazines (called **'zines**) are available on the Internet. An abbreviated list of the most interesting e-journals and 'zines in the criminology and criminal justice area follows.

ALL LAW (LAW JOURNALS ON-LINE):
http://www.AllLaw.com/Journals.html

ALABAMA LAW REVIEW: http://boots.law.ua.edu/lawreview

AMERICAN JOURNAL OF CRIMINAL JUSTICE:
http://www.louisville.edu/journal/ajcj

AMERICAN UNIVERSITY LAW REVIEW:
http://www.wcl.american.edu/pub/journals/lawrev/aulrhome.htm

CARDOZO ELECTRONIC LAW BULLETIN:
http://www.gelso.unitn.it/card-adm/Welcome.html

CORNELL LAW REVIEW: http://www.law.cornell.edu/clr

FLORIDA LAW WEEKLY: http://www.polaris.net/~flw/flw.htm

FLORIDA STATE LAW REVIEW:
http://www.law.fsu.edu/lawreview/index.html

INDIANA JOURNAL OF GLOBAL LEGAL STUDIES:
http://www.law.indiana.edu/glsj/glsj.html

INTERNATIONAL JOURNAL OF DRUG TESTING:
http://big.stpt.usf.edu/~journal

JOURNAL OF ONLINE LAW:
http://warthog.cc.wm.edu/law/publications/jol

LAW JOURNAL EXTRA: http://www.ljx.com

NATIONAL LAW JOURNAL: http://www.ljextra.com/nlj

STANFORD JOURNAL OF INTERNATIONAL LAW:
http://www-leland.stanford.edu/group/SJIL

UNIVERSITY OF COLORADO LAW REVIEW:
http://stripe.Colorado.EDU/~cololrev/Home.html

VILLANOVA LAW REVIEW:
http://vls.law.vill.edu/students/orgs/law-review

WASHBURN LAW JOURNAL: http://washburnlaw.edu/wlj

WASHINGTON LAW REVIEW: http://www.law.washington.edu/~wlr

WASHINGTON AND LEE LAW REVIEW: http://www.wlu.edu/~lawrev

WEB JOURNAL OF CURRENT LEGAL ISSUES:
http://www.ncl.ac.uk/~nlawwww A bimonthly electronic journal
published by Blackstone Press, Ltd., in the United Kingdom, focus-
ing on current legal issues, including judicial decisions, law reform,
legislation, legal research, policy-related socio-legal research, legal
information, and information technology and practice.

WORLDWIDE CRIMINOLOGY JOURNAL: Subscribe by sending e-mail to
Signe Bengtsson, the journal's originator at: **stockholms.institute.of**
.criminology@stockholms-kriminologiska-institut.se

 USING THE WEB

Join at least one of the e-mail discussion lists described in this chapter, and
subscribe to at least one of the newsgroups. Then do the following:

1. Read the messages being posted to both the discussion list and the
   newsgroup. What topics are being discussed? Are the discussions
   focused? Could they be better focused? How?

2. If you were to begin your own discussion list or newsgroup, what
   would it be about? What rules might you set for discussants to be
   sure that they stick to the theme of the list/group? How would you
   enforce those rules?

CHAPTER VI

SEARCH ENGINES AND WEB MAPS

I have found that a great part of the information I have was acquired by looking for something and finding something else on the way.

—*Franklin P. Adams*

Men don't stop to ask for directions on the Information Superhighway either!

—*Anonymous*

CHAPTER OUTLINE

INTRODUCTION

The Web is a huge place. With nearly 100 million Web pages residing on servers all over the world, and with millions more being added every year, it can be extremely difficult to find what you're looking for. Imagine the Library of Congress after an earthquake, when all the books have fallen off the shelves and the power has gone out. What chance would you have of finding a particular book if you were rummaging around through the tumbled books at night? Even a flashlight wouldn't help much. In fact, under such circumstances, you could spend a lifetime searching through all of the books in the library and still might not find what you're looking for!

Fortunately for Web surfers, a number of search services, sometimes called *search engines*, have already done the job of categorizing most of the

Web's content—and they continue to index new pages almost as fast as they are added. Better yet, almost all of these services are free!

Search engines index Web pages using a number of strategies. Some, called *spiders* or *crawlers,* literally crawl across the Web and poll every site they find in order to determine that site's content. Others depend on human input (either from Web site designers, a staff of Web searchers, or both) to create directories of Web sites.

Technically speaking (although we don't want to get *too* technical), there are two main type of search facilities available on the web: **search engines** and **directories.** True search engines create their listings automatically, by crawling through the Web and indexing what they find. Directories depend on human input for the data they contain. Some search sites, of course, are hybridized—that is, they use both strategies in developing their content. For our purposes we will not distinguish between true search engines and directories, although you should be aware that the difference exists.

This chapter contains a list of most major search sites, along with another list of sites that are essentially lists of lists. We call the latter *maps* of the Web, although they are not necessarily available in the form of image maps, which we discussed earlier. Before you can use a search engine, however, it is best that you know some rules about how they work.

SEARCH ENGINE: site-specific software and hardware that create indexes of Internet sites based on the titles of files, keywords, or the full text of files. Also, a tool for searching for information on the Internet by topic.

It is very important to remember that individual search engines have their own rules about how you should enter the information you are looking for. Most such engines are built around Boolean logic. **Boolean logic** was created by the English mathematician, George Boole, who developed a kind of algebra of logic. Boolean logic has become the basis for most computer database searches. It uses words called *operators* to determine whether a statement is true or false. Common Boolean operators are AND, OR, and NOT. Proper use of these three words can make your search far more fruitful than it might otherwise be. They can also save you an enormous amount of frustration when trying to find what you want.

If, for example, you want to learn more about crime rates in the United States, you might search for the term *crime* on the Web using a popular search engine. Doing so, however, will probably return thousands of hits. Another way to submit your search would be to type *crime* AND *rates* into the search field. Using the operator AND means that the search engine you are using will return the names and locations of documents containing both of the words *crime* and *rates*. If you were to type in *crime* OR *rates*, however, you would be inundated with a plethora of hits containing *either* the word *crime* or the word *rates*. You can also use the operator NOT as follows: *crime* NOT *England*. You will still receive many documents containing the word *crime*, but none that contain the word *England*. The NOT operator allows you to restrict your search.

Keep in mind that search sites differ, and that this general guide to using search engines may not apply to all sites. Some sites, for example, use the minus sign (–) instead of NOT, and some use the plus sign (+) in place of AND.

Many search sites allow you to search using a phrase. Some (but not all) require that you enclose the phrase in quotation marks. Hence, searching for the phrase "crime in the United States" might give you a better chance of finding the information you are looking for than looking for just *crime* AND *rates*. Of course, you might also want to search again using the phrase "crime in the U.S." since that is how the phrase might appear on a number of sites containing the data you seek.

Once the search site has returned a list of hits, you can click on the document that interests you the most. You can always use the "back" button on your browser to return to the results list provided by the search engine.

Some search facilities are topic-specific and limit searches to documents and information contained on that particular site. The interfaces used by such search facilities are generally far simpler than those that you will see when you visit major search engines. Even so, the principles that apply to site-specific searches are usually much the same as those that apply to searches of the entire Web. The NCJRS document database search page is shown, by way of example, in Figure 6-1.

As mentioned previously, sites differ as to how they expect you to phrase your search. It is best to check with the search site to see what they require. Here, for example, is what the Justice Information Center has to say about conducting a search on the NCJRS Abstracts Data Base:

About this Data Base

The National Criminal Justice Reference Service Abstracts Data Base contains summaries of more than 140,000 publications on criminal justice, including Federal, state, and local government reports, books, research reports, journal articles, and unpublished research. Subject areas include corrections, courts, drugs and crime, law enforcement, juvenile justice, crime statistics, and victims of crime. The time period covered is from the early 1970's to the present. The Data Base is also available on CD-ROM and as a file on the DIALOG service.

Search the NCJRS Abstracts Database

The National Criminal Justice Reference Service Abstracts Database contains summaries of more than 140,000 criminal justice publications, including Federal, State, and local government reports, books, research reports, journal articles, and unpublished research. Click here for more information about this Data Base.

Do a Global Search to search all parts of the data base, or choose one of the other options:

- ⦿ Global Search help
- ⦾ Subject Search (searches title, short summary, and subject terms) help
- ⦾ Author Search (searches author and corporate author) help
- ⦾ NCJ Number Search help

If you would like to select publications issued between two dates,

enter start date using the YY format: ☐

and enter end date using the YY format: ☐

To search, type the word or words that describe your topic into the box and click on Submit.
You may use and, or and not to combine words or phrases.

[Submit] [Clear]

OR click on one of these topics for searches already performed by NCJRS:

Corrections	Law Enforcement
Drugs and Crime	Statistics
Juvenile Justice	Victims

See Obtaining documents found in this Data Base for more information.

This Data Base is under development. Please sign the Guest Book.

FIGURE 6-1

The NCJRS Abstracts database search page: http://www.ncjrs.org/cgi/database/ncjpubs.cgi.

The Abstracts Data Base is produced by NCJRS, a service of the National Institute of Justice, with the Office of Juvenile Justice and Delinquency Prevention, Office for Victims of Crime, Bureau of Justice Statistics, and Bureau of Justice Assistance, all part of the Office of Justice Programs, U.S. Department of Justice, and the Office of National Drug Control Policy.

Hints on Searching

To search, simply type the word or words that describe your topic into the open search box. Then click on the submit button.

- Combining Terms

You can combine your search words with AND, OR, and NOT as well as parentheses (). For example, if you are searching for information on HIV/AIDS in correctional facilities, you could type:

(AIDS or HIV) AND (prison or jail or correctional)

Do not enclose your search terms in "quotes" unless quotes are a part of the expression for which you are searching. Examples:

community policing and california

criminal law review

- "Wildcard" searching or "truncating"

To search on a word root with a variety of endings, use the $. For example, correction$ will find the words correction, corrections, or correctional. Also use the $ to allow for plurals: for example, type juvenile$ to find the words juvenile or juveniles.

- If You Find Too Much

Instead of using the Global search function, use the Search only by titles, short summaries, and subject terms option.
Limit your search by date.
Make your wording more specific. Remember that all of the publications in this Data Base deal with criminal justice, so searching for words like crime or justice will bring back too much.
Add another term into the open search box. For example, instead of entering corrections AND treatment, type in corrections AND treatment AND mental health.

- If You Find Too Little

Remove one of the terms from your search. If you are using too many terms, you may be restricting your search too much.
Change one of the terms to a broader term. For example, replace juvenile gangs with gangs.
Try to think of synonyms or related words, and combine them with OR. For example:

death penalty OR capital punishment

(police or law enforcement) AND madison

(narcotics or drugs) and (adolescents or juveniles)

Look for misspellings in the terms you have entered.
Allow for plurals with the $. For example, prison$ will find prison or prisons (as well as prisoners, etc.).

Northern Light, on the other hand, one of the Web's newer search sites, uses a somewhat different set of search rules. Here's a few of the instructions you can find on the Northern Light help page on how to enter searches.[19]

Search Help

To increase the precision of your search results, Northern Light requires most of the words in your search to be present in the result documents. To gain more control over your results, please read through the rest of these hints.

Use many words in your search. The more words you give us, the more on target your results will be. Examples:

ski resorts Vermont rather than skiing

ergonomic workstation mouse keyboard rather than ergonomics

Use OR to retrieve documents that include any of the search words (rather than most), or use NOT to indicate a word that must not appear in the documents. (Please Note: Northern Light does not currently support full Boolean expressions, though we will in the future). Examples:

encryption OR cryptography

dolphins NOT NFL

Use QUOTES around specific phrases to focus your search on occurrences of the actual phrase. Examples:

recipes for "chocolate cake"

"General Dynamics"

A word of warning is in order about any information you get off of the Internet: It may not be reliable. Keep in mind that anyone can publish literally anything on the Net—and frequently they do. The reliability and authenticity of information posted on the Net is always in question. Unless the information is posted by a well-known source such as the Department of Justice or the National Criminal Justice Reference Service, it is best to either double-check the information before you use it or add a disclaimer to any material you produce that uses the information. If you are writing a term paper, for example, your instructor may ask that you use only sources on the Web known to be reliable and to note the source of all information you gather from the Web. We don't have the space to discuss Internet citations in detail. Some manuals are starting to list the proper format for Web citations. Generally, however, Web materials may be cited as follows:

The Justice Research Association, "Rules for Posting." Web posted at http://talkjustice.com/rules.htm. Accessed April 2, 1998.

Finally, you should keep in mind that Web search tools differ in a number of other ways. Some search only top-level domains, meaning that they don't look at Web pages in subdirectories. Others index every word on every page they can find (regardless of level). Still others attempt to index images, video, and audio files as well as text. It is best to familiarize yourself with the various search sites that are available and to learn something about the kinds of results they can be expected to return, along with their rules for entering search terms, before you decide which is right for you. If you would like to learn more about how search engines work, try this site:

HOW SEARCH ENGINES WORK:
http://searchenginewatch.internet.com/webmasters/work.html

If you are interested in how some of the major search sites compare, a few statistics are shown in Figure 6-2.[20]

WEB SEARCH ENGINES
All-in-One Search Engines

http://www.albany.net/allinone A variety of ways to search the Web.

ALTA VISTA: **http://www.altavista.digital.com** Digital Computer's high-speed search engine.

Search Engine	AltaVista	Excite	HotBot	InfoSeek	Lycos	Northern Light	Web Crawler
Size (pages in mills)	Big (100)	Big (55)	Big (80)	Medium (30)	Medium (30)	Big (30 to 50)	Small (2)
Pages crawled per day	10 million	3 million	Up to 10 million	—	6 to 10 million	—	—
Freshness	1 day to 3 months	1 to 3 weeks	1 day to 2 weeks	Minutes to 2 months	1 to 2 weeks	2 weeks	Updated weekly
Date	Yes	No	File Date	No	Yes (via detailed display)	File Date	No

FIGURE 6-2

A comparison of major search engines. Excerpted from Search Engine Watch, Search Engine Features Chart, http://searchenginewatch.com/features.htm, by Danny Sullivan, April 1998. Copyright © 1998 Mecklermedia Corporation, 20 Ketchum Street, Westport, CT 06880; http://www.internet.com. All rights reserved. Reprinted with permission.

ARGUS CLEARINGHOUSE: **http://www.clearinghouse.net** Good for searching broad subject areas.

CNET SEARCH ENGINES: **http://www.search.com** Lists almost all available search engines on the Web.

EXCITE!: **http://www.excite.com** Searches and site reviews. If you are using Windows 95, Windows 98, or Windows NT, Excite! provides free software for integration into your browser. The software, called Excite! Direct, adds an Excite! logo to your browser toolbar and allows you to search Excite! quickly and conveniently without having to visit excite.com first. You can download the free software by visiting http://www.excite.com/direct.

HOTBOT: **http://www.hotbot.com** A relatively new standard for Web search engines.

I FIND: **http://www.inference.com/ifind** An "intelligent massively fast parallel" Web searcher.

INFOSEEK: **http://www.infoseek.com** A solid searcher.

LISZT: **http://www.liszt.com** A good place to search for newsgroups.

LYCOS: **http://www.lycos.com** A venerable and reliable search site.

MAGELLAN: **http://www.mckinley.com** One of the first search sites.

NETFIND: **http://www.aol.com/netfind** A Net search service sponsored by America Online.

NORTHERN LIGHT: **http://www.nlsearch.com** A relatively new search service that uses "Custom Search Folders" and an integrated results list of Web and premium information.

OPEN TEXT: **http://pinstripe.opentext.com/search** A great, but little known, searcher.

SAVVY SEARCH: **http://www.cs.colostate.edu/~dreiling/smartform.html** A new parallel multiple search engine.

SHAREWARE SEARCH: **http://www.shareware.com/sw/search/quick** A shareware finder.

WEBCRAWLER: http://webcrawler.com

WEBSEEK: http://www.ctr.columbia.edu/webseek

YAHOO!: http://www.yahoo.com Searches, people finder, chat, and more.

ZAMBONI'S SEARCHERS: http://www.iglou.com/zamboni/search.html
A collection of search engines.

Site Lists and Web Maps

ATLAS OF THE WORLD WIDE WEB:
http://www.rhythm.com/~bpowell/Atlas/realAtlasHome.html

GATEWAY TO THE WORLD: http://www.netusa.com/weblist.htm
An international WWW resource.

HANDILINKS: http://ahandyguide.com

HOTSHEET: http://www.tstimpreso.com/hotsheet

LIBRARIAN'S INDEX TO THE INTERNET: http://sunsite.berkeley.edu/
InternetIndex

LINKMASTER: http://www.linkmaster.com

WHAT'S NEW TOO: http://newtoo.manifest.com/WhatsNewToo
A comprehensive list of new Web sites.

METASEARCHING

Metasearchers, also known as multisearchers or parallel search engines, poll many search engines with whatever search term or phrase you enter. If you use these combination search services you are said to be "conducting a metasearch," or **metasearching.** Metasearchers are a lot like huge search engines in that they help compile results from many different sources. Metasearchers organize their results into a uniform format, which they then display to you.

METASEARCHER: a search engine that searches many different search sites simultaneously.

A list of most metasearchers is available via one Web page, Dr. Webster's Big Page of Search Engines, which can be reached at http://www.123go

.com/drw/search/metasearch.htm. A second source for metasearchers is the Web Developer's Virtual Library at http://www.stars.com/Location/Meta/Searchers.html. Of course, you can also visit *Talk Justice* to view a page that contains an up-to-date list of metasearchers. A site that allows you to metasearch the metasearchers is MetaPleth by SpaceSearch Lite. You can reach MetaPleth at http://www.ee.surrey.ac.uk/Personal/L.Wood/spacesearch/metapleth.

METASEARCHERS

Here's a list of metasearchers that you should find useful.

CYBER411 PARALLEL SEARCH ENGINE:
http://helios.unive.it/~franz/cyber.html Cyber411 sends your query to 15 different search engines simultaneously.

DOGPILE: http://www.dogpile.com A respected metasearcher with an unusual name.

HIGHWAY 61: http://www.highway61.com Submits your query to the six largest search engines simultaneously.

INFERENCE FIND: http://www.inference.com/ifind A great meta-searching tool that queries the major search engines, merges the results, removes redundancies, and gathers the hits into groups of links based on your request.

MAMMA: http://www.mamma.com A smart parallel search engine.

MEGAWEB: http://stoat.shef.ac.uk:8080/megaweb Allows you to choose from specific categories of search tools. A multilingual inter-face is available.

METACRAWLER: http://www.metacrawler.com MetaCrawler sends your queries to many different search engines, including Alta Vista, Excite!, InfoSeek, Lycos, WebCrawler, and Yahoo.

METAFIND: http://search.metafind.com Organizes results in an easy-to-use manner.

THE MOTHER LOAD (TML): http://www.cosmix.com/motherload
TML offers three search modes:

THE INSANE SEARCH: http://www.cosmix.com/motherload/insane
This is the most thorough metasearch mode available at TML.

THE WEB SEARCH: http://www.cosmix.com/motherload/#websearch
A simplified metasearch.

THE MOTHER LOAD SEARCH:
http://www.cosmix.com/motherload/#mlsearch A local directory
search of Mother Load–indexed items.

SAVVYSEARCH: http://www.cs.colostate.edu/~dreiling/smartform.html
SavvySearch allows you to conduct searches in a wide variety of languages, including English, French, German, Italian, Portuguese,
Spanish, Dutch, Norwegian, Korean, Russian, Esperanto, Swedish,
and Danish.

SEARCH ONRAMP: http://search.onramp.net Ranks and scores the results of a simultaneous search of many engines.

STARTING POINT: http://www.stpt.com

A number of proprietary software tools are available today that can perform metasearches, but with more personal precision than you can specify
in Web-based metasearches. Programs like Quarterdeck's Web Compass®
and Blue Sky's Web Seeker® turn your computer into a personal metasearcher. They also give you the ability to browse the results returned by
your search, even allowing you to save metasearch results on your computer as HTML files for later use. These software tools can also be set to
routinely go out and automatically search and update your disk-based
index, working transparently in the background while you use your computer for other things.

It is, however, not necessary to purchase software to conduct effective
searches. Most likely, a simple but effective way to search the Web already
exists right on your desktop. That's because most of today's major
browsers have a search feature built in. The feature is usually displayed
right on the browser's toolbar. Both Explorer and Navigator label the feature plainly enough, calling it "search." Navigator symbolizes the search
function with a flashlight, while Explorer uses a globe. Although such
built-in search features do not have the full functionality of metabrowsers,
they do provide you with easy access to most of the major search engines.
Click the "search" button on your browser and you will see what we mean!

USING THE WEB

Visit three of the search sites and three of the metasearch engines listed in this chapter. At each site, search for a topic of special interest, such as "international criminal justice," "community policing," or the "classical school of criminology." Then answer these questions:

1. What did you learn about phrasing your searches? Is it best to search for a single word, to combine words with AND, or to use a search phrase?

2. If you want to use a phrase, how does each site require you to enter it? What are the differences between each of the sites in this regard?

3. Did you find that metasearch engines worked better than stand-alone search sites? On what do you base your answer?

Chapter VII

Netiquette and Web Manners

Technology is driving the future; the steering is up to us.
—*Computer Professionals for Social Responsibility*[21]

When thou enter a city abide by its customs.
—*The Talmud*

CHAPTER OUTLINE

- Introduction
- What Is Netiquette?
    E-Mail
    Mailing Lists and Newsgroups
    Internet Relay Chat (IRC)
- Netiquette Resources
- Using the Web

INTRODUCTION

The early days of the personal computer brought with them efforts by a number of concerned groups to educate computer owners in how to use their machines ethically and with a sense of social responsibility. The Computer Ethics Institute,[22] for example, issued its "Ten Commandments for Computer Ethics" a number of years ago. The commandments[23] are reproduced in Figure 7-1.

The advent of the Internet has made ethical issues associated with the use of computers far more important today than they were in the early days of personal computing. That is because the Net is largely an ungoverned entity—making the need for self-control and an awareness of social responsibility a crucial issue among Net surfers. Today's Net citizens and Web site builders have a great deal of freedom as to what they can post

THE TEN COMMANDMENTS FOR COMPUTER ETHICS

by the Computer Ethics Institute

1. Thou shalt not use a computer to harm other people.
2. Thou shalt not interfere with other people's computer work.
3. Thou shalt not snoop around in other people's files.
4. Thou shalt not use a computer to steal.
5. Thou shalt not use a computer to bear false witness.
6. Thou shalt not use or copy software for which you have not paid.
7. Thou shalt not use other people's computer resources without authorization.
8. Thou shalt not appropriate other people's intellectual output.
9. Thou shalt think about the social consequences of the program you write.
10. Thou shalt use a computer in ways that show consideration and respect.

FIGURE 7-1

Source: Computer Ethics Institute: http://cpsr.org/dox/cei.html.

on the Web, what kinds of e-mail messages they can send, what kind of Web sites they build, and the content they choose to contribute to news-groups.

Today's ethical questions take many forms: (1) What's the purpose of the Internet and the Web? What should they be used for? (2) Should there be limits on how they are used? Should anybody be able to use the Net for anything they choose—so long as it is not blatantly criminal in purpose? (3) What is proper conduct for individual members of the on-line commu-nity? (4) How can informal standards be established and communicated? (5) How can they be enforced? Should they be? (6) How much influence should the government have over Web content and personal on-line com-munications?

A serious ethical problem facing today's Net citizens, for example, is the huge amount of junk e-mail making its way into e-mail boxes everywhere. It is not unusual for anyone with an e-mail address to constantly receive numerous e-mail messages advertising get-rich schemes and a huge array of products that almost no one wants. Junk e-mail is not yet against the law (although legislation is being drafted in various jurisdictions to control e-mail abuses). Some people receive hundreds of junk e-mail messages a day as a result of their e-mail address having ended up on some mass-mailing list used by **spammers.** Spammers are people who sell mailing lists to one another, and if you end up on one spammer's list, you can sure that you will soon be on many others. If that happens, the amount of junk e-mail you receive can grow to astronomical proportions—causing legitimate e-mail to get lost in the flood of messages received.

SPAMMERS: unscrupulous individuals and companies who clutter the Net with unsolicited junk e-mail.

To address the problem, most e-mail software allows you to set filters, rejecting messages with certain keywords or key phrases in their subject lines (e.g., "get rich quick") or mail coming from certain addresses. Of course, spammers are smart enough to regularly change their e-mail addresses and to use a wide variety of catchy phrases in the subject lines of their messages, making it difficult to filter out all unwanted mail. If you are unable to end or significantly reduce the amount of **spam** you receive, you may find it necessary to change e-mail accounts. If you set too many filters in your e-mail program, you may successfully limit spam—but may end up filtering out much legitimate mail as well!

SPAM: junk e-mail indiscriminately sent to a lot of people. The process of sending such messages is called *spamming*.

Many other potential ethical and interpersonal problems permeate the Net. Sex sites, offering total nudity, live sex acts via computer, and perverted sexual antics, abound. Some people say that there are more sex sites on the Web than any other category of site, and such sites are reputed to be the biggest moneymakers on the Web. Whether or not triple-X content should be available on the Web and whether it should be available to all those (even children) who surf the Web is an important issue that is receiving much attention today. The Communications Decency Act, passed by Congress a few years ago in an effort to control such sites, was largely overturned by the U.S. Supreme Court in 1997. Other efforts are now under way in Congress to establish a rating system for all Web sites. Sites would be required to display their assigned ratings prominently on their home pages. Browsers could then read a site's rating and could be set by concerned parents, employers, and others to prevent access to certain types of sites.

Another area—that of interpersonal communications—provides an especially difficult challenge from an ethical standpoint. Some people misrepresent themselves during e-mail communications. They may claim, for example, to be female when they are actually male (and vice versa). Others may claim to be looking for love even though they are married. A few people offer sexual services for sale, and still others attempt to gain sympathy in order to receive money and donations. Some send bogus e-mail designed to have recipients relinquish their charge-card numbers or bank account information. They then sell this information to criminals who use the acquired charge-card numbers to make fraudulent purchases. Quite a few unethical Net citizens run scams, selling nonexistent products in bogus schemes to get money. Just about any kind of illegal scam you can think of that has been perpetrated among people in the physical world can be found in cyberspace today.

By far the most common problem on the Net today is the relatively uninhibited flow of hostile and/or obscene interpersonal communications. People in discussion groups are especially likely to receive abusive messages when they post opinions that may be unpopular with others. E-mail messages that berate other people, often with obscene terminology, are called **flames,** and the process of sending such messages is called **flaming.**

> **FLAMES:** abusive, obscene, and distasteful messages generally directed at a particular individual. The process of sending such messages is called *flaming.*

Anyone interested in exploring computer ethics in more detail can visit the computer ethics site of Tom Engel, M.D., at Yale University School of Medicine: http://gasnet.med.yale.edu/software/EthicsDescription.html. Dr. Engel has developed computer ethics software (called "Computer Ethics Questions") in the form of a tutorial capable of running on both Macintosh and Windows platforms. You can download the free software from his site or from the *Talk Justice* Cybrary. Dr. Engel gives permission to users to modify the question bank to fit their needs, although modification of the software itself is prohibited. Engel's software, which is oriented toward the medical field, contains the following scenarios:

- Has computer software ever killed anyone?
- Is personal electronic mail private?
- Is electronic mail anonymous?
- Is electronic mail identified by institution?
- Is it appropriate to use strong language in computer discussion?
- Is it appropriate to encrypt electronic mail or other files?
- Is it appropriate to explore a computer network?
- Is it appropriate to use someone else's computer password?

- Is it easy to select good computer passwords?

- Is it appropriate to read someone else's computer files without permission?

- Is it appropriate to read grades or salaries or other personal information on computers?

- Is it appropriate to circumvent computer security arrangements?

- Is it appropriate to call up records for a patient other than your own?

- Is it appropriate to access pornography on a network?

- Is it appropriate to copy computer programs or other files?

- Is the Internet free?

- Are ethical issues involving computers different from other ethical situations?

WHAT IS NETIQUETTE?

Not all of the Net's problems can be solved overnight. Nonetheless, there is much that you, as an individual, can do *now* to improve the Net. By following a few simple rules of **netiquette,** you can make the Net a much better place for yourself and others. The term *netiquette* refers to a set of rules for behaving properly on-line, and most netiquette is concerned with on-line communications. Figure 7-2 displays what Virginia Shea, a prolific writer in the area of netiquette, calls the "core rules of netiquette."

NETIQUETTE: network etiquette, the dos and don'ts of on-line communication.[24] Also, the etiquette of cyberspace.

Shea says that all 10 rules essentially boil down to one: *Remember the human.* By that she means that we must always remember that when we are on-line we are not interacting merely with impersonal computers or with an impersonal network. At the other end of our e-mail messages or discussion group contributions, says Shea, there are always other human beings. We cannot treat those human being as though they are machines without feelings. In other words, if we are to be ethical actors in cyberspace, we cannot confuse the impersonal medium of the Internet with the people who populate it.

Remember the human is a good rule. It is easy to be offensive on-line, however, without meaning to be. That is because cyberspace, like anyplace else with a unique culture, has its own set of rules and standards. Violate them and you will be considered rude or offensive.

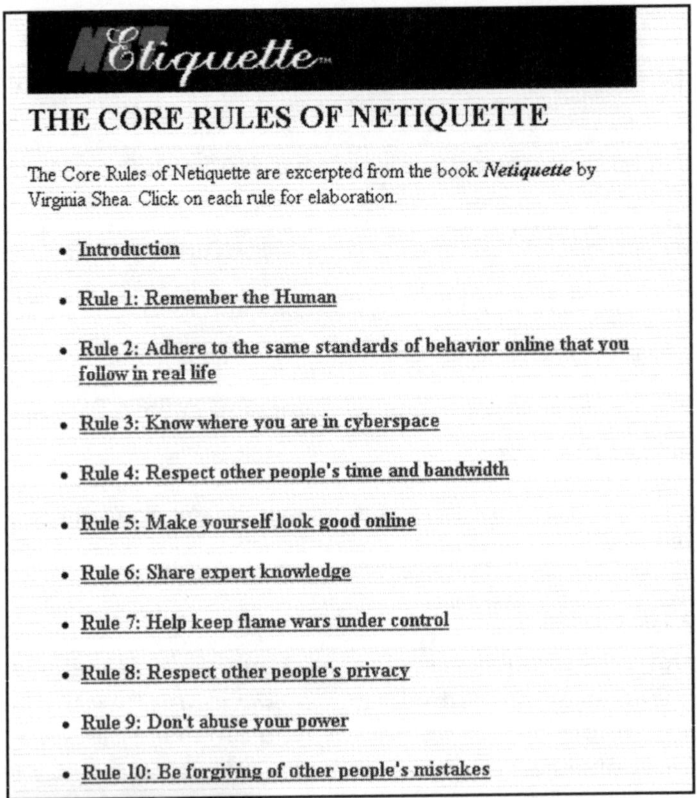

Netiquette™

THE CORE RULES OF NETIQUETTE

The Core Rules of Netiquette are excerpted from the book *Netiquette* by Virginia Shea. Click on each rule for elaboration.

- Introduction

- Rule 1: Remember the Human

- Rule 2: Adhere to the same standards of behavior online that you follow in real life

- Rule 3: Know where you are in cyberspace

- Rule 4: Respect other people's time and bandwidth

- Rule 5: Make yourself look good online

- Rule 6: Share expert knowledge

- Rule 7: Help keep flame wars under control

- Rule 8: Respect other people's privacy

- Rule 9: Don't abuse your power

- Rule 10: Be forgiving of other people's mistakes

FIGURE 7-2

The core rules of netiquette. Web posted at http://www.albion .com/netiquette/corerules.html. Source: Screenshot courtesy of Albion.com. See http://www.albion.com/netiquette/index.html for more Netiquette information.

What follows is a short summary of netiquette guidelines. This summary has been adapted from RFC 1855, a working document posted on the Web by personnel at Intel Corporation to stimulate thought about ethical behavior on the Net. The guidelines printed here deal with three areas of Net use: (1) e-mail communications, (2) mailing lists and newsgroups, and (3) other interactive services such as Internet Relay Chat. You can find the full 20-page text of RFC 1855 in the *Talk Justice* Cybrary. The recommendations that follow are not rules, but are meant only to advise you on how to conduct yourself on the Net.

E-Mail

If your Internet access is through a corporate account, check with your employer about his or her policy regarding private e-mail.

Don't assume any Internet communication is completely secure. Never include in an e-mail message anything you would not put on a postcard.

Independently verify any suspect mail you receive—especially if it contains important content—as e-mail return addresses can easily be forged.

If you are forwarding or reposting a message, don't change the original wording.

Remember that it is considered very impolite to forward someone's e-mail message to another person without the author's permission.

When responding to a previous post, include the relevant parts of the original message. That way it will be clear what you are responding to.

If you are replying to a message, quote only the relevant parts—not the entire message (especially if it is a very lengthy message you are responding to).

Do not send chain letters, especially those involving moneymaking pyramid schemes. They are highly frowned upon by Internet culture and can make you look like a fool.

Do not send abusive or heated messages (flames) or obscenity over the Internet.

Don't send flame bait. That is, don't send messages that are sure to offend people you are communicating with.

If you receive a flame, it is best to ignore it.

Be careful about using sarcasm or irony. Readers can't see your facial expressions or hear your tone of voice. Statements that you intend as jokes can be taken seriously.

Remember that no one can hear your tone of voice. Use **emoticons** to express what you are feeling. Signal jokes by using a smiley such as :-). However, do *not* overuse emoticons.

Use only e-mail abbreviations that you are sure of, or you may have readers ROTFL (rolling on the floor laughing).

Take care with addressing mail. Carefully read the "To:" and "Cc:" lines in your message before you send it. You can easily send mail to unintended recipients if you are not careful. *That* can be embarrassing.

Allow time for mail to be received and replied to before sending a follow-up message. Keep in mind that mail messages do not necessarily move as fast as spoken words on the telephone and that people's work schedules and time differences around the world can result in delays.

Don't make your mail too long, unless the recipient is expecting a verbose message or unless a long message is truly necessary given the subject matter. Under normal circumstances an e-mail message longer than 100 lines of text is too long.

If you use a signature file, keep it short. Four to six lines is usually enough. Elaborate signatures with multiple addresses, lengthy quotations, and/or ASCII artwork just take up space in your recipients' mailboxes.

Remember, the Internet is a global community, and other people's values and outlook on life may be different from your own. Be tolerant in what you say and in how you respond to what others say.

Be careful with slang or phrases that may offend or that may not be understood in another region or country.

Use mixed-case letters when you type. UPPERCASE LOOKS AS IF YOU ARE SHOUTING and is generally considered offensive.

Use asterisks (*) before and after a word to give it emphasis.

Always include a subject header in your mail messages in order to let recipients know what the message is about before they read it.

If you have more than one topic to write about, send separate messages.

Spelling mistakes are distracting. Most e-mail software programs today have built-in spell checkers. Use the one in your program before posting your message.

Proofread. Grammatical problems are equally annoying.

Remember that unsolicited e-mail, especially if it contains advertising, is generally unwelcome (and is lawfully forbidden in some countries).

Know how your mail program works. Some mail and news editors, for example, only *appear* to insert line breaks—but actually don't. Your message recipients might see every paragraph as one immense line that scrolls far off their screens. You can learn what your mail and news editors do by sending a message to yourself (or by posting it to the newsgroup alt.test) and then reading the message in a couple of newsreaders.

When attaching files to your e-mail messages, try to keep them reasonably sized. You should consider using a compression program (like PKZIP) to reduce the size of files before sending them.

Mailing Lists and Newsgroups

Remember that messages posted to mailing lists and newsgroups are read by a large number of people.

Before joining a newsgroup or mailing list, you may want to be a **lurker.** That is, you might read what others in the list or group are saying in order to get a feel for the nature of the group before jumping in.

If posting to newsgroups, be aware that many are archived, and the archives are available for a very long time. Don't say anything that might come back to haunt you years down the road. It is generally not possible to retrieve messages once they have been sent.

Be very careful about advertising. Most groups look highly askance at anyone who posts advertisements to their group.

Do not make statements that can be interpreted as official positions of your organization or offers to do business.

Read FAQs (Frequently Asked Questions), if they are available, before posting a question to the group.

Keep your messages concise, and make them relevant to the group and to the topics being discussed by the group.

Don't post messages to inappropriate newsgroups.

Don't get involved in or respond to flame wars.

If you find a newsgroup or a topic offensive, avoid it or leave the group.

Keep private messages private. Don't post them to the group; send them instead to the person's private e-mail address.

Don't betray confidences. It's all too easy to quote a personal message by mistake in a message to the entire group.

Internet Relay Chat (IRC)

Internet Relay Chat (IRC) allows participants to enter into live, real-time conversations with other Internet users. Participants generally join a **channel** or a **chat room** centered on a shared topic of interest. The *Talk Justice* site, for example, makes real-time chat available to anyone with an interest in criminal and social justice.

Netiquette surrounding participation in **IRC** demands that you behave appropriately:

- Respect the standards of the group you are talking to. It is generally a good idea to listen to a channel before participating in order to get a feel for the ground rules. After only a few minutes of listening, you should have an idea of what is and is not acceptable.

- Remember, the world is a big place full of very different people. If you find subject matter that offends you, then don't join that chat channel.

- Leave a channel that becomes offensive to you after you joined. Sometimes the course of a discussion changes, new people enter a chat area, or the purpose of the channel changes. All these can have an adverse affect on how comfortable you feel in the chat channel.

- Understand that unacceptable behavior on your part may get you banned from a channel or from the chat area.

NETIQUETTE RESOURCES

Some interesting netiquette sites can be found at the following addresses.

ALBION.COM: http://www.albion.com/netiquette/index.html Albion's highly recommended Netiquette Home Page contains the following information: (1) links to both summary and detailed information about netiquette; (2) netiquette basics; (3) an overview of network etiquette excerpted from the book *Netiquette* by Virginia Shea (Shea has been called "the Ms. Manners of the Internet"); (4) a netiquette quiz designed to test your etiquette knowledge (requires a Java-compatible browser); (5) a netiquette table of contents with links to a wealth of netiquette information; and (6) a netiquette catalog page where you can order Virginia Shea's Net classic *Netiquette*. Albion also supports the "Netiquette Mailing List." In order to join the list, send e-mail to netiquette-request@albion.com with the words "subscribe YourFirstName YourLastName" as the *subject* of the message.

ARLENE H. RINALDI NETIQUETTE HOME PAGE:
http://www.fau.edu/~rinaldi/netiquette.html Rinaldi is a professor at Florida Atlantic University.

EMILY POSTNEWS: http://www.clari.net/brad/emily.html Some well-considered ideas on how to behave on the Net.

NETIQUETTE IN BRIEF:
http://www.wiu.edu/users/mfbhl/wiu/netiquette.htm A summary of netiquette principles.

THE NETIQUETTE QUIZ:
http://www.albion.com/netiquette/netiquiz.html If your browser supports Java, you can test your netiquette knowledge at this site.

Books available on the subject of netiquette include the following.

Tracey LaQuey, *The Internet Companion* (Reading, MA: Addison-Wesley Publishing Company, 1994).

David Angel and Brent Heslop, *The Elements of E-mail Style* (Reading, MA: Addison-Wesley Publishing Company, 1994).

 USING THE WEB

In this chapter we were able to spend only a brief amount of time discussing netiquette. In order to gain a more complete knowledge of the subject, you should visit three of the five netiquette resource sites described in this chapter. Then answer the following questions:

1. What significant areas of netiquette information were excluded from this chapter (but found at the sites)? Describe each area in some detail.

2. Do you disagree with any of the principles of netiquette listed on any of these sites? If so, why? With which do you most agree? Why?

3. Are there any forms of netiquette that you feel have not been addressed by this guide and the sites you visited? If so, what are they?

CHAPTER VIII

CRIMINAL JUSTICE CAREERS ON-LINE

Work is life, you know, and without it, there's nothing but fear and insecurity.
—*John Lennon (1940–80), British rock musician*[25]

Work expands so as to fill the time available for its completion.
—*Parkinson's Law*[26]

CHAPTER OUTLINE

- Finding Employment On-Line
- General Listings
- Government Jobs
    State Job Listings
    Membership Sites
- General Employment Services on the Web
- Career Advice and Resume Posting Services
- Using the Web

FINDING EMPLOYMENT ON-LINE

Not long ago, finding a job took a lot of legwork. Job seekers had to read newspapers, subscribe to special employment services, and sometimes travel considerable distances to investigate local job markets. While applying for a job today is still one of the most daunting experiences facing recent college graduates, the process has been made a lot easier by on-line job banks and electronic employment services.

Some sites, such as Government Jobs.Com, are designed to make your job search efficient. No fees are charged to search the site. Job openings are posted primarily by government agencies, including those at federal, state, and local levels. Job search firms and advertising agencies also advertise vacant positions on the service. Although employers must pay a fee to advertise, potential employees can search all job vacancies for free.[27]

Each Government Jobs.Com Web listing includes the position title, a description of the position, job requirements (education, special skills, etc.), duties/responsibilities, salary if given, closing date, name of agency, and any other information pertinent to the position. In addition to job listings, Government Jobs.Com provides job resource information by state, including job-line phone numbers, city and county leagues and associations, statewide newspapers, and so forth. It also includes links to municipal and county government Web sites.

The federal government maintains a number of job-listing services on the Web and uses such sites as recruitment tools. One of the most popular is FedWorld (you can reach the jobs page at http://www.fedworld.gov/jobs/jobsearch.html). If you visit FedWorld you can also click on a selection that reads "Sign up to get FedWorld Vacancy Announcements via Email." Fill out the form that appears, send it to the FedWorld server, and you will quickly find job announcements appearing in your e-mail box. FedWorld also makes available some shareware software packages containing federal job application forms OF612 and SF171, which many folks use to apply for federal jobs.

A number of individual criminal justice agencies also post job requirements on the Web. The FBI special agent information page, for example, reads as follows:

Entry Requirements

To qualify for training as an FBI Agent, a candidate must:

1. be a U.S. citizen;
2. be between the ages of 23 and 37 when entering on duty;
3. hold a bachelor's degree obtained in an accredited four-year resident program at a college or university; and
4. have three years full-time work experience (law school graduates, graduates with a degree in accounting or a fluency in a foreign language for which the Bureau has a need may not need the three years work experience).

All newly appointed Special Agents must complete 15 weeks of intensive training at the FBI Academy in Quantico, Virginia. Classroom hours are spent by studying a variety of academic and investigative subjects accompanied by fitness, defensive tactics, and firearms training. Emphasis is placed on developing investigative techniques, as well as skills in interviewing, interrogation, and gathering intelligence information.

After graduation from the FBI Academy, a new Special Agent is assigned to an FBI field office. This assignment is determined by the individual's special skills and the needs of the Bureau. As part of their duties, Special Agents are required to relocate during their careers.

Salary and Career Paths—Special Agents

Special Agents enter service in Grade GS 10 on the federal government's General Schedule pay scale and can advance to Grade GS 13 in field assignments. Promotions to supervisory, management, and executive positions are available in Grades GS 14 and GS 15, as well as in the Senior Executive Service. All Special Agents may qualify for overtime compensation.

Finally, some agencies are now posting job application forms directly on the Web. You can complete these forms on-line, click the "submit" button at the end of the form, and apply for a job without ever leaving your chair in front of your computer. Figure 8-1, for example, shows an on-line application form for employment as a U.S. Border Patrol agent. You can find the form at http://www.usajobs.opm.gov/BPA1.HTM.

GENERAL LISTINGS

General job-listing services frequently provide up-to-date information on positions that are available *now*. They are a lot like "help wanted" sections in newspapers or trade journals. These sites, however, do not necessarily provide other services to the job seeker beyond simple lists.

CORRECTIONS JOBS: **http://www.corrections.com/jobs** The Corrections Connection job-listing service.

PUBLIC SAFETY RECRUITMENT: **http://www.psrjobs.com/lawrecru.htm** Established in 1993 to help you reach your law enforcement career goals, PSR provides information from thousands of paid law enforcement agencies from across the nation.

POLICE JOBS: **http://www.tap.net/~hyslo/poljobs.htm** Extensive list of police employment sites.

GOVERNMENT JOBS

Anyone seeking a career in state or federal government would be well advised to check out the following government jobs listing services.

FBI PERSONNEL AND EMPLOYMENT PAGE: **http://www.fbi.gov/over/ personel.htm** Information on hiring, recruitment, salaries, and

Border Patrol Agent On-Line Application

Welcome. You have reached the U.S. Government's World Wide Web application processing system. We are now accepting applications for Border Patrol Agent positions with the United States Immigration and Naturalization Service.

The vacancies to be filled are General Schedule grades 5 and 7. You will be presented with a series of questions that must be answered. Some questions will require a simple Yes or No response, while others may require you to select from a list of options, or require you to type information using the keyboard.

Please enter your 3-digit extension number now. If you do not know the extension number, please enter 999.

We are interested in knowing how you heard about this recruitment announcement for Border Patrol Agent positions. Indicate only one of the following numbers which was your primary source of information.

Ad in area newspaper.

INS employee.

INS Human Resources or Personnel Office

Ad in military base newspaper.

Ad in college newspaper.

College Career Planning Office, College Job Fair, or Faculty Member.

USAJOBS, Federal Job Opportunities Board, Federal Job Information Touch Screen Computer Kiosk, or Career America Connection.

INS or U.S. Border Patrol's internet web sites.

OPM's USAJOBS internet web site.

Other internet web sites.

State Employment Office.

Job announcement on DOD Transition Bulletin Board.

Exiting military personnel job fair.

Other job fairs.

Other sources.

FIGURE 8-1

Border Patrol agent application form available on-line. You may complete the form on-line and submit it via the Net.

employment statistics. Figure 8-2 shows the opening page for FBI employment information.

THE U.S. OFFICE OF PERSONNEL MANAGEMENT:
http://www.usajobs.opm.gov The United States Office of Personnel Management runs a *huge* jobs Web site at this address. All kinds of jobs are listed, but a search feature makes it possible to easily find jobs in the criminal justice area.

FEDWORLD JOBS: **http://www.fedworld.gov/jobs/jobsearch.html** This
Web site contains a series of database files using input from hundreds of human resources people in the federal government. The

We request the following information in order to evaluate our efforts to recruit minorities and women. Providing this information is voluntary. This information will not be use to make selections nor will your chances for employment be affected if you do not answer these questions. Additionally, we treat the information that you provide to us as confidential, and we protect it from disclosure under the Privacy Act at 5 U.S.C. Section 552a(b). OMB Clearance Number 1115-0188, Expiration Date October 31, 1999.

A. Gender

    ○ Male   ○ Female

B. National Origin

    Are you of Hispanic/Latino Origin?   ○ Yes ○ No

C. Race

    ○ White?
    ○ African-American?
    ○ American Indian or Alaskan Native?
    ○ Asian or Pacific Islander?

D. Veteran Status

    Are you a Veteran of the U.S. armed forces who was discharged under honorable conditions?   ○ Yes ○ No

We need your Social Security Number to maintain your records. Executive Order 9397 authorizes the Office of Personnel Management to use this number in keeping records. We may also use this number to make requests for information about you from employers, schools, banks and others. Giving us your Social Security Number is voluntary; however, we cannot process your application without it."

It is important that you enter your Social Security Number correctly. FAILURE TO DO SO WILL PROHIBIT OR DELAY THE PROCESSING OF YOUR APPLICATION AND WRITTEN TEST.

Now enter your Social Security Number: □ - □ - □

You must be available for employment within the next six months. If you will not be available during this time ○ Yes ○ No frame, you will not be considered. Are you available for employment within the next six months?

When you have completed this portion of your application, click on the **SUBMIT APPLICATION** button. Your application will be reviewed for completeness. If it is complete, you will get the next part of the application. If there are errors, your application form will be returned with a list of the errors so you can correct and re-submit it. This may take from 10 to 30 seconds. Please be patient.

SUBMIT APPLICATION

TOP

FIGURE 8-1

(continued)

database allows you to search abstracts of open U.S. federal government jobs, and it is updated every Tuesday through Saturday at 9:30 A.M. EST. The FedWorld Jobs opening screen is shown in Figure 8-3.

GOVERNMENT JOBS DATABASE OF CRIMINAL JUSTICE EMPLOYMENT OPPORTU-NITIES: http://www.govtjobs.com/crim/index.html One of the latest

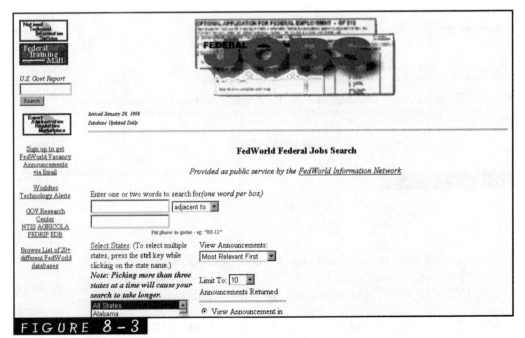

FBI Personnel and Employment

- Current Hiring Activity and Salaries and Wages
- Recruitment
  - Special Agent
  - Support Personnel
    - Laboratory Examiner Positions
- Equal Employment Opportunity Affairs
- Employee Statistics

The FBI is a unique institution in the federal government in that it is responsible for sensitive foreign counterintelligence matters, important civil investigations, background inquiries on persons nominated for high public office, and criminal investigations which may involve prominent figures in both the public and private sectors. In recognition of these diverse responsibilities, the FBI has traditionally been provided broader discretion in personnel matters than is afforded most other federal agencies.

All persons and positions in the FBI are in the excepted service (Title 28, USC, Section 536). This places all FBI employees outside the general civil service population and allows the Director to take various personnel actions relating to hiring, promotion, qualifications, discipline, and other matters with a greater degree of discretion than would be the case if FBI were personnel included in the competitive service.

Positions in the FBI work force are governed by regulations issued by the Office of Personnel Management (OPM), an independent agency in the Executive Branch of the federal government. Most of the FBI's positions are white-collar occupations and can be classified into five broad white-collar job categories established by OPM:

- Professional
- Administrative
- Technical
- Clerical

FIGURE 8-2

FBI employment announcements on the Web: http://www.fbi.gov/over/personel.htm.

The FedWorld Jobs opening page: http://www.fedworld.gov/jobs.

FIGURE 8-3

and most up-to-date listings of criminal justice job opportunities. A screen capture of a page from Govtjobs.com is shown in Figure 8-4.

IRA WILSKER'S LAW ENFORCEMENT EMPLOYMENT PAGE:
http://www.ih2000.net/ira/ira2.htm#jobs An excellent, information-rich, jobs site!

LAW ENFORCEMENT CAREERS: http://www.gate.net/~fcfjobs A full-service career site for those seeking employment in the law enforcement field. Law Enforcement Careers categorizes job information as follows: (1) Federal Law Enforcement Careers, (2) State Trooper Careers, and (3) Correctional Officer Careers. The site also provides separate testing guides, including the "Federal Law Enforcement Testing Guide" and the "State and Local Law Enforcement Testing Guide."

THE POLICE OFFICERS' INTERNET DIRECTORY JOBS PAGE: http://www.officer.com/jobs.htm A very comprehensive listing of current law enforcement jobs. Highly recommended for those seeking law enforcement employment.

A sample page from the Government Jobs site. Reprinted with permission: http://www.govtjobs.com.

THE STATE POLICE INFORMATION CENTER:

http://www.internetwks.com/officers A nationwide provider of state and federal law enforcement career information. The interface for this site may be a bit tricky.

State Job Listings

This listing of state-level job opportunities in the criminal justice field is not meant to be comprehensive. The list, however, provides a representative sample of state careers resources.

California

CRIMINAL JUSTICE EMPLOYMENT OPPORTUNITIES IN CALIFORNIA:
http://robles.callutheran.edu/scj/employ.html

BERKELEY POLICE DEPARTMENT:
http://www.ci.berkeley.ca.us/bpd/join.html

LOS ANGELES POLICE DEPARTMENT:
http://www.ci.la.ca.us/dept/PER/polrecru.htm

SACRAMENTO POLICE DEPARTMENT:
http://www.sacpd.org/emp_inf.html

Florida

FLORIDA MARINE PATROL RECRUITMENT INFORMATION:
http://www.dep.state.fl.us/law/fmp/recruit1.html

Maryland

BALTIMORE COUNTY: http://www.access.digex.net:80/~issd/career.html

Tennessee

NASHVILLE POLICE:
http://www.nashville.org/pl/job_opportunities.html

Washington

SPOKANE POLICE DEPARTMENT: http://www.ior.com/~spd/employ.html

Membership Sites

At membership sites, some services are free, but you may have to first register on-line or join the sponsoring association to gain full access to these sites. Here's a brief list of such sites.

FEDERAL SUPPORT SERVICES:
http://www.federalsupportservices.com/fssframe.html This site tells visitors that the federal government employs approximately 100,000 law enforcement personnel and hires *hundreds,* even *thousands,* of personnel each year! Unfortunately, the site provides little help to job seekers beyond attempting to sell visitors printed packages to assist them in job searches. It does, however, contain links to a number of other useful sites.

NATIONAL DIRECTORY OF EMERGENCY SERVICES: http://www1.policejobs .com/ndes/phome.html Your up-to-the-minute source for police department employment opportunities.

THE PUBLIC SAFETY EXECUTIVE ASSOCIATION (PSEA): http://www .policechief.com/default.htm A membership site that helps members who are beginning careers in the field of public safety.

GENERAL EMPLOYMENT SERVICES ON THE WEB

A number of employment sites on the Web go beyond a mere listing of available jobs. They offer general jobs information, frequently including lots of links to potential employers. We call these sites "general employment services." A number of them are listed here.

CAREER MAGAZINE: http://www.careermag.com A comprehensive resource designed to meet the individual needs of networked job seekers.

CAREERNET: http://www.careers.org A listing of over 11,000 links to jobs, employers, business, education, and career service professionals and over 6,000 links to employment-related resources.

CAREERSITE: http://www.careersite.com A comprehensive list for job seekers and employers.

CAREERWEB: http://www.cweb.com A free place to store your resume on-line. Uses a job-match function to track your targeted job preferences with e-mail notification.

JOBTRAK: http://www.jobtrak.com A job-listing service that partners with hundreds of college and university career centers. It is used by over 200,000 employers.

CAREER ADVICE AND RESUME POSTING SERVICES

A relatively new idea in seeking criminal justice jobs exists in the form of sites that help you prepare a resume, advise you on how to submit it to agencies that are currently hiring, or list your resume and credentials on-line for potential employers to see. You may want to consider posting your own resume on-line and then directing potential employers to it. Doing so can demonstrate your technical and computer prowess. You can view the on-line resume of Dr. Schmalleger, our director, by visiting one of the Justice Research Association servers at http://cjcentral.com/resume. Although it is unlikely that your resume will be nearly as lengthy as Dr. Schmalleger's, this page should give you an idea of how to build your own on-line resume. The following sites provide criminal justice career services, including help with resume construction.

CAREER SHOP: **http://www.tenkey.com**

DR. CARLIE'S ADVISENET:
http://www.smsu.edu/contrib/soc/advnet/advnet.htm A new concept in on-line advising for criminal justice students. Provides users with advice on where the field is going, where to find jobs (includes many job search engines), and additional useful information for students at *any* university. The site is maintained by Dr. Mike Carlie of Southwest Missouri State University.

INTELLIMATCH: **http://www.intellimatch.com** Matches your resume with the needs of prospective employers.

LAW ENFORCEMENT EMPLOYMENT SERVICES:
http://www.xensei.com/users/hubcom/prodemp.htm

POLICE CAREERS: **http://www.policecareer.com/employment.html**
A professional police resume and career service company.

THE MONSTERBOARD: **http://www.monster.com**

If you are uncertain whether you want to enter the law enforcement profession, you can see what it is like to attend a police academy in cyberspace by visiting *The New Blue Line. The New Blue Line* traces an officer's steps through the Virginia Beach, Virginia, Police Academy from the day of arrival through graduation. The project is the work of *Virginian-Pilot* reporter Mike Mather, who attended the academy to see what it would be like and then wrote about his experiences. The newspaper describes the resulting on-line experience this way: "Spend five months inside the Virginia Beach Police Academy. Follow three recruits as they face the grueling physical regimen, the nerve-wracking firing-range test . . . and the terror of The Redman. Two recruits will survive. One will fail. Would you?" The site makes for an interesting experience! *The New Blue Line* can be reached at http://www.pilotonline.com/special/blueline.

 ## USING THE WEB

Visit some of the federal job sites described in this chapter. Once there, search for jobs in the area of law enforcement. Look for jobs in corrections. Then answer the following questions:

1. Which sites did you visit? What made you choose those sites?

2. Which site do you consider to be the best for job searches? Why?

3. What search terms did you use? Are there other, alternative, terms that you might have used? If so, what are they?

4. If you were seeking employment in one of these fields (police work or corrections), which three of the jobs you found listed would you apply for? What makes those jobs attractive?

CHAPTER IX

SECURITY ISSUES

As surely as the future will bring new forms of technology, it will bring new forms of crime.

—Cynthia Mason and Charles Ardai[28]

Thou shalt not steal thy neighbor's data.

—InterLock® security devices advertisement

CHAPTER OUTLINE

- Security on the Internet
- Security Companies and Related Sites
- Security Information
- Viruses
    Antivirus Sites and Information
    Antivirus Software on the Web
    Macintosh Antivirus Utilities
- Using the Web

SECURITY ON THE INTERNET

You have probably heard quite a bit about security on the Internet. Security is important because there are a number of unscrupulous people (sometimes called *crackers* because they work to crack codes, passwords, etc.), well versed in technology, who spend time and money trying to steal personal information from other Internet users. Such high-tech criminals often try to grab passwords, credit card numbers, personal banking information, and other types of valuable data (including business plans for new products, government plans for military action, etc.) from the Internet. They do so by using their computers and special software to secretly enter Internet information pipelines. Then they watch the flow of information along those pipelines, looking for valuable data that is unencrypted.

One of the most basic types of security about which you should be concerned involves keeping your password a secret. If others acquire your password, they can use it to masquerade as you, enter your Internet or on-line account, and leave you with the bill for their on-line activities. Worse, once they have logged on as you, they can change your password—effectively locking you out of your own accounts!

You can protect your password by remembering a few basic tips:

- Do not share your password with *anyone*. Of course you have trusted friends. But even trusted friends may inadvertently share information with others, while some may not be as dependable as you thought. You should be especially attentive to the need to keep your password private while you are on-line. *Never* give your password to anyone who sends you an e-mail message asking for it unless you are sure you know the requester. Even then, if you e-mail a password to a trusted friend, your e-mail message could be intercepted by a cracker sitting on an Internet node looking for just such information. Members of the America Online service, for example, often receive "instant messages" (IMs) from other members masquerading as system administrators for AOL. Those fraudulent IMs sometimes request passwords and other personal information. Although AOL has worked hard to eliminate this security problem, it is still occurring at the time of this writing.

- Do not write your password for on-line access or on-line accounts in any place that is easily visible. One person at the Justice Research Association, for example, got into the habit of writing her password on yellow sticky tabs, which she then posted on the edges of her computer monitor. While it may be okay to use sticky tabs to remind you of your mother's birthday, it is *not* a good idea to paste tabs containing passwords anywhere they can be seen by others.

- Change your password on a regular basis. Some people recommend changing your password every month; others suggest every six months. The point to keep in mind is that the longer you use the same password, the more likely it is to be "broken" or to fall into the hands of an unscrupulous person. Crackers may be trying to break your password without your knowledge by using software to contact your ISP or on-line service repeatedly, each time randomly trying a computer-generated password and waiting until the system lets them in.

- Use a password that is at least eight characters long and that is made up of a mix of letters and numbers.

✔ Do not use a password that someone who knows you could easily guess (like the name of your dog or cat or the name of your boyfriend or girl-friend).

✔ Do not use an English-language word as your password. Given the technology available to crackers, they are the easiest passwords to break.

✔ Do not allow anyone to watch as you type in your password. This is the most common way that passwords are compromised.

✔ Do not use your username or user ID as your password. Both are required to log on, and many people ask, "Why remember two words when I can type the same one in twice?" People who receive e-mail from you may be able to learn your username or ID, and they may try using it as your password.

✔ Do *not* use well-known abbreviations, names of fictional characters, or names of television or movie heroes or heroines.

Given all this advice on what *not* to use as a password, what *should* you use? Some people suggest using a sentence that is easy to remember and then creating a password based on that sentence. For example, "My daughter is four years old" is easy to remember and can be used as the basis for a password like "mdis4yrold." Another password might come from the sentence, "The Justice Research Association was created in 1978" (jrain1978). In case you are wondering, no, we don't use that password at the Justice Research Association.

Whether you follow this advice or not, if you notice that strange things are happening with your account you should contact your ISP or on-line service immediately. *And* you should immediately change your password.

Beyond passwords, there are other security issues of which you should be aware. Most of today's popular browsers have a number of important security features built in. In order to use many of them, however, you must be connected to a site that runs on a secure server, or you must have **security certificates** installed on your own computer. A *security certificate* is a file that electronically identifies a person or an organization. Browsers use certificates to encrypt information. You can use a certificate to check the identity of the certificate's owner. You should trust a certificate only if you trust the person or organization that issued it.

Some sites run on secure servers, which will automatically encrypt any information you send back to them via an HTML form. An HTML form is a Web page sent to you by the secure server that you can fill out and send back to that same server. Secure servers make it possible for you to engage in secure transactions and to exchange information over the Web without the need for any special security software on your own machine. Forms sent to you by secure servers usually contain wording that looks something like this: "First, click here to activate SSL [Secure Sockets Layer] protocol. All of the information you will enter will then be securely transferred using RSA encryption." Rather than RSA encryption,[29] they might refer to DES (Data Encryption Standard) security or some other form of encryption security, or simply tell you that the HTML form you are working with is a secure document. Another way to tell if you are sending information in a secure mode initiated by the server you are in contact with is to look at the URL in your browser's location field. Secure connections will usually be indicated by the preface "https://" rather than the usual "http://."

DATA ENCRYPTION: methods used to encode computerized information, making the data inaccessible to unauthorized individuals.

You can also set your browser to alert you if you are about to send sensitive information to a nonsecure site or if you are about to send sensitive information that is not encrypted. Encrypted information can be read only by someone who has a decryption key, such as a password that you provide to them. Most browsers set the alert to display by default. You can disable alerts by choosing the "options" or "preferences" selections in your browser, finding the security section, and clicking on the checkbox "display security warnings" (or similar wording). Clicking on the checkbox should remove the existing checkmark, thus disabling the warnings.

Most browsers make it easy to tell if you are about to send or receive information from a secure site (such as a banking institution that makes your personal financial files available to you on-line). Navigator, for example, displays a screen like the one that follows to let you know that you can have confidence in the security of your Internet connection.

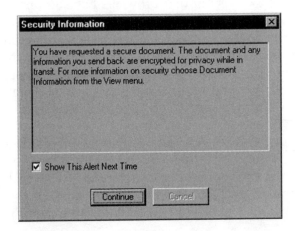

If, however, you see a security information statement such as this and you decide to uncheck the "Show This Alert Next Time" box, then you will have to depend on other indicators (such as the "https://" prefix to URLs mentioned earlier) to let you know when you are working with a secure HTML document.

Navigator categorizes security certificates into four groups: (1) Yours (your own certificates), (2) People (certificates sent to you from other people or organizations), (3) Web Sites (certificates sent to you from Web sites), and (4) Signers (certificates from certificate signers, also known as ("Certificate Authorities").

One especially important provider of digital authentication products and services is VeriSign Corporation. As the first commercial Certificate Authority, VeriSign has issued Digital IDs for almost every secure Internet server worldwide. Strict verification and security practices, enforced through automated background checks and state-of-the-art security systems, ensure the integrity of every VeriSign Digital ID. Visit the VeriSign Digital ID issuing center at http://www.verisign.com/idcenter/new/idplus.html for additional information.

While space does not permit discussion of all the potential security issues involved in use of the Internet, the following letter from Senator Patrick Leahy (D-VT) indicates the growing importance of this issue. The letter was sent by Senator Leahy to various organizations and mailing list forums, including the Electronic Frontier Foundation's "ACTION" list.

From: Senator_Leahy@leahy.senate.gov

Date: May 2, 1996, 12:02:02 EST

Subject: Letter From Senator Patrick Leahy (D-VT) On Encryption

To: action@eff.org (action mailing list) Please post where appropriate

------BEGIN PRETTY GOOD PRIVACY SIGNED MESSAGE------

Dear Friends:

Today, a bipartisan group of Senators has joined me in supporting legislation to encourage the development and use of strong, privacy-enhancing technologies for the Internet by rolling back the out-dated restrictions on the export of strong cryptography. In an effort to demonstrate one of the more practical uses of encryption technology (and so that you all know this message actually came from me), I have signed this message using a digital signature generated by the popular encryption program PGP [Pretty Good Privacy].

I am proud to be the first member of Congress to utilize encryption and digital signatures to post a message to the Internet. As a fellow

Internet user, I care deeply about protecting individual privacy and encouraging the development of the Net as a secure and trusted communications medium. I do not need to tell you that current export restrictions only allow American companies to export primarily weak encryption technology.

The current strength of encryption the U.S. government will allow out of the country is so weak that, according to a January 1996 study conducted by world-renowned cryptographers, a pedestrian hacker can crack the codes in a matter of hours! A foreign intelligence agency can crack the current 40-bit codes in seconds.

Perhaps more importantly, the increasing use of the Internet and similar interactive communications technologies by Americans to obtain critical medical services, to conduct business, to be entertained and communicate with their friends, raises special concerns about the privacy and confidentiality of those communications.

I have long been concerned about these issues, and have worked over the past decade to protect privacy and security for our wire and electronic communications. Encryption technology provides an effective way to ensure that only the people we choose can read our communications. I have read horror stories sent to me over the Internet about how human rights groups in the Balkans have had their computers confiscated during raids by security police seeking to find out the identities of people who have complained about abuses.

Thanks to PGP, the encrypted files were undecipherable by the police and the names of the people who entrusted their lives to the human rights groups were safe. The new bill, called the "Promotion of Commerce On-Line in the Digital Era (PRO-CODE) Act of 1996," would: (1) bar any government-mandated use of any particular encryption system, including key escrow systems, and affirm the right of American citizens to use whatever form of encryption they choose domestically; (2) loosen export restrictions on encryption products so that American companies are able to export any generally available or mass market encryption products without obtaining government approval; and (3) limit the authority of the federal government to set standards for encryption products used by businesses and individuals, particularly standards which result in products with limited key lengths and key escrow.

This is the second encryption bill I have introduced with Senator Burns and other congressional colleagues this year. Both bills call for an overhaul of this country's export restrictions on encryption, and, if enacted, would quickly result in the widespread availability of strong, privacy protecting technologies. Both bills also prohibit a government-mandated key escrow encryption system. While PRO-CODE would limit the authority of the Commerce Department to set encryption standards for use by private individuals and businesses, the first bill we introduced, called the "Encrypted Communications Privacy Act," S.1587, would set up stringent procedures for law enforcement to follow to obtain decoding keys or decryption assistance to read the plain text of encrypted communications obtained under court order or other lawful process. It is clear that the current policy towards encryption exports is hopelessly outdated, and fails to account for the real needs of individuals and businesses in the global marketplace. Encryption expert Matt Blaze, in a recent letter to me, noted that current U.S. regulations governing the use and export of encryption are having a "deleterious effect . . . on our country's ability to develop a reliable and trustworthy information infrastructure." The time is right for Congress to take steps to put our national encryption policy on the right course. I am looking forward to hearing from you on this important issue. Throughout the course of the recent debate on the Communications Decency Act, the input from Internet users was very valuable to me and some of my Senate colleagues. You can find out more about the issue at my World Wide Web homepage (http://www.leahy.senate.gov/) [if this address does not work, try http://www.senate.gov/member/vt/leahy/general/ or http://www.senate.gov/~leahy] and at the Encryption Policy Resource Page (http://www.crypto.com/). Over the coming months, I look forward to the help of the Net community in convincing other Members of Congress and the Administration of the need to reform our nation's cryptography policy.

Sincerely,
Patrick Leahy
United States Senator

If you want to learn more about Internet security you should visit the Computer Crime and Investigations Center at http://www.ovnet.com/~dckinder/crime.htm, or you can go to the Computer Emergency Response Team (CERT®) Coordination Center at http://www.cert.org. The CERT Coordination Center, located at Carnegie Mellon University in Pittsburgh, Pennsylvania, studies Internet security vulnerabilities, provides incident response services to sites that have been the victims of attack, publishes a variety of security alerts, researches security and survivability in wide-area-networked computing, and develops information to help Web developers improve security at your site.[30]

Another excellent source of Web security information is the World Wide Web Security FAQ (Frequently Asked Questions) site at http://www.w3.org/Security/Faq/. You might also check out the home page of Pretty Good Privacy (PGP) software at http://www.pgp.com. PGP allows you to encode your e-mail and protect its contents against prying eyes anywhere on the Net. PGP also allows you to encrypt and decrypt files that are stored on your own computer to prevent others from accessing them. An on-line walk-through of PGP features for Windows users is available at http://www.pgp.com/products/50demos/windows. PGP freeware (for use only within the United States) can be found at http://web.mit.edu/network/pgp.html and at the PGP Web site. If you visit the PGP site, you will see this reminder: "Please remember that all cryptographic software is classified as export-controlled by the U.S. Department of Commerce. If you are a citizen of the USA or Canada, or have permanent alien resident status in the U.S., you may legally purchase and download the software." The same restrictions apply to PGP freeware.

It is not our purpose to discuss Net security in great detail in this short guide. If you are interested in further study, you might review some of the sources for information on Net security that follow. Keep in mind that some of the information found at these sites can be very technical. Other sites contain primarily political information (that is, arguments for and against the use of various forms of data security).

SECURITY COMPANIES AND RELATED SITES

THE CERT COORDINATION CENTER: http://www.cert.org The CERT home page. CERT focuses on computer security concerns for Internet users.

CISCO SYSTEMS NETWORK ENCRYPTION SERVICES: http://www.cisco.com/warp/public/732/Security/ncryp_wp.htm Cisco Systems, Inc., builds most of the routers that make the Internet possible. This site describes the uses of cryptography in data networking. (Note the underscore in the site name.)

CRYPTOGRAPHY FOR ENCRYPTION, DIGITAL SIGNATURES, AND AUTHENTICATION PAGE: http://www.ozemail.com.au/~firstpr/crypto Contains links to information on cryptography, a tutorial on public-key encryption for secrecy, and a discussion of the debate regarding government control of cryptography.

THE ELECTRONIC FRONTIER FOUNDATION (EFF): http://www.eff.org The Electronic Frontier Foundation is the civil liberties union of cyberspace.

NATIONAL INSTITUTE OF STANDARDS AND TECHNOLOGY COMPUTER SECURITY RESOURCE CLEARINGHOUSE: http://csrc.ncsl.nist.gov NIST's computer security resource clearinghouse contains information on numerous security topics, as well as alerts about viruses and other security threats.

RSA DATA SECURITY: http://www.rsa.com Site of RSA Data Security, Inc., creators of the RSA encryption technology used in Netscape Navigator, Quicken, Lotus Notes, and hundreds of other products.

VERISIGN CORPORATION: http://www.verisign.com The world leader in encryption technologies for individual and commercial use.

SECURITY INFORMATION

THE CASE FOR CLIPPER: http://www.mit.edu/afs/athena/org/t/ techreview/www/articles/july95/Denning.html An article that appeared in the July 1995 issue of the *MIT Technology Review*. It was written by Dorothy Denning, a professor of computer science at Georgetown University.

CES COMMUNICATIONS: http://www.cescomm.co.nz CES home page. CES is a supplier of voice and fax encryptors and data security products.

CLINTON ADMINISTRATION STATEMENT ON COMMERCIAL ENCRYPTION POLICIES: http://www.epic.org/crypto/key_escrow/wh_cke_796.html This statement describes what it claims is a proposed framework that would encourage the use of strong encryption in commerce and private communications while protecting the public safety and national security. Also provided is a section on the U.S. Cryptography Policy.

CRYPTOGRAPHIC PRODUCT SURVEY: http://www.tis.com/research/crypto/crypt_surv.html Results of a worldwide survey of cryptographic products.

CRYPTOGRAPHY ARCHIVE: http://www.austinlinks.com/Crypto An extensive archive containing links to information on the Clipper chip, computer security issues, encryption policy resources, information liberation organizations, and the Macintosh Cryptography Interface Project.

DATA ENCRYPTION METHODS: http://www.catalog.com/sft/encrypt.html A Web-posted paper discussing the many methods used to encrypt data.

DIGITAL DELIVERY, INC.: http://www.digitaldelivery.com The site of Digital Delivery, Inc., a supplier of encryption tools for documents and software.

DIGITAL SIGNATURES: HOW THEY WORK
http://www.zdnet.com/pcmag/issues/1507/pcmag0090.htm *A PC Magazine* article exploring principles of digital authenticity and the U.S. government's proposed Digital Signature Standard.

ENTRUST TECHNOLOGIES: http://www.entrust.com
Entrust Technologies develops software security products for encryption and digital signature. Its home page provides links to product information, a resource library, company press releases, partners, events, FAQs, and Web security references.

FACT SHEET—PUBLIC ENCRYPTION MANAGEMENT:
http://ftp.eff.org/pub/Privacy/Clipper/wh_clipper.factsheet This fact sheet, from the White House, includes the President's directive for "Public Encryption Management."

INTERNATIONAL CRYPTOGRAPHY: http://www.cs.hut.fi/ssh/crypto
A site listing international sources of cryptographic software, information on cryptographic methods, algorithms, and protocols. Materials cover encryption, decryption, cryptanalysis, steganography (hiding information), software, tools, information, and assessments about cryptographic methods.

INTERNATIONAL PGP HOME PAGE: http://www.pgpi.com
Provides up-to-date information about PGP, FAQs, bugs, documentation, and links regarding the latest international PGP versions.

NETWORK SECURITY BUYER'S GUIDE: http://www.netsecurityguide.com
Provides information about network security, utilities, and virus protection. Offers a searchable database of products, links to vendor sites, and a library of white papers, press releases, and product presentations.

PAPER ON KEY ESCROW ENCRYPTION SYSTEMS: http://www.cosc.georgetown.edu/~denning/crypto/Taxonomy.html
For the technically minded.

QUADRALAY'S CRYPTOGRAPHY ARCHIVE:
http://www.austinlinks.com/Crypto This archive is a collection of links relating to electronic privacy and cryptography.

SECURITY INFORMATION AND TOOLS: http://www.geocities.com/CapeCanaveral/4716
Contains information on security issues,

encryption news, and tools for Unix and Windows NT, as well as several publications from the National Computer Security Center (NCSC).

VERISIGN'S SECURE E-MAIL REFERENCE GUIDE:
http://www.verisign.com/securemail/guide

WEBLOCK ENCRYPTION: http://www.perint.com Provides information about WebLock, a software-based encryption process from Peregrine International.

WHITE HOUSE CLIPPER STATEMENT, OCTOBER 1996:
http://www.epic.org/crypto/key_escrow/clipper4_statement.html
This announcement, from Vice President Al Gore, describes the latest version of the key escrow—now called the *key recovery*—plan intended to promote legalized government access to encoded communications.

VIRUSES

One of the perils of surfing the Web is the possibility that your computer (or your network, if your machine is part of one) may become infected by computer viruses. A virus is a malicious and generally quite small software program designed and written to adversely affect your computer by altering the way it works without your knowledge or permission.[31] Viruses work secretly by implanting themselves into one or more of your files and then spreading quietly from one file to another when the originally infected file is accessed or read. They are written by human beings, *not* by computers, and are apparently intended to demonstrate the code writer's skills.

> **VIRUS:** a malicious and generally quite small software program designed and written to adversely affect your computer by altering the way it works without your knowledge or permission.

The reason that viruses are so called is because they have the ability to self-replicate and to propagate within one computer and across networks (like the Internet). Viruses often lurk in memory, waiting to infect the next program that is run or the next disk that is accessed.

Virus infections can come from a number of different sources, but the most common are shared disks (floppy or otherwise), the Internet, and infected computers on local area networks (LANs).

A few years ago viruses could be attached only to executable programs (those that actually run on your machine). Newer viruses, however, are much more insidious. Some, called **macro viruses,** including the **concept virus,** can attach themselves to Microsoft Word® files. Others can make their way into your computer through small programs called *scripts* that are downloaded to your machine while you browse the Web. Some of the most recent viral codes have been found hidden within Java scripts, ActiveX applets, and Shockwave programs—small scripts written by Web site designers to provide motion and interactivity on their Web sites. **Cookies,** small programs that are sent to your machine by sites you visit, may also contain viruses.

> **COOKIES:** The collective name for files stored on your hard drive by your Web browser that hold information about your browsing habits (which sites you have visited, which newsgroups you have read, etc.). Cookies are sent to your computer by sites that you visit.

Viruses may activate immediately upon download, or may be set to activate on a certain date (such as the Michelangelo virus, which runs when your computer's internal clock reaches the artist's birth date). They may also activate after a certain period of time or during a given activity, called a *trigger,* performed by the user. A trigger may be something as simple as attempting to save a certain kind of file. The important thing to realize is that you can easily download a virus off the Web without being aware of it. Once that happens, the virus will patiently wait in your computer until the conditions specified by the program's author manifest.

Some viruses are relatively harmless and do little more than take over the computer screen in order to display a leering graphic or a phrase like "gotcha." These are called **benign viruses.** Others, called **malignant viruses,** are more insidious and can cause letters and words on your screen to crumble or fall to pieces. The worst of the malignant viruses can corrupt selected files, delete important operating files from your disk, fill up your hard drives and computer memory (thereby slowing your machine to a crawl), or reformat your entire hard disk—destroying all of the information in your computer or making it inaccessible to you.[32]

Viruses fall into four general categories, depending on how they work inside your machine. The first are **file infectors.** These are viruses that attach themselves to, or replace, **executable files** with name extensions like "COM," "EXE," "SYS," "DRV," "BIN," or "OVL." The file that runs Windows, for example, is called "windows.com," and has been a frequent target of virus writers.

EXECUTABLE FILES: program files that actually run on your machine and generally do not change in size, as opposed to text, document, or data files, which are routinely modified as you work with them.

A second viral category is that of **boot sector infectors.** Boot sector infectors work by attacking the boot sector on floppy disks or hard drives. (They may also infect removable storage media, such as Iomega Zip® and Jaz® drives, although those types of drives are rarely used to boot machines.) All disks have a boot sector, even those that cannot be used to start, or boot, your machine. Boot sector viruses spread when users leave an infected diskette in a drive and attempt to boot or reboot their machines. Even though the disk may appear to be an empty floppy disk, when the machine attempts to boot, the first thing that it will do is try to read and execute the boot sector. The virus is then read into the machine's memory and infects the hard drive. Although it is easy to acquire a boot sector infection, it is not easy to tell when it has occurred. Attempting to boot from an infected disk will result in the message, "Non-System Disk." Even though you may pop the infected floppy out of your floppy drive and proceed to boot normally from your hard drive, infection has already occurred.

A third category of viruses is called **master boot record infectors** (MBRIs). MBRIs infect what is called the *master boot program* on the hard drive(s) in your computer. Since your computer will read the boot program at startup time, it will also run whatever instructions are included in the MBRI virus. Finally, **multipartite viruses** comprise the fourth category of virus. They are simply a combination of two or more of the types already discussed.

Although not a separate category, it is important to realize that certain kinds of viruses, called *stealth viruses* and *polymorphic viruses,* are smart enough to change themselves slightly each time they infect a new machine. Because most antivirus programs depend largely on a database of known viruses (called a *virus signature file*) and compare files they find on your machine with known virus codes, polymorphic and stealth viruses can easily elude some of the best antivirus software available today. Many advanced antivirus programs, however, offer you the choice of inoculating the important files in your computer. The strategy behind inoculation is simple: The antivirus program simply records the size of the inoculated file (using only executable files that are not supposed to change), and periodically compares the recorded size with the current size of the file. Executable files that have changed in size are suspected of harboring a virus.

Antivirus Sites and Information

ANTIVIRUS RESOURCES: http://www.hitchhikers.net/av.shtml A wealth of on-line information about the virus problem, with access to recommended antivirus shareware and trial software.

ANTIVIRUS TOOLKIT PRO® (ATP) VIRUS ENCYCLOPEDIA: http://www.metro.ch/avpve Anything you ever wanted to know about hundreds of viruses.

DR. SOLOMON'S ANTIVIRUS® SITE: www.drsolomon.com A comprehensive site with software, virus news, and listings of the most common viruses. This worthwhile site can be difficult to reach because of the large number visitors it serves.

HITCHHIKERS: www.hitchhikers.net/av.shtml

NEW MEXICO HIGHLANDS UNIVERSITY'S COMPUTER VIRUS INFORMATION PAGE: http://jaring.nmhu.edu/virus.htm Many different types of antivirus information. The site's motto is "Practice Safe Computing."

SOPHOS ANTIVIRUS CENTER: http://www.sophos.com/virusinfo Includes a virus encyclopedia, virus hoaxes, antivirus software tools, and many other features.

SYMANTEC CORPORATION'S NORTON ANTIVIRUS® CENTER: http://www.sarc.com Rated as one of the most comprehensive antivirus centers on the Web. The site is searchable by keyword.

UNIVERSITY OF MICHIGAN'S VIRUS BUSTERS PAGE: http://www.umich.edu/~wwwitd/virus-busters This site's theme is "We ain't 'fraid 'o No Virus!"

Antivirus Software on the Web

DR. SOLOMON'S ANTIVIRUS TOOLKIT: http://www.drsolomon.com A popular program. May run a bit slowly on some machines.

F-PROT AND F-PROT PROFESSIONAL: http://www.f-prot.com Top-rated, popular antiviral program.

INOCULAN: http://www.cheyenne.com/virusinfo/trymebuyme.html Cheyenne Corporation's latest entry into the antivirus market.

MCAFEE ANTIVIRUS: **http://www.mcafee.com** One of the best DOS and Windows products available. Shareware.

NORTON ANTIVIRUS: **http://www.symantec.com** Proprietary software, which in version 4.0 and later may be the most effective antivirus software available.

PC-CILLIN: **http://www.antivirus.com** A Trend Micro site. Scan-mail antivirus software is also available to protect your incoming e-mail messages.

IBM ANTIVIRUS: **http://www.av.ibm.com/IBMAntiVirus** For many different operating systems.

INTEGRITY MASTER: **http://www.stiller.com/stiller.htm** A Stiller Research product. Includes lots of antivirus information.

LANDESK:
http://web.jf.intel.com/support/landesk/virusprotect/4x/software .htm An antivirus program from Intel. Choose the one that is right for your hardware and software.

XSCAN: **http://www.helpvirus.com**

Macintosh Antivirus Utilities

DR. SOLOMON'S FIND VIRUS: **http://www.drsolomon.com/download** Evaluation version.

MCAFEE VIRUSCAN FOR MAC: **http://www.mcafee.com**

MACINTOSH ANTIVIRUS: **http://www.cc.umanitoba.ca/campus/acn/ docs/indexes/macvirus.html**

NORTON/SYMANTEC ANTIVIRUS:
http://www.symantec.com/avcenter/download.html

SIMTEL: **http://oak.oakland.edu/simtel.net/msdos/virus.html** One of the largest collections of antiviral software anywhere. Some files are dated.

THUNDERBYTE ANTI-VIRUS: **http://www.thunderbyte.com**

USING THE WEB

Visit three of the antivirus sites described in this chapter. Once there, find the product descriptions for antivirus software available through these sites. Then answer the following questions:

1. Which sites did you visit? What made you choose those sites?

2. Compare the features of the antivirus products you found. How do they differ? How are they similar?

3. Which site offers the best antivirus software? Why do you think that particular product is the best?

CHAPTER X

USING THE TALK JUSTICE SITE

Justice is Truth in action!

—Benjamin Disraeli

Injustice anywhere is a threat to justice everywhere!

—M. L. King

CHAPTER OUTLINE

- The Purpose of the Site
- The Justice Research Association
- The Criminal Justice Distance Learning Consortium
- Using the Web

THE PURPOSE OF THE SITE

A dedicated Web site supports this guide (see Figure 10-1). Available 24 hours a day, the site is sponsored by the Justice Research Association with support from Prentice Hall Publishing Company. The name of the site is *Talk Justice*. You can reach *Talk Justice* by using this URL:

http://talkjustice.com

Figure 10-1 shows the *Talk Justice* home page.

Talk Justice gives you the tools you need to keep up with the constantly changing world of URLs and the Internet. Visit *Talk Justice* for the latest Web addresses for sites discussed in this guide (and others), to access ongoing message boards focused on criminal justice issues, and to participate in real-time chat with other *Talk Justice* users. Central features of the site include the following:

📌 **Discussion Forums** *Talk Justice* discussion forums exist in the form of message boards. You can access the message boards by clicking on the

Welcome to

Talk Justice
On the World Wide Web

An on-line forum dedicated to discussion of crime and justice issues.

This site is supported by the *Talk Justice* Web Guide. Get your copy *now!*

Enter the *Talk Justice* Message Boards by Clicking Below

Frames-challenged browsers click here
for a non-frames version of this site.

View Our:

Criminal Justice Image Map

Click Below to Enter the *Talk Justice* Chat Room

Talk Justice Chat!

CLICK HERE to listen to an Introduction from Frank Schmalleger,
Director of the Justice Research Association — the sponsoring agency of *Talk Justice*.
(Requires Real Audio)

FIGURE 10-1

The Talk Justice *home page at http://talkjustice.com.*

twinkling "begin" button on the opening page. Once in the message area, you can search messages, browse message threads, or contribute your own new message(s).

The Criminal Justice Image Map   The criminal justice image map is an innovative feature that diagrammatically represents processing through the criminal justice system. The map contains hot spots that lead to links for further exploring topical areas on the map. Try it! You'll like it!

🖚 **Real-Time Chat**   The *Talk Justice* chat room allows you to join other *Talk Justice* users in a real-time chat area. Try the chat room at various times. Sometimes it is full of people chatting with one another, but at other times it is empty. If you find that you are the only person in the chat area, you might wait a few minutes and see if other people join you. Finally, remember that the chat facility takes a while to load on most computers. The time required for the chat facility to load depends on the speed of your Internet connection and how busy the Net is. If you are working from a university computer center connected to a fast T1 line (or using an even faster T3 connection), you may not even notice the time it takes to enter the chat area. If you are connecting to *Talk Justice* through a modem, however, it may take up to two minutes for the chat feature to load, depending on your modem's speed.

🖚 **RealAudio Introduction to *Talk Justice***   You can click on the "Real-Audio" icon to listen to a few brief introductory comments from Dr. Frank Schmalleger, Director of the Justice Research Association (the sponsoring agency of *Talk Justice*). This feature requires that the Real-Audio player be installed as a plug-in on your computer.

🖚 **Rules for Posting on *Talk Justice***   *Talk Justice* began as a message-posting facility for those interested in criminal justice. It quickly became obvious, however, that not all posters respected other discussion group members. That made it necessary to institute rules for posting messages—which can be viewed by clicking on this hyperlink. The rules are not overly demanding. They are built on the netiquette principles discussed in Chapter 7 and ask mostly that you respect other *Talk Justice* users.

🖚 **The *Talk Justice* Cybrary**   The Cybrary is an electronic library. The *Talk Justice* Cybrary is built around the Web listings found in Chapter 3 of this guide. It is constantly updated, ensuring that you will find the most current links available for the information you seek. The Cybrary also expands on the materials provided in Chapter 3, allowing you to check out additional criminal justice resources and site listings.

🖚 **E-Jokes**   "Tired of Work? Computer got you down? Then take a break with some e-jokes!" That's how the introduction to our E-Jokes section begins. These are computer jokes reputedly based on true stories. We think you will like them!

THE JUSTICE RESEARCH ASSOCIATION

A link on the *Talk Justice* home page takes you to the Justice Research Association (JRA), which sponsors the *Talk Justice* site. There you can learn about the association's involvement in distance learning. JRA sponsors the *Talk Justice* Web site, the Criminal Justice Distance Learning Consortium (CJDLC), and supports efforts by colleges and universities to utilize the latest communications technology in the service of higher education in the criminal justice area.

Other activities undertaken by JRA include research in criminal justice, the creation and maintenance of Web sites relevant to criminal justice and criminology, and the ongoing development of a criminal justice Cybrary—a Web-based cyberlibrary with links to criminal justice sites throughout the world. You can reach JRA on the Web at http://www.cjcentral.com/jra. The JRA home page is shown in Figure 10-2.

THE CRIMINAL JUSTICE DISTANCE LEARNING CONSORTIUM

The Criminal Justice Distance Learning Consortium (CJDLC), provides resources to college and university criminal justice programs interested in distance learning. CJDLC facilitates distance education efforts through its on-line resource base, which includes links to Web sites supporting criminal justice distance learning technology. CJDLC also evaluates existing resources in support of teaching and is in the process of developing electronic classrooms for use by institutions lacking such facilities.

Membership in CJDLC is free and is open to both criminal justice instructors and institutions. Members receive a bimonthly e-newsletter, and they can have their e-mail addresses and links to their sites posted on the CJDLC site. CJDLC also provides a place for the electronic posting of articles and papers on distance learning. In this regard, CJDLC serves as a clearinghouse of information on distance learning in the criminal justice area. The CJDLC home page is shown in Figure 10-3.

USING THE WEB

Visit the *Talk Justice* site at http://talkjustice.com. Once there, explore the site's features. Then answer the following questions:

1. What does this site have to offer? Provide a list of features available on *Talk Justice*.

FIGURE 10-2

The home page of the Justice Research Association at http://cjcentral.com/jra.

The Justice Research Association

The Corporate Sponsor of

The Criminal Justice Distance Learning Consortium

~ What We Do ~

The Justice Research Association (JRA) sponsors both the Talk Justice web site, and the Criminal Justice Distance Learning Consortium (CJDLC). Through these projects, JRA supports efforts by colleges and universities to utilize the latest communications technology in the service of higher education in the criminal justice area. JRA is also the developer of The Definitive Guide to Criminal Justice & Criminology on the World Wide Web.

New → Sample Chapter from The Definitive Guide to Criminal Justice & Criminology on the World Wide Web!

PROJECT AREAS

 Research Projects and Research Possibilities

 View Excerpts from the Definitive Guide to Criminal Justice and Criminology on the WWW

 The Criminal Justice Distance Learning Consortium!

 Check out our Huge Cyber Library -- The Cybrary!!

 Visit TALKJUSTICE.COM our on-line CJ Forum

 Funding Opportunities in Criminal Justice

 Sites of Related Interest

Meet The Director

Frank Schmalleger, Ph.D., Executive Director

Call, e-mail, or write us to discuss your criminal justice distance learning needs.

For Additional Information, Call, Write, or e-mail:

```
The Justice Research Association
        P.O. Drawer 23557
   Hilton Head Island, SC 29925
     Phone: 803-689-6298
       FAX:  803-342-2552
```

Begun in 1978 as Southern Planning Consultants

The Justice Research Association became a Delaware corporation in 1994.

WELCOME

The Criminal Justice
Distance Learning
Consortium

Consortium

NEW! We are the corporate author of the new *Definitive Guide to Criminal Justice and Criminology on the World Wide Web* (© 1999). If you teach in a college or university, community college, training academy, or high school you may be eligible to receive a free copy of the 200 page guide. Instructor's wishing to receive a free copy of the guide for adoption consideration should send e-mail to admin@cjcentral.com stating their request. Please tell us your name, your phone number, the name of your school, the name of your class, approximate enrollment, and date of offering. Shipments can be made to school addresses only.

 View Excerpts from the Definitive Guide
to Criminal Justice and Criminology on the WWW

FREE! Join the Consortium

   Criminal Justice and Criminology
Distance Learning Tools and Resources

 Check out our Huge Cyber Library -- The Cybrary!!

 Visit TALKJUSTICE.COM our on-line CJ Forum

 Read our Mission Statement. Really! It's exciting!

Stay Tuned for CJDLC Virtual Classrooms -- Opening in 1999!

The Criminal Justice
Distance Learning
Consortium is dedicated to
improving instruction in
Criminal Justice and
Criminology wherever
and whenever it occurs.
Join us in our quest for
improved instruction and
new distance learning
standards and
technologies.

 E-Mail

Send e-mail

See and hear a
message from
our director.

FIGURE 10-3

The home page of the Criminal Justice Distance Learning Consortium at http://cjcentral.com/cjdlc.

2. How do the message boards differ from the chat area? Which did you find more useful? Why?

3. How do you think the _Talk Justice_ site can best be used in your studies? Why?

4. Click on the Criminal Justice Distance Learning Consortium link on the _Talk Justice_ page. After visiting the Criminal Justice Distance Learning Consortium, describe what it offers.

INTERNET GLOSSARY

This glossary is made available through the courtesy of SquareOne Technology and is reprinted with the permission of SquareOne. All rights are reserved by SquareOne Technology, http://www.squareonetech.com. Terms added to the SquareOne Glossary by the Criminal Justice Distance Learning Consortium are indicated with an asterisk (*).

ADD-IN: A miniprogram that runs in conjunction with a Web browser or other application that enhances the functionality of that program. In order for the add-in to run, the main application must be running as well.

ADDRESS: The location of an Internet resource. An e-mail address may take the form of joeschmoe@somecompany.com. A Web address looks something like http://www.squareonetech.com.

ANCHOR: Either the starting point or destination of a hyperlink. The letters at the top of this page are all anchors—clicking one takes you to another part of this page.

ANONYMOUS FTP: An anonymous FTP site allows Internet users to log in and download files from the computer without having a private userid and password. To log in, you typically enter anonymous as the userid and your e-mail address as the password.

APPLET: A program that can be downloaded over a network and launched on the user's computer. See **Java**.

ARCHIE: The system used in searching FTP sites for files. Also Veronica's boyfriend.

ASCII: American Standard Code for Information Interchange. A set of 128 alphanumeric and special control characters. ASCII files are also known as plain text files.

AU (.au)—a common audio file format for Unix systems.

AVI: Audio/Video Interleaved—a common video file format (.avi). Video quality can be very good at smaller resolutions, but files tend to be rather large.

BANDWIDTH: A measurement of the volume of information that can be transmitted over a network at a given time. Think of a network as a water pipe—the higher the bandwidth (the larger the diameter of the pipe), the more data (water) can pass over the network (through the pipe).

BINARY: The system by which combinations of 0s and 1s are used to represent any type of data stored on a computer.

BITMAP FILE: A common image format (.bmp) defined by a rectangular pattern of pixels.

BOOKMARK: A pointer to a particular Web site. Within browsers, you can bookmark interesting pages so you can return to them easily.

BPS: Bits per second—a measurement of the volume of data that a modem is capable of transmitting. Typical modem speeds today are 14.4 Kbps (14,400 bits per second) and 28.8 Kbps. ISDN offers transfer rates of 128 Kbps.

BROWSER: A program run on a client computer for viewing World Wide Web pages. Examples include Netscape, Microsoft's Internet Explorer, and Mosaic.

CACHE: A region of memory where frequently accessed data can be stored for rapid access.

CGI: Common Gateway Interface—the specification for how an HTTP server should communicate with server gateway applications.

CHAT: A system that allows for on-line communication between Internet users. See **IRC.**

CLIENT: A program (like a Web browser) that connects to and requests information from a server.

CLIENT/SERVER PROTOCOL: A communication protocol between networked computers in which the services of one computer (the server) are requested by the other (the client).

COMPRESSED: Data files available for download from the Internet are typically compacted in order to save server space and reduce transfer times. Typical file extensions for compressed files include zip (DOS/Windows) and tar (Unix).

COOKIES: Sweet snacks. Also the collective name for files stored on your hard drive by your Web browser that hold information about your browsing habits, like what sites you have visited, which newsgroups you have read, etc. Many view cookies as an invasion of privacy. To learn about ways to protect your privacy, visit this site for software and information.

CYBERSPACE*: The computer-created matrix of virtual possibilities, including on-line services, wherein human beings interact with each other and with technology itself.

DIAL-UP CONNECTION: A connection to the Internet via phone and modem. Connection types include PPP and SLIP.

DIRECT CONNECTION: A connection made directly to the Internet—much faster than a dial-up connection.

DISCUSSION GROUP: A particular section within the USENET system typically, though not always, dedicated to a particular subject of interest. Also known as a *newsgroup.*

DOMAIN: The Internet is divided into smaller sets known as domains, including .com (business), .gov (government), .edu (educational), and others.

DOMAIN NAME: Allows you to reference Internet sites without knowing the true numerical address.

DOWNLOAD: The process of copying data file(s) from a remote computer to a local computer. The opposite action is upload, where a local file is copied to a server.

E-MAIL: Electronic mail.

EMOTICON: A combination of characters that form a facial expression. For example, if you turn your head sideways, the characters :) make a smiley face, and the characters 8) make a four-eyed smiley. Frequently used in e-mail messages to convey a particular tone. If you wanted to jokingly insult somebody, without starting a flame war, you could write, "I think you are a total loser :)".

EUDORA: A popular freeware and commercial e-mail management program.

EXCHANGE: Microsoft's integrated fax and e-mail program designed for Windows 95.

FAQ: Frequently Asked Questions—a collection of common questions and answers on a particular subject.

FLAME: An insulting message exchanged via e-mail or within newsgroups. A series of flames is known as a *flame war.*

FREEWARE: Software that is available for download and unlimited use without charge. Compare to **shareware.**

FTP: File Transfer Protocol—a set of rules for exchanging files between computers via the Internet.

GATEWAY: Computer hardware and software that allow users to connect from one network to another.

GIF: Graphics Interchange Format—a common image format. Most images seen on Web pages are GIF files.

GOPHER: A system allowing users to search for files via menus or directory structures. Uses plain-English names and is text based only.

HELPER APPLICATION: A program allowing you to view multimedia files that your Web browser cannot handle internally, such as images, audio and video files. The file must be downloaded before it will be displayed/played. Plug-ins allow you to actually view the file over the Internet without downloading first.

HOME PAGE: The opening page of a Web site. Also, the Web site that automatically loads each time you launch your browser.

HOST: The name of a specific machine within a larger domain.

HotJava: A Web browser developed by Sun Microsystems that takes full advantage of applets written in the Java programming language.

HTML: HyperText Markup Language—a collection of tags typically used in the development of Web pages.

HTTP: HyperText Transfer Protocol—a set of instructions for communication between a server and a World Wide Web client.

HYPERLINK: A connection between two anchors. Clicking on one anchor will take you to the linked anchor. Can be within the same document/page or two totally different documents.

HYPERTEXT: A document that contains links to other documents, commonly seen in Web pages and help files.

INFORMATION SUPERHIGHWAY/INFOBAHN: The terms were coined to describe a possible upgrade to the existing Internet through the use of fiber-optic and/or coaxial cable to allow for high-speed data transmission. This highway does not exist—the Internet of today is not an information superhighway.

IRC: Internet Relay Chat—the system allowing Internet users to conduct on-line text-based communication with one or more other users.

ISDN: Integrated Services Digital Network—a system of all-digital, high-bandwidth telephone lines allowing for the simultaneous delivery of audio, video, and data. Data travels at 128 Kbps.

ISP: Internet service provider—the company that provides you with a connection to the Internet via either a dial-up connection or a direct connection.

IP ADDRESS: Internet Protocol address—every computer on the Internet has a unique identifying number, like 209.37.81.17.

INTERNET: The worldwide network of computers communicating via an agreed-upon set of Internet protocols. Odds are that if you are reading this document, you are probably on the Internet right now (just in case you didn't know).

JAVA: A programming language, similar to C++, created by Sun Microsystems for developing applets that are capable of running on any computer regardless of the operating system.

JPEG: Joint Photographic Experts Group—a common image format. Most of the images you see embedded into Web pages are GIFs, but sometimes, especially in art or photographic Web sites, you can click on the image to bring up a higher-resolution (larger) JPEG version of the same image.

KILL FILE: Found within newsreaders, a list of undesirable authors or threads to filter out.

KNOWBOT: A system for finding Internet user's e-mail addresses via their first and last names. Due to the rapid growth in the volume of e-mail users, this system is not perfect.

LAN: Local area network—a network of computers confined within a small area, such as an office building.

LINK: Another name for a hyperlink.

LISTSERV: An electronic mailing list typically used by a broad range of discussion groups. When you subscribe to a listserv, you will receive periodic e-mail messages about the topic you have requested.

LURKING: The act of reading through mail lists and newsgroups without posting any messages. Considered good netiquette to get the feel of the topic before adding your own two cents.

LYNX: A popular text (nongraphical) World Wide Web Browser.

MAILING LIST: A list of e-mail addresses to which messages are sent. You can subscribe to a mailing lists typically by sending an e-mail to the contact address with the following in the body of the message: the word *subscribe,* the name of the list, and your e-mail address.

MICROSOFT: C'mon, everybody has heard of Microsoft! Home of Bill Gates. The world's largest operating system and application software development company. Products include Windows 95, NT, the MS Office suite, MS Internet Explorer, and far too many others to list here.

MIDI: Musical Instrument Digital Interface—a high-quality audio file format.

MIME: Multipurpose Internet Mail Extensions, a protocol for allowing e-mail messages to contain various types of media (text, audio, video, images, etc.).

MIRROR SITE: An Internet site set up as an alternative to a busy site; contains copies of all the files stored at the primary location.

MOSAIC: One of the first graphical World Wide Web browsers developed at NCSA.

MPEG: Motion Picture Experts Group—a video file format offering excellent quality in a relatively small file. Video files found on the Internet are frequently stored in the MPEG format. Full-length movies (like *Top Gun*) are available on CD and are stored in the MPEG format.

MULTIMEDIA: A combination of media types on a single document, including text, graphics, animation, audio, and video.

NAME SERVER: A computer running a program that converts domain names into appropriate IP addresses and vice versa.

NCSA: National Center for Supercomputing Applications—an organization headquartered at the University of Illinois. Researchers here created the Mosaic and HTTPD server programs.

NETIQUETTE: Emily Post meets the Internet. Short for Internet etiquette.

NETSCAPE: Netscape dominates the market for World Wide Web browsers and servers.

NETWORK: A system of connected computers exchanging information with each other. A LAN is a relatively smaller form of a network in comparison to the Internet, a worldwide network of computers.

NEWBIE: A new Internet user. If you are reading this definition, you probably are one (or at least were one before you read this).

NEWSGROUP: A particular section within the USENET system typically, though not always, dedicated to a particular subject of interest. Also known as *discussion groups.*

NEWSREADER: A program designed for organizing the threads received from a mailing list or newsgroup.

ON-LINE: When you connect to the Internet, you are on-line.

ON-LINE SERVICE: Services such as America Online, CompuServe, Prodigy, and the Microsoft Network that provide content to subscribers and usually connections to the Internet, though sometimes limited. For instance, on-line services just recently added Web browsing ability. If you spend a lot of time on the Internet, the fees these services charge add up rapidly.

PACKET: A chunk of data. The TCP/IP protocol breaks large data files into smaller "packets" for transmission. When the data reaches its destination, the protocol makes sure that all packets have arrived without error.

PAGE: An HTML document, or Web site.

PGP: Pretty Good Privacy—an encryption scheme that uses the "public key" approach—messages are encrypted using the publicly available key, but can only be deciphered by the intended recipient via the private key.

PING: Packet Internet Groper. A program for determining if another computer is presently connected to the Internet.

PIXEL: Short for picture element—the smallest unit of resolution on a monitor. Commonly used as a unit of measurement.

PKZIP: A widely available shareware utility allowing users to compress and de-compress data files. Helps reduce storage space and transfer times.

PLUG-IN: A small application that extends the built-in capabilities of your Web browser. Examples include Macromedia's Shockwave, providing animation, and RealAudio, offering streamed sound files over the Internet. Compared to helpers, the multimedia files do not need to be downloaded before shown or played.

POP: Post Office Protocol—a method of storing and returning e-mail.

POST: To send a message to a mailing list or newsgroup.

PPP: Point-to-Point Protocol—a protocol for converting a dial-up connection to a point-to-point connection over the Internet. Frequently used for accessing the World Wide Web over phone lines. Considered more stable than a SLIP connection.

PROTOCOL: An agreed-upon set of rules by which computers exchange information.

PROVIDER: An Internet service provider, or ISP.

QUEUE: A list of e-mail messages that will be distributed next time you log on to the Internet.

QUICKTIME: A common video file format created by Apple Computer. Video files found on the Internet are often stored in the QuickTime format—they require a special viewer program for playback.

REGISTER: With shareware, when you contact the vendor and pay for the product, you are registering. In return, you will receive either a password to turn off the nag notices or a copy of the full commercial version.

ROBOT: A program that automatically searches the World Wide Web for files.

SEARCH ENGINE: A tool for searching for information on the Internet by topic. Popular engines include InfoSeek, Inktomi (Alta Vista), and Web Crawler.

SERVER: One-half of the client/server protocol, runs on a networked computer and responds to requests submitted by the client. Your World Wide Web browser is a client of a World Wide Web server.

SGML: Standard General Markup Language—a standard for markup languages. HTML is one version of SGML.

SHAREWARE: Software that is available on a free, limited-trial basis. Sometimes this is a fully featured product, other times it lacks some of the features of the commercial version. If you find the product useful, you are expected to register the software, for which in return you will receive the full-featured commercial version.

SIGNATURE: A personal tag automatically appended to an e-mail message. May be short, such as the author's name, or quite long, such as a favorite quote.

SITE: A single Web page or a collection of related Web pages.

SLIP: Serial Line Internet Protocol—a protocol allowing you to use a dial-up connection as an Internet connection. Similar to a PPP connection, though far less stable.

SMTP: Simple Mail Transfer Protocol—a protocol dictating how e-mail messages are exchanged over the Internet.

SNAIL MAIL: Plain old paper mail. United States Post Office. Cliff Claven delivered snail mail when he wasn't drinking with Norm at Cheers.

SPAM: *Non-Internet:* Delicious "meat" in a can! *Internet:* Sending multiple, some-times thousands, of unwelcome messages to a newsgroup or mailing list to pro-mote a commercial product or web site.

SUBSCRIBE: To become of a member of. One can subscribe to a mailing list, a news-group, an on-line service, or an Internet service.

T1: A category of leased telephone line service allowing transfer rates of 1.5 Mbps (megabytes per second) over the Internet. Too expensive for home users (around $2,000 per month), but commonly found in business environments.

TAR: Tape archive—a compression format commonly used in the transfer and stor-age of files residing on Unix computers.

TCP/IP: Transmission Control Protocol/Internet Protocol—this protocol is the foundation of the Internet, an agreed-upon set of rules directing computers on how to exchange information with each other. Other Internet protocols, such as FTP, Gopher, and HTTP, sit on top of TCP/IP.

TELNET: A protocol for logging on to remote computers from anywhere on the In-ternet.

THREAD: An ongoing message-based conversation on a single subject.

TIFF: Tagged Image File Format—a popular graphic image file format.

TROLLING: Deliberately posting false information in order to elicit responses from people who really want to help. A typical response might be, "No, Bart Simpson was NOT one of our founding fathers."

UNIX: A powerful operating system used on the backbone machines of the Inter-net. World Wide Web servers frequently run on Unix.

UPLOAD: To copy a file from a local computer connected to the Internet to a remote computer. Opposite is download.

URL: Uniform Resource Locator—the method by which Internet sites are addressed. An example would be "http://www.squareone.com," the address of the this home page.

USENET: Short for user's network. The collection of the thousands of bulletin boards residing on the Internet. Each bulletin board contains discussion groups, or newsgroups, dedicated to a myriad of topics. Messages are posted and responded to by readers either as public or private e-mails.

VERONICA: The system used in searching Gopher menus for topics. Also Archie's girlfriend.

VIRUS*: A malicious and generally quite small software program designed and written to adversely affect your computer by altering the way it works without your knowledge or permission.

VISIT: Synonymous with viewing a World Wide Web site.

WAIS: Wide Area Information Server—a system of searchable text databases.

WAN: Wide area network—a system of connected computers spanning a large geographical area.

WAV: Waveform audio (.wav)—a common audio file format for DOS/Windows computers.

WINSOCK: A Microsoft Windows DLL file that provides the interface to TCP/IP services, essentially allowing Windows to use Web browsers, FTP programs, and others.

WWW: World Wide Web, or simply Web. A subset of the Internet which uses a combination of text, graphics, audio, and video (multimedia) to provide information on almost every subject imaginable.

X BITMAP: An uncompressed black-and-white-image file format (.xbm).

X PIXELMAP: An uncompressed color-image file format (.xpm).

YAHOO: A Web directory created by a couple of guys from Stanford who now have more money than the entire state of Arkansas. Rumor has it they own one business suit between them. Their site is constantly updated and provides an easy way of finding almost any Web page. Check it out for yourself at www.yahoo.com.

ZIP: A compressed file format (.zip). Many files available on the Internet are compressed or zipped in order to reduce storage space and transfer times. To uncompress the file, you need a utility like PKZIP (DOS) or WinZip (Windows).

ENDNOTES

1. Adam Gaffin, *The Electronic Frontier Foundation's Guide to the Internet*, Version 3.20 (December 11, 1996).
2. Michael Hanrahan, "History of the Internet," Web posted at http://www.wayoutthere.com/idrc/history/index.html.
3. Tracy LaQuey and Jeanne C. Ryer, *The Internet Companion: A Beginner's Guide to Global Networking* (Addison-Wesley, 1993), on-line version.
4. Gregory R. Gromov, "History of Internet and WWW: The Roads and Crossroads of Internet's History," Web posted at: http://www.internetvalley.com/intval.html.
5. Many of the definitions in this manual are adapted from SquareOne Technology's *Internet Glossary*, which is reprinted as a glossary in this book.
6. Zakon, Robert Hobbes. "Hobbes' Internet Timeline v2.4a." February 22, 1996, p. 2. Web posted at http://info.isoc.org/guest/zakon/Internet/History/HIT.html.
7. "Technology," Clinton Campaign Position Paper, September 16, 1992.
8. The assignment of IP addresses is made through a central Internet Registry, which is separate from the InterNIC.
9. Berners-Lee, Tim and Robert Cailliau. "WorldWideWeb: Proposal for a HyperText Project," p. 2. Undated. Web posted at http://www.w3.org/pub/WWW/Proposal. (According to Robert Cailliau's "A Little History of the World Wide Web," October 3, 1995—Web posted at http://www.w3.org/pub/WWW/History.html—the proposal was submitted in October 1990.)
10. February 1996 issue.
11. SquareOne Technology, "How Do I Locate and Use a Helper Application?" Web posted at http://www.squareonetech.com/helper.html.
12. Cecil Greek, "Using the Internet as a Newsmaking Criminology Tool." Presentation given at the American Society of Criminology annual meeting, San Diego, CA, November 20, 1997. Web posted at http://www.fsu.edu/~crimdo/asc-sd.htm.
13. See G. Martin Lively and Judy A. Reardon, "Justice on the Net: The National Institute of Justice Promotes Internet Services," an *NIJ Research in Action* bulletin. March 1996.

14. Richard Castagna, Lynn Ginsburg, and Cynthia Morgan, "Stop the E-mail Madness," *Windows Magazine*, October 1997.

15. Internet telephony, or the use of Internet services to carry voice communications, is still in its infancy. In the not-too-distant future, however, many people will be able to talk over the Internet in much the same way that they send e-mail or participate in chat rooms today.

16. *Essays*, bk. 3, ch. 9, "Of Vanity" (1588).

17. We should say "easily available," since messages are routinely stored on listservers for a period of time and *can* be accessed by anyone with sufficient expertise at issuing listserv commands. Most, however, would not regard the process as easy.

18. See the Leathernet.Com Glossary at http://www.learnthenet.com/english/index.html.

19. Northern Light search help and tips. Web posted at http://www.nlsearch.com/docs/bigfaq.htm#simplesearch. Accessed June 1, 1998.

20. Published by Search Engine Watch, owned by Mecklermedia. Web posted at http://searchenginewatch.com/features.htm. Accessed April 3, 1998.

21. Visit CPSR at http://www.cpsr.org.

22. The Computer Ethics Institute may be reached at Computer Ethics Institute, 11 Dupont Circle, NW, Suite 900, Washington, DC 20036.

23. From the classic guide by Arlene Rinaldi, *The Net: User Guidelines and Netiquette*, Web posted at http://www.fau.edu/rinaldi/net/ten.html.

24. See Albion.com's netiquette section at http://www.albion.com/netiquette/index.html.

25. *Twenty-Four Hours*, 15 Dec. 1969, BBC-TV. From *The Columbia Dictionary of Quotations*. Copyright © 1993 by Columbia University Press.

26. C. Northcote Parkinson, *The Pursuit of Progress* (1958).

27. Information derived and partially quoted from govtjobs.com. Web posted at http://www.govtjobs.com/index.html. Accessed March 5, 1998.

28. Cynthia Mason and Charles Ardai, *Future Crime: An Anthology of the Shape of Crime to Come* (New York: Donald I. Fine, 1992), p. xiii.

29. The company that created the RSA standard is RSA Data Security, Inc. It is based in Redwood City, California, and can be reached at (415) 595-8782 or at http://www.rsa.com.

30. See the CERT® home page, http://www.cert.org.

31. Definition adapted from Norton AntiVirus Web site. See http://www.norton.com.

32. While there are sometimes ways to recover from these kinds of viral attacks, they are best left to professionals.

INDEX

student study
ART NOTEBOOK

Inquiry into Life

Seventh Edition

Sylvia S. Mader

WCB **Wm. C. Brown Publishers**

Dubuque, Iowa · Melbourne, Australia · Oxford, England

Book Team

Editor *Colin H. Wheatley*
Developmental Editor *Kristine M. Noel*
Production Editor *Catherine S. Di Pasquale*
Designer *Anna C. Manhart*
Art Editor *Joseph P. O'Connell*
Photo Editor *Lori Hancock*
Permissions Coordinator *Karen L. Storlie*

Wm. C. Brown Publishers
A Division of Wm. C. Brown Communications, Inc.

Vice President and General Manager *Beverly Kolz*
Vice President, Publisher *Kevin Kane*
Vice President, Director of Sales and Marketing *Virginia S. Moffat*
National Sales Manager *Douglas J. DiNardo*
Marketing Manager *Craig Johnson*
Advertising Manager *Janelle Keeffer*
Director of Production *Colleen A. Yonda*
Publishing Services Manager *Karen J. Slaght*
Permissions/Records Manager *Connie Allendorf*

Wm. C. Brown Communications, Inc.

President and Chief Executive Officer *G. Franklin Lewis*
Corporate Senior Vice President, President of WCB Manufacturing *Roger Meyer*
Corporate Senior Vice President and Chief Financial Officer *Robert Chesterman*

Cover photo © Art Wolfe

The credits section for this book begins on page 199 and is
considered an extension of the copyright page.

A Times Mirror Company

ISBN 0-697-23117-8

Printed in the United States of America by Wm. C. Brown Communications, Inc.,
2460 Kerper Boulevard, Dubuque, IA 52001

10 9 8 7 6 5 4 3 2

TO INSTRUCTORS AND STUDENTS

This Student Study Art Notebook is a gratis ancillary to assist students in note taking during lectures. On each page, there are one, two, or sometimes three figures faithfully reproduced from the textbook. Each figure also corresponds to one of the 250 acetates available to instructors who adopt this textbook.

The intention is to place the acetate art in front of students (via the notebook) as the instructor uses the overhead during lectures. The advantage to the student is that he/she will be able to see all labels clearly, and take meaningful notes without having to make hurried sketches of the acetate figure.

The pages of the Art Notebook are perforated and three-hole punched, so they can be removed and placed in a personal binder for specific study and review, or to create space for additional notes.

DIRECTORY OF NOTEBOOK FIGURES

TO ACCOMPANY

INQUIRY INTO LIFE, 7/E BY SYLVIA S. MADER

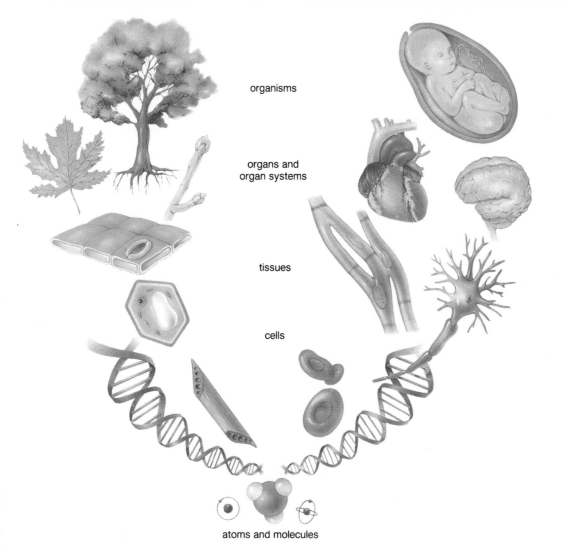

organisms

organs and
organ systems

tissues

cells

atoms and molecules

Levels of Organization
Figure 1.2

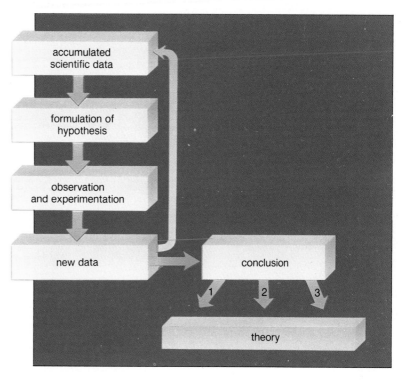

accumulated
scientific data

formulation of
hypothesis

observation
and experimentation

new data

conclusion

1   2   3

theory

The Scientific Method
Figure 1.8

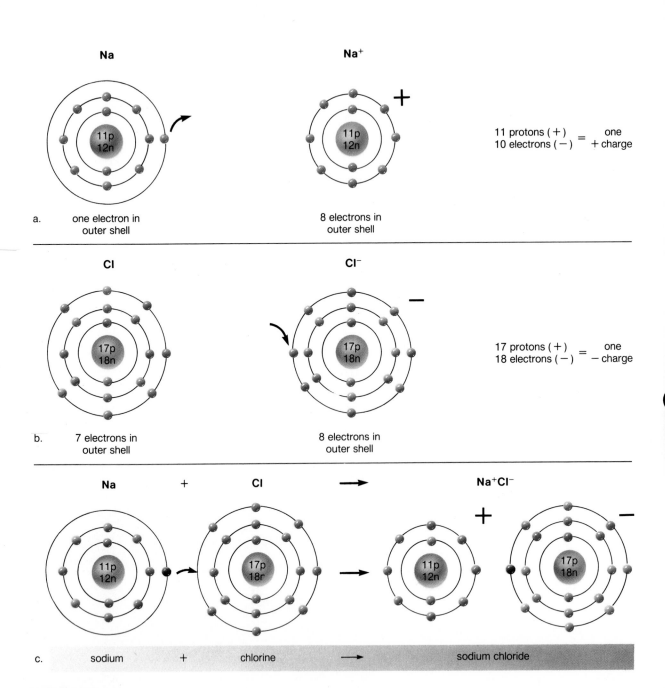

Na   **Na⁺**

a. one electron in   8 electrons in
    outer shell   outer shell

11 protons ($+$)   =   one
10 electrons ($-$) $+$ charge

Cl   **Cl⁻**

b. 7 electrons in   8 electrons in
    outer shell   outer shell

17 protons ($+$)   =   one
18 electrons ($-$) $-$ charge

Na $+$ **Cl** $\longrightarrow$ **Na⁺Cl⁻**

c. sodium $+$ chlorine $\longrightarrow$ sodium chloride

Ionic Reactions
Figure 2.4

2

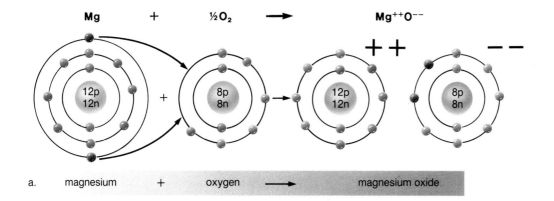

Mg   +   **½O₂**   ➞   **Mg⁺⁺O⁻⁻**

a.   magnesium   +   oxygen   ➞   magnesium oxide

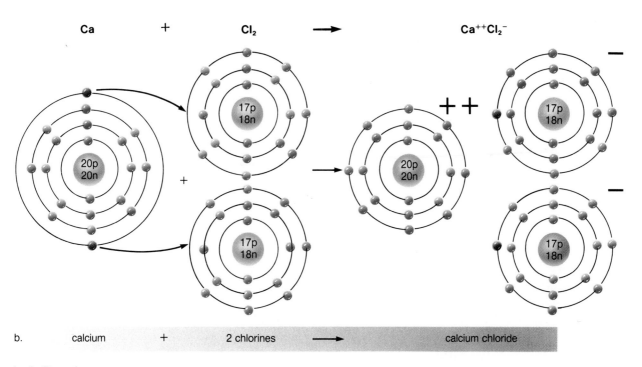

Ca   +   **Cl₂**   ➞   **Ca⁺⁺Cl₂⁻**

b.   calcium   +   2 chlorines   ➞   calcium chloride

Ionic Reactions
Figure 2.5

3

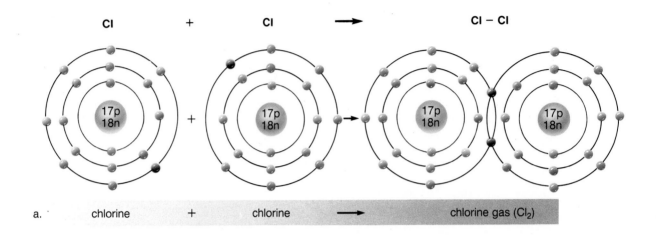

Cl + **Cl** ⟶ **Cl – Cl**

a.   chlorine   +   chlorine   ⟶   chlorine gas (Cl_2)

N + **N** ⟶ **N≡N**

b.   nitrogen   +   nitrogen   ⟶   nitrogen gas (N_2)

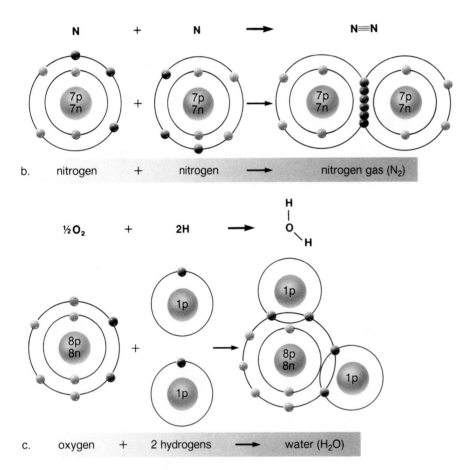

$\frac{1}{2}O_2$ + **2H** ⟶

$$\begin{array}{c} H \\ | \\ O \\ \diagdown \\ \quad H \end{array}$$

c.   oxygen   +   2 hydrogens   ⟶   water (H_2O)

Covalent Reactions
Figure 2.6

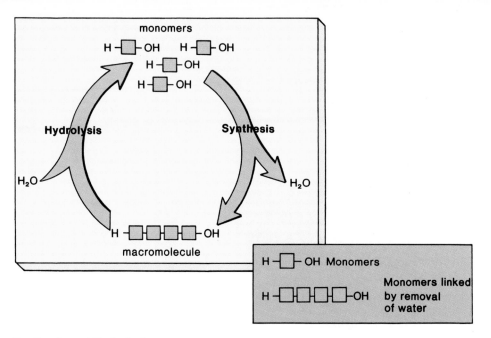

Synthesis and Hydrolysis
Figure 2.14

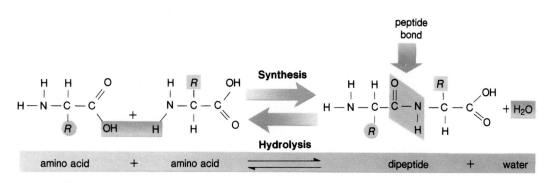

Dipeptide Formation
Figure 2.16

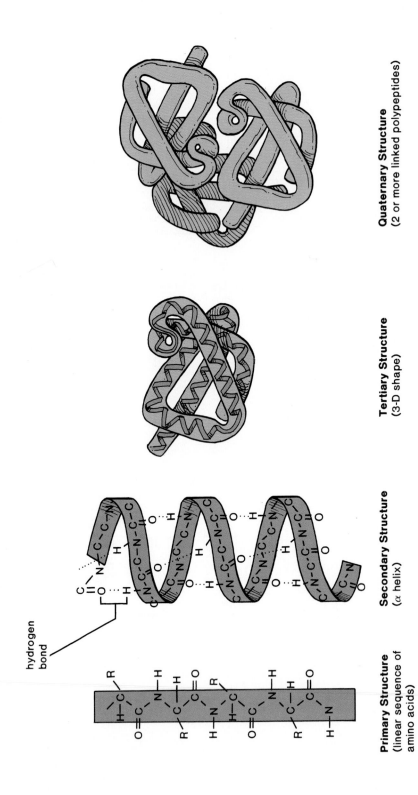

Primary Structure
(linear sequence of amino acids)

hydrogen bond

Secondary Structure
(α helix)

Tertiary Structure
(3-D shape)

Quaternary Structure
(2 or more linked polypeptides)

Levels of Structure in a Protein
Figure 2.17

6

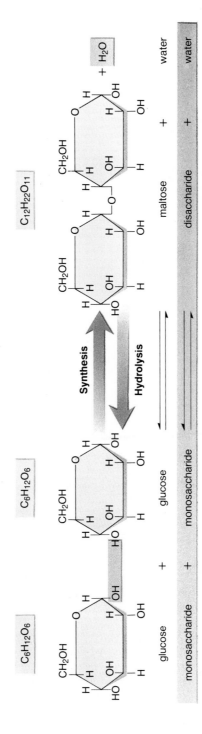

Disaccharide Formation
Figure 2.20

7

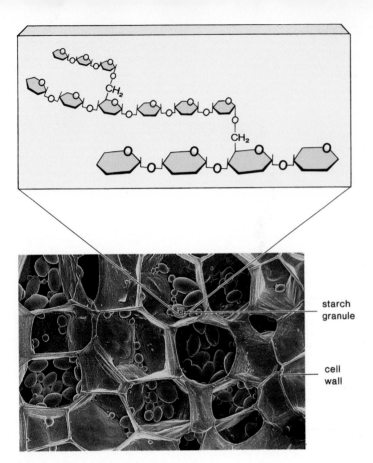

Starch Structure and Function
Figure 2.21

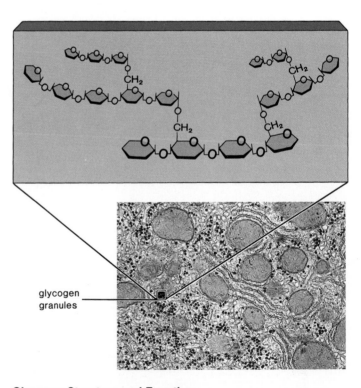

Glycogen Structure and Function
Figure 2.22

8

Cellulose Structure and Function
Figure 2.23

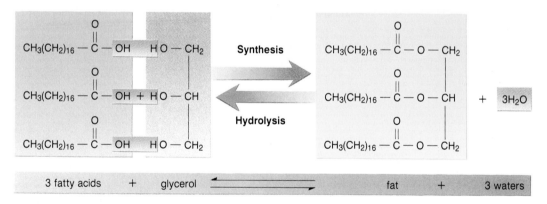

Fat Formation
Figure 2.24

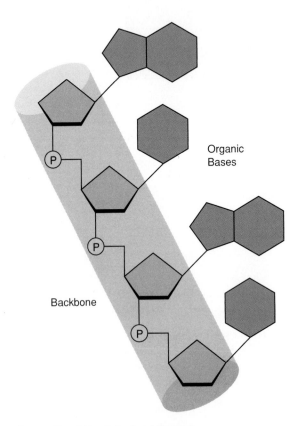

Organic
Bases

Backbone

Generalized Nucleic Acid Strand
Figure 2.30

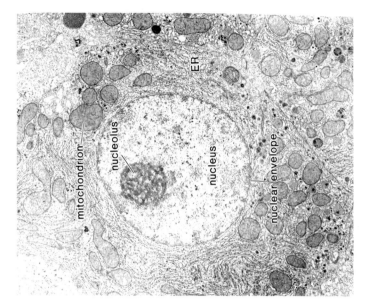

Animal Cell
Figure 3.4a

mitochondrion

nucleolus

nucleus

nuclear envelope

ER

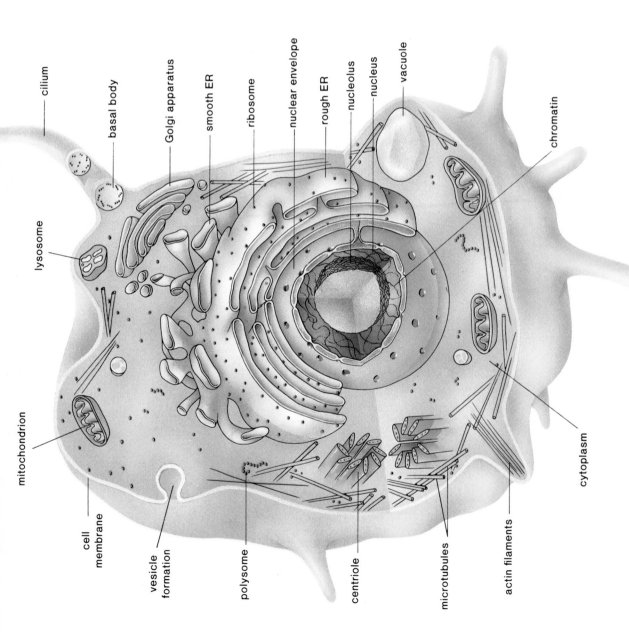

cilium

basal body

Golgi apparatus

smooth ER

ribosome

nuclear envelope

rough ER

nucleolus

nucleus

vacuole

chromatin

lysosome

mitochondrion

cell membrane

vesicle formation

polysome

centriole

microtubules

actin filaments

cytoplasm

11

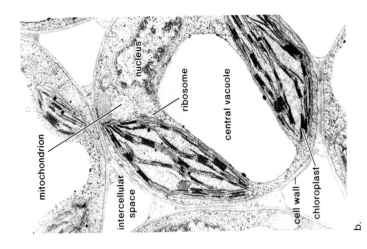

nucleus

ribosome

mitochondrion

intercellular
space

central vacuole

cell wall
chloroplast

b.

Plant Cell
Figure 3.4b

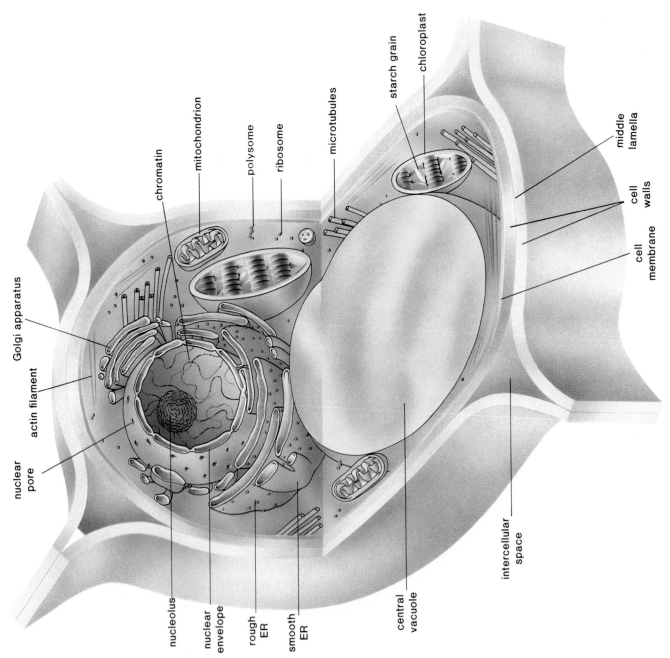

Golgi apparatus

actin filament

nuclear
pore

nucleolus

nuclear
envelope

rough
ER

smooth
ER

central
vacuole

intercellular
space

chromatin

mitochondrion

polysome

ribosome

microtubules

starch grain

chloroplast

middle
lamella

cell
walls

cell
membrane

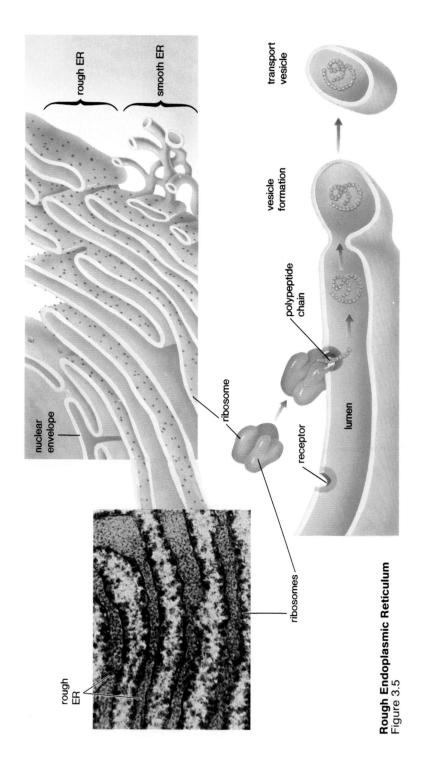

Rough Endoplasmic Reticulum
Figure 3.5

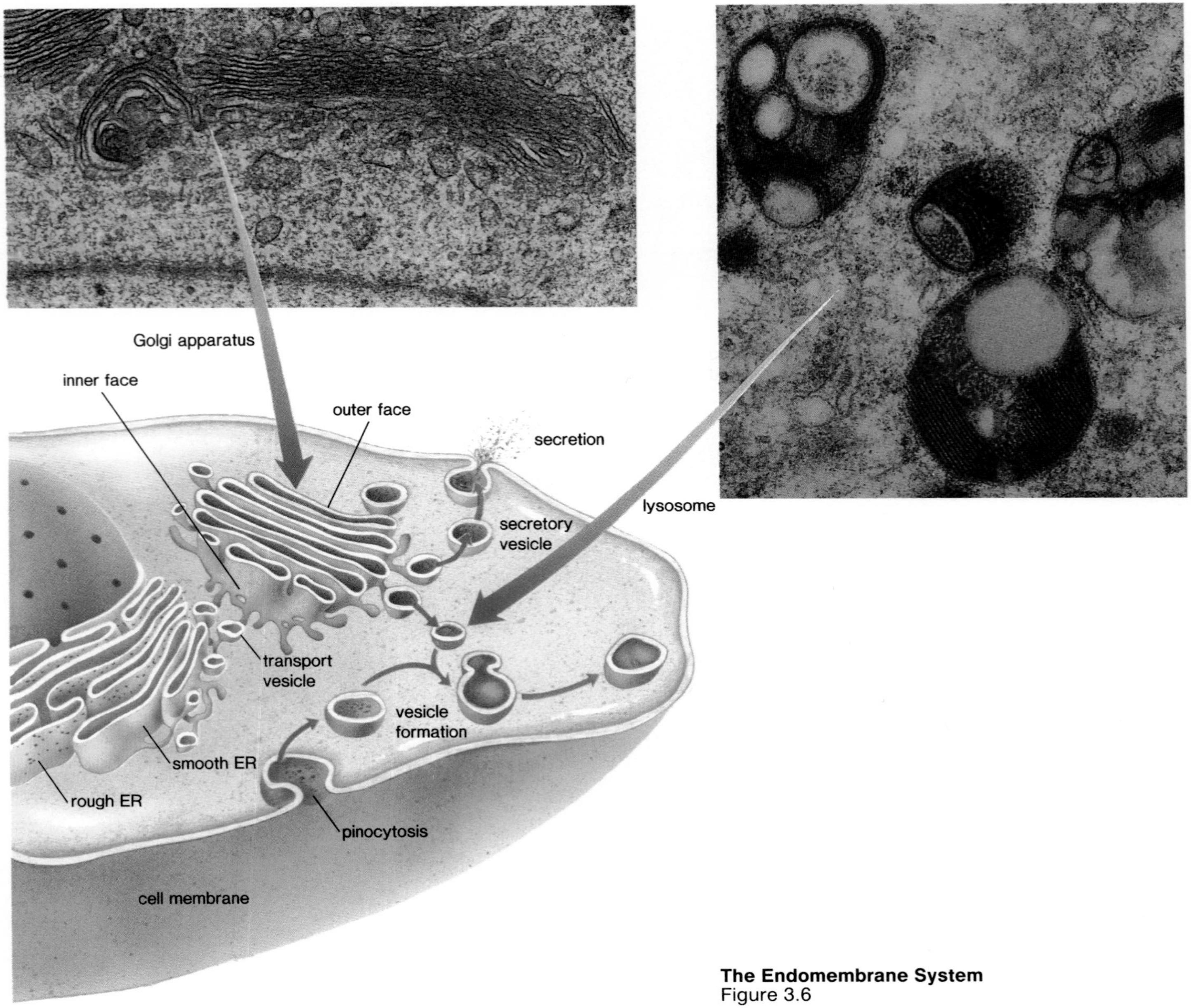

The Endomembrane System
Figure 3.6

lysosome

secretion

secretory
vesicle

outer face

Golgi apparatus

inner face

transport
vesicle

vesicle
formation

pinocytosis

smooth ER

rough ER

cell membrane

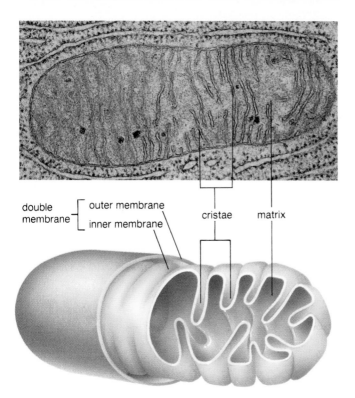

double membrane { outer membrane
                  inner membrane

cristae   matrix

Mitochondrial Structure
Figure 3.7

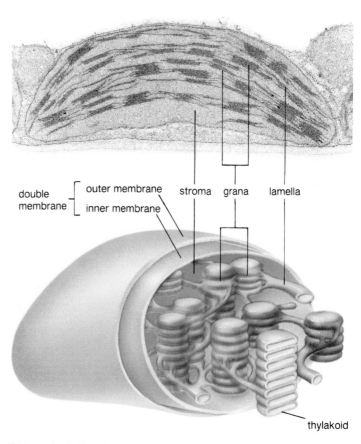

double membrane { outer membrane
                  inner membrane

stroma   grana   lamella

thylakoid

Chloroplast Structure
Figure 3.8

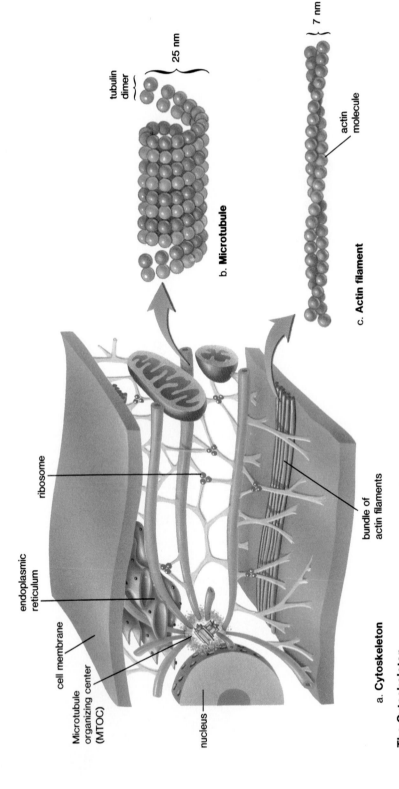

tubulin
dimer

25 nm

b. **Microtubule**

7 nm

actin
molecule

c. **Actin filament**

ribosome

endoplasmic
reticulum

cell membrane

Microtubule
organizing center
(MTOC)

nucleus

bundle of
actin filaments

a. **Cytoskeleton**

The Cytoskeleton
Figure 3.9

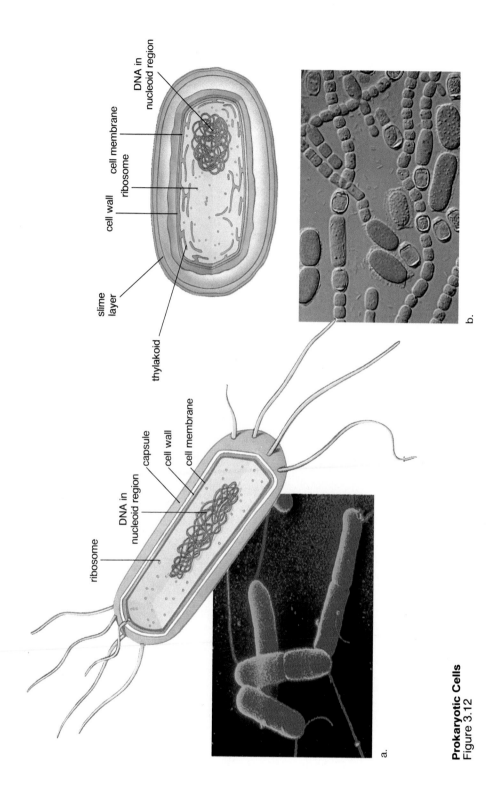

Prokaryotic Cells
Figure 3.12

DNA in nucleoid region

cell membrane

cell wall   ribosome

cell wall

slime layer

thylakoid

b.

capsule

cell wall

cell membrane

DNA in nucleoid region

ribosome

a.

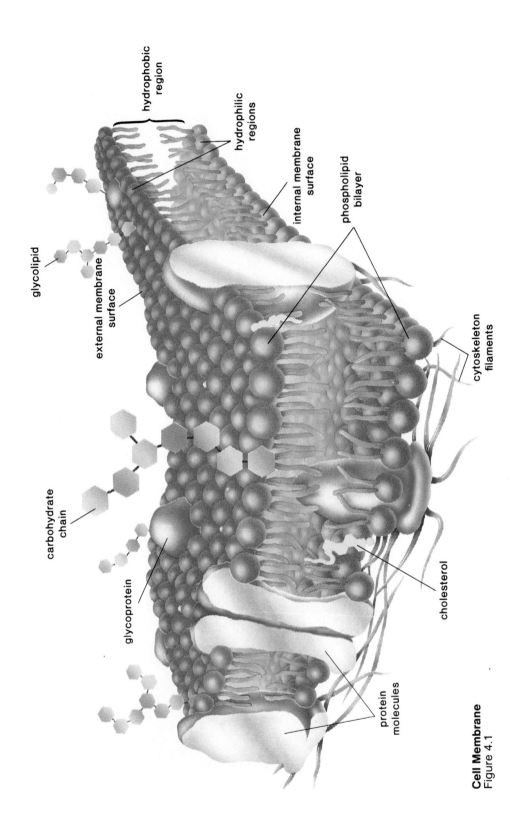

Cell Membrane
Figure 4.1

hydrophobic region

hydrophilic regions

internal membrane surface

phospholipid bilayer

glycolipid

external membrane surface

cytoskeleton filaments

carbohydrate chain

glycoprotein

cholesterol

protein molecules

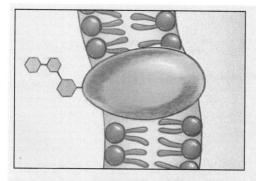

Cell-recognition protein

A glycoprotein that identifies the cell. For example, the MHC (major histocompatibility complex) glycoproteins are different for each person; thus, organ transplants are risky and relatively infrequent. Cells with foreign MHC glycoproteins are attacked by blood cells responsible for immunity.

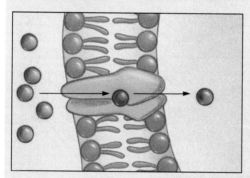

Outside of Cell

cell membrane

Inside of Cell

Channel protein

A protein that allows a particular molecule or ion to freely cross the cell membrane as it enters or exits the cell. Recently, it has been shown that cystic fibrosis, an inherited disorder, is caused by faulty chloride ion (Cl^-) channels. When these channels are not functioning normally, a thick mucus collects in airways and in pancreatic and liver ducts.

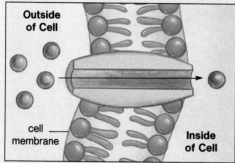

Carrier protein

A protein that selectively interacts with a specific molecule or ion so that it can cross the cell membrane to enter or exit the cell. The carrier protein that transports sodium ions (Na^+) and potassium ions (K^+) across the cell membrane requires ATP energy. The inability of some persons to use up energy for sodium-potassium transport has been suggested as the cause of their obesity.

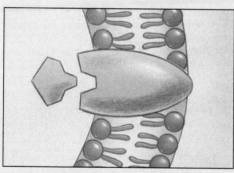

Receptor protein

A protein that is shaped in such a way that a specific molecule can bind to it. Recently, it has been shown that Pygmies are short not because they do not produce enough growth hormone, but because their cell membrane growth hormone receptors are faulty and cannot interact with the hormone.

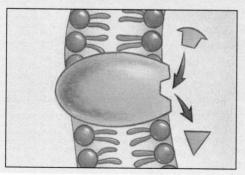

Enzymatic protein

A protein that catalyzes a specific reaction. For example, adenylate cyclase is a cell membrane protein that is involved in ATP metabolism. Polluted water may contain cholera bacteria, which release a toxin that interferes with the proper function of adenylate cyclase. Sodium ions and water leave intestinal cells in such volume that the individual dies from severe diarrhea.

Membrane Protein Diversity
Figure 4.2

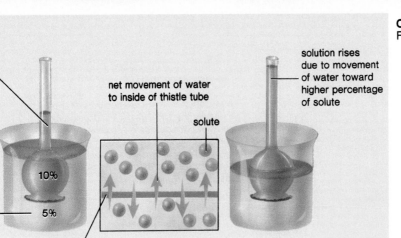

less water (higher percentage of solute)

net movement of water to inside of thistle tube

solute

solution rises due to movement of water toward higher percentage of solute

more water (lower percentage of solute)

10%

5%

membrane

a. In the beginning   b. In the meantime   c. In the end

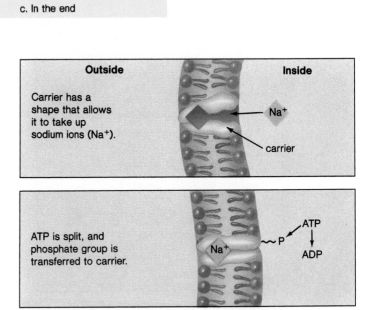

Outside   Inside

Carrier has a shape that allows it to take up sodium ions (Na^+).

Na^+

carrier

ATP is split, and phosphate group is transferred to carrier.

Na^+

$\sim P$

ATP

ADP

Change in shape results that causes carrier to release sodium ions (Na^+) outside the cell. New shape allows carrier to take up potassium ions (K^+).

Na^+

K^+

$\sim P$

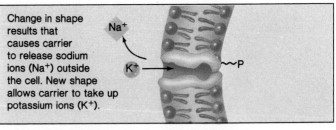

Phosphate group is released from carrier.

K^+

P

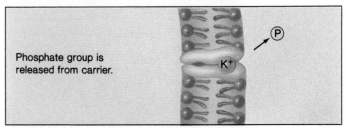

Change in shape results that causes carrier to release potassium ions (K^+) inside the cell. New shape is suitable to take up sodium ions (Na^+) once again.

K^+

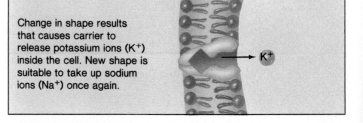

Sodium-Potassium Pump
Figure 4.9

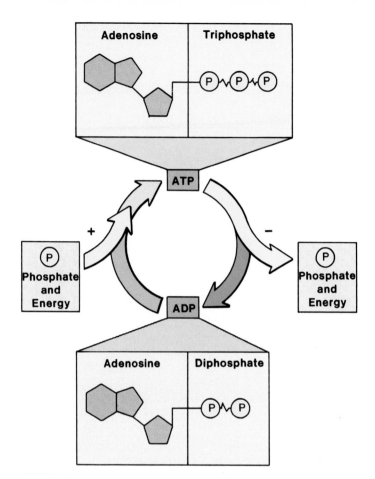

ATP Cycle
Figure 5.2

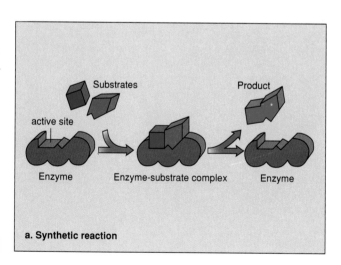

a. Synthetic reaction

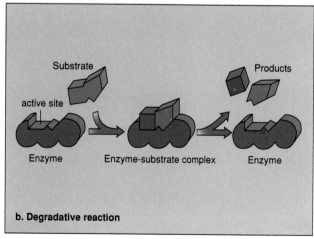

b. Degradative reaction

Enzymatic Action
Figure 5.4

21

Chloroplast Structure and Function
Figure 6.1

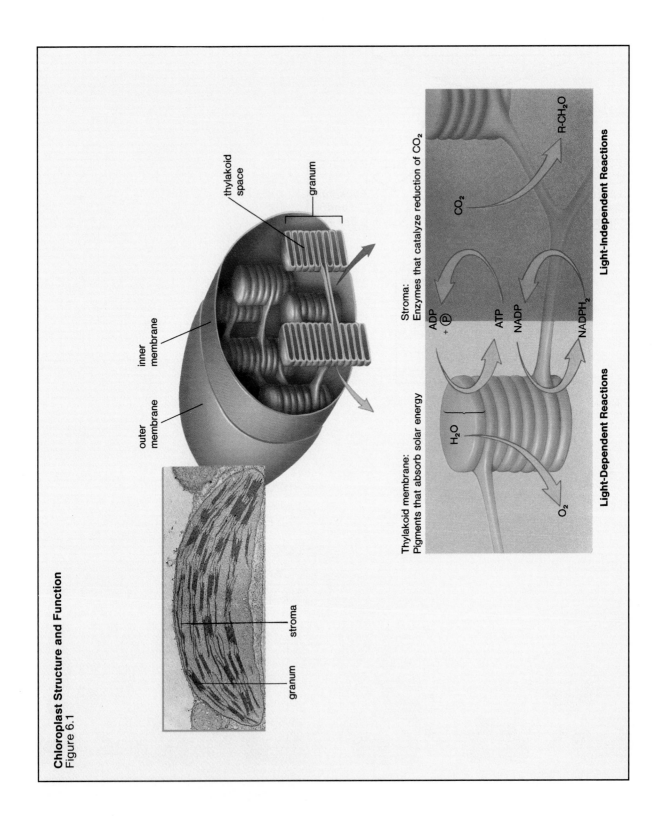

outer membrane

inner membrane

thylakoid space

granum

stroma

granum

Stroma:
Enzymes that catalyze reduction of CO_2

Thylakoid membrane:
Pigments that absorb solar energy

CO_2

R-CH$_2$O

ADP + (P)

ATP

NADP

NADPH$_2$

H_2O

O_2

Light-Dependent Reactions

Light-Independent Reactions

Noncyclic Electron Pathway
Figure 6.3

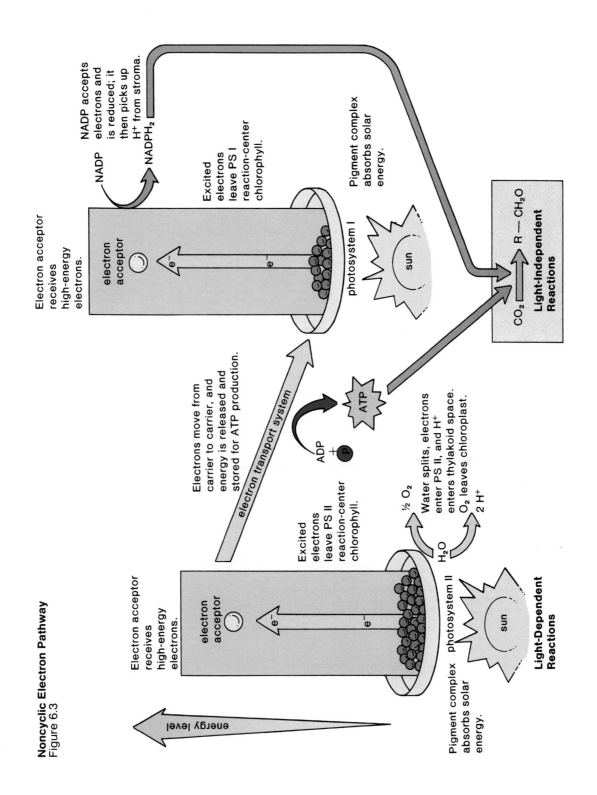

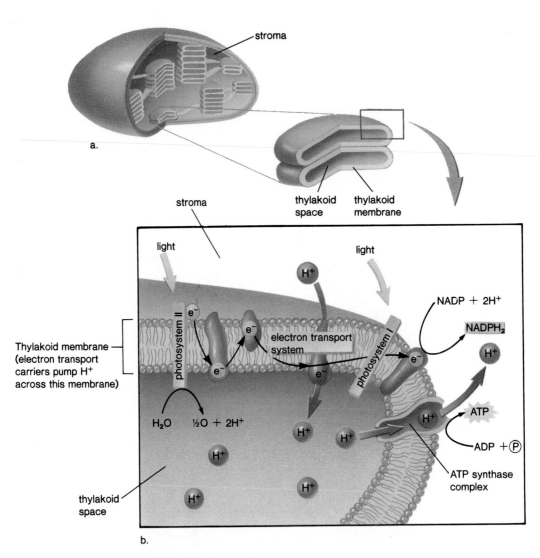

Electron Transport System and Chemiosmosis
Figure 6.4

Light-Independent Reactions
Figure 6.5

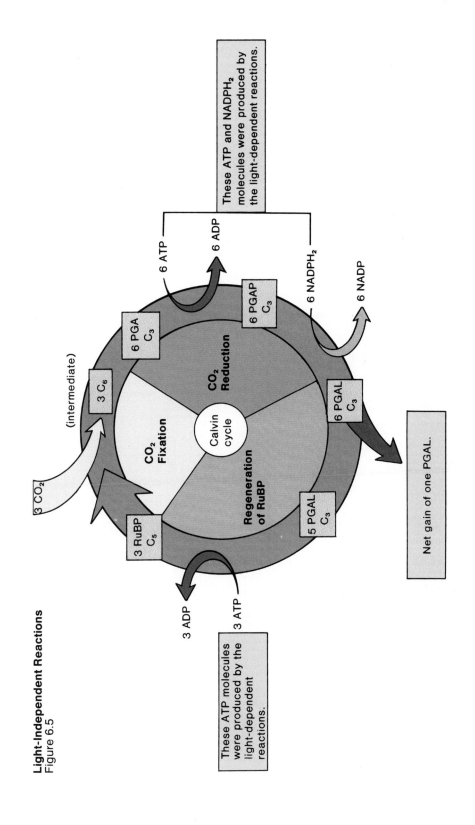

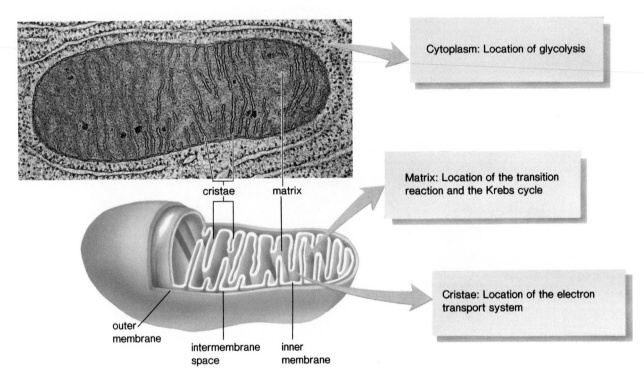

cristae   matrix

Cytoplasm: Location of glycolysis

Matrix: Location of the transition reaction and the Krebs cycle

Cristae: Location of the electron transport system

outer membrane

intermembrane space

inner membrane

Mitochondrion Structure and Function
Figure 6.6

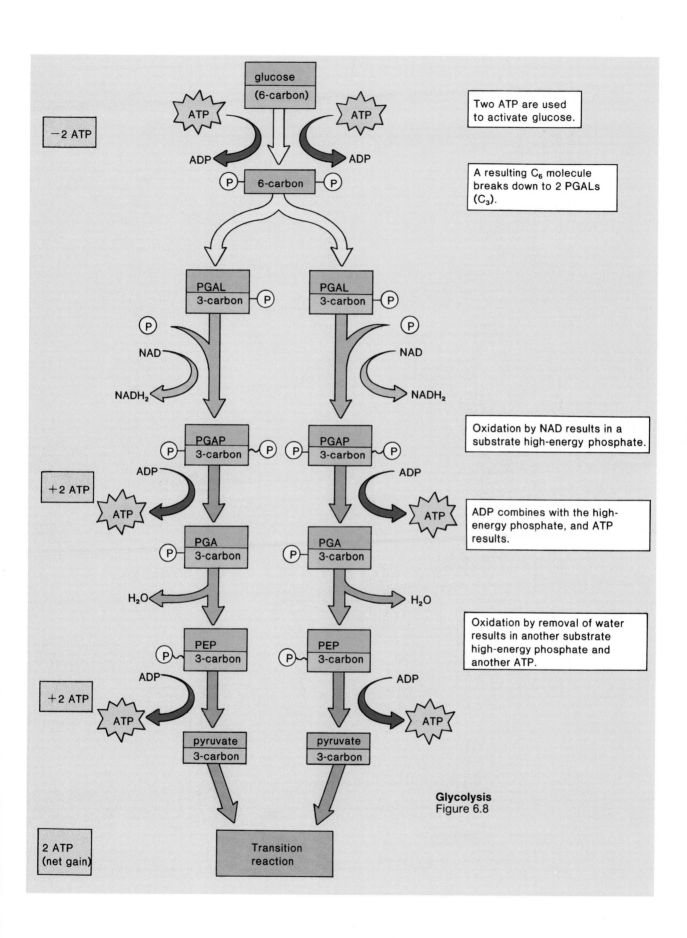

Glycolysis
Figure 6.8

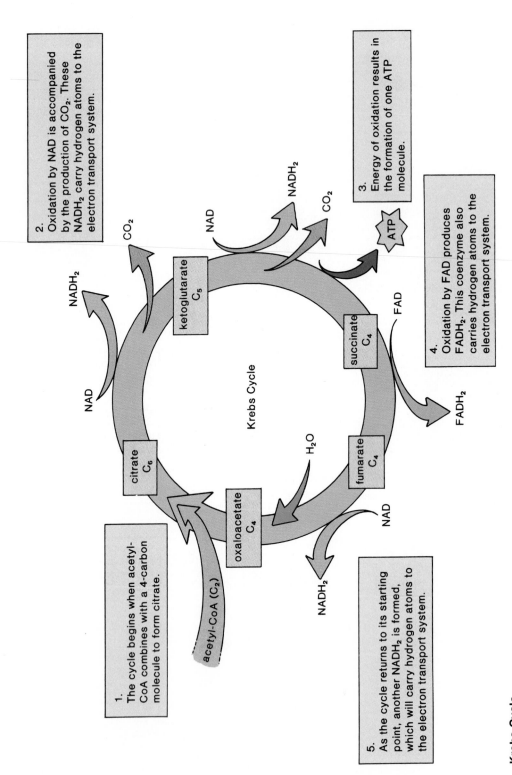

2.
Oxidation by NAD is accompanied by the production of CO_2. These $NADH_2$ carry hydrogen atoms to the electron transport system.

3.
Energy of oxidation results in the formation of one ATP molecule.

4.
Oxidation by FAD produces $FADH_2$. This coenzyme also carries hydrogen atoms to the electron transport system.

1.
The cycle begins when acetyl-CoA combines with a 4-carbon molecule to form citrate.

5.
As the cycle returns to its starting point, another $NADH_2$ is formed, which will carry hydrogen atoms to the electron transport system.

CO_2

$NADH_2$

NAD

ketoglutarate
C_5

NAD

citrate
C_6

Krebs Cycle

oxaloacetate
C_4

acetyl-CoA (C_2)

H_2O

fumarate
C_4

NAD

$NADH_2$

succinate
C_4

FAD

$FADH_2$

$NADH_2$

CO_2

ATP

Krebs Cycle
Figure 6.9

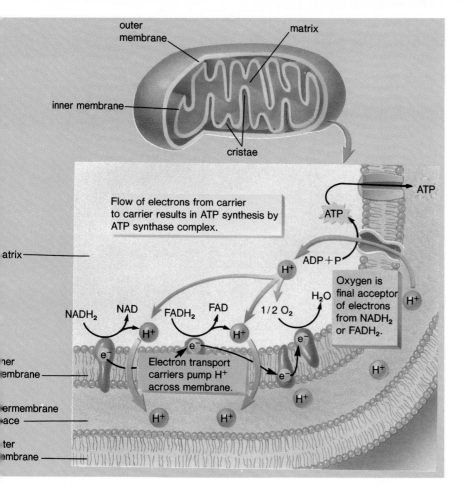

Flow of electrons from carrier to carrier results in ATP synthesis by ATP synthase complex.

ATP

ATP

ADP + P

matrix

H⁺

Oxygen is final acceptor of electrons from NADH₂ or FADH₂.

H⁺

NADH₂   NAD   FADH₂   FAD   1/2 O₂   H₂O

$NADH_2$ NAD $FADH_2$ FAD $1/2\ O_2$ H_2O

H⁺   H⁺   H⁺

inner membrane

e⁻

Electron transport carriers pump H⁺ across membrane.

e⁻   e⁻   e⁻

H⁺

intermembrane space

H⁺   H⁺   H⁺

outer membrane

outer membrane
inner membrane
matrix
cristae

Electron Transport System
Figure 6.10

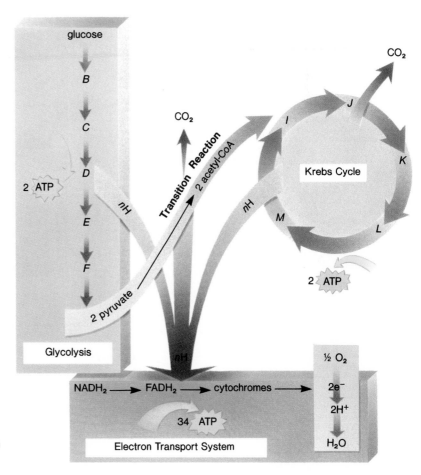

glucose

B

C

D nH

E

F

2 ATP

2 pyruvate

Glycolysis

CO_2

Transition Reaction

2 acetyl-CoA

nH

CO_2

I   J

K

Krebs Cycle

M   L

2 ATP

nH

NADH₂ → FADH₂ → cytochromes

½ O₂

2e⁻

2H⁺

H₂O

34 ATP

Electron Transport System

Pathways of Aerobic Cellular Respiration
Figure 6.11

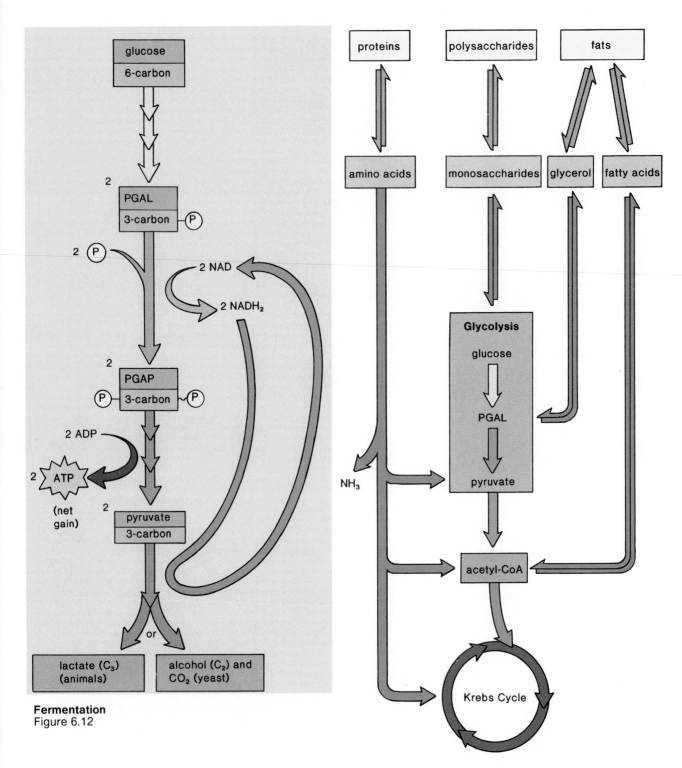

Fermentation
Figure 6.12

Interrelationship of Metabolic Pathways
Figure 6.13

Photosynthesis vs. Cellular Respiration
Figure 6.14

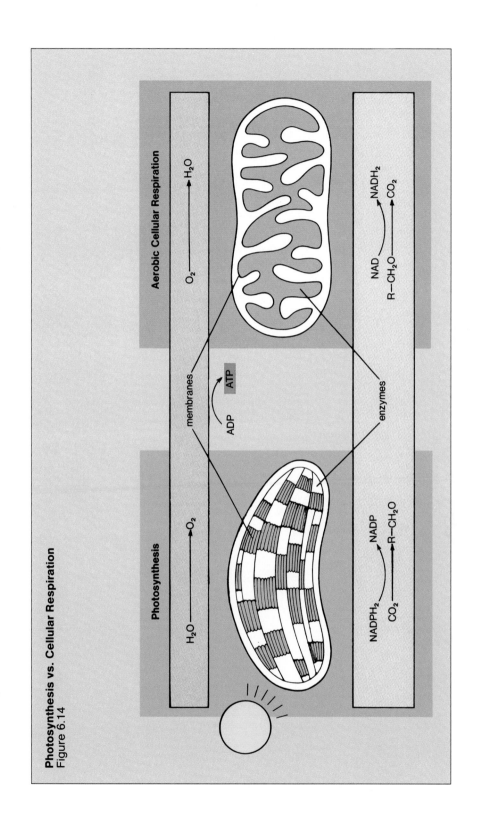

Photosynthesis

Aerobic Cellular Respiration

H$_2$O ⟶ O$_2$

O$_2$ ⟶ H$_2$O

membranes

ADP

ATP

enzymes

NADPH$_2$ ⟶ NADP
CO$_2$ ⟶ R–CH$_2$O

NAD ⟶ NADH$_2$
R–CH$_2$O ⟶ CO$_2$

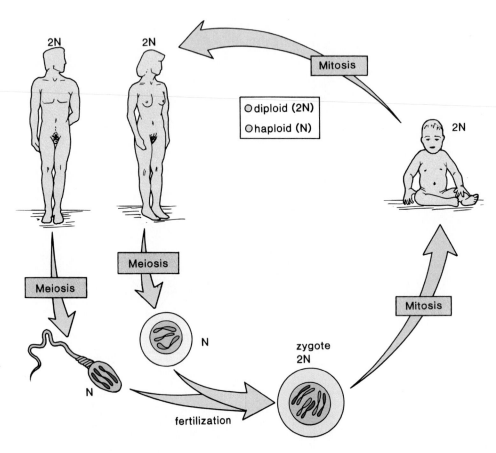

2N

2N

Mitosis

○ diploid (2N)
○ haploid (N)

2N

Meiosis

Meiosis

Mitosis

N

N

zygote
2N

fertilization

Life Cycle of Humans
Figure 7.2

Mitosis Overview
Figure 7.4

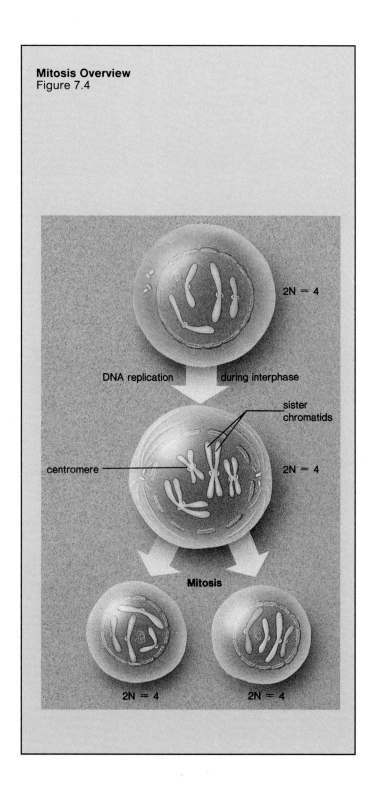

2N = 4

DNA replication   during interphase

sister
chromatids

centromere

2N = 4

Mitosis

2N = 4   2N = 4

Mitosis

Late Interphase

Chromosomes have 2 sister chromatids following DNA replication.

Parent cell

centrioles

chromatin

nucleolus

nuclear envelope

Prophase

Chromosomes are distinct and randomly placed in the cell. Spindle fibers appear, nuclear envelope fragments; nucleolus disappears.

chromosome

centromere

Metaphase

Chromosomes (each having 2 sister chromatids) are at the equator (center of fully formed spindle).

spindle fibers

equator

pole

aster

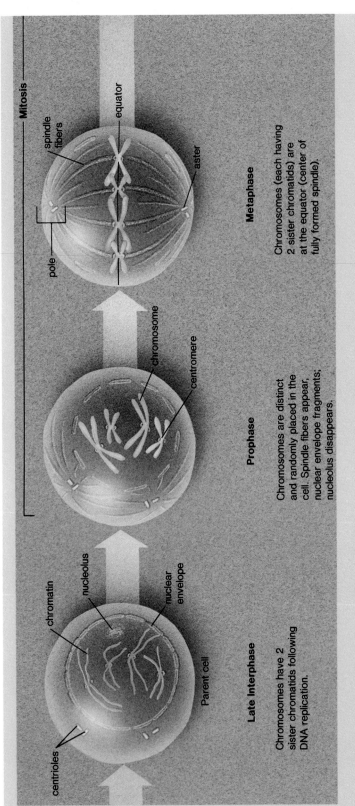

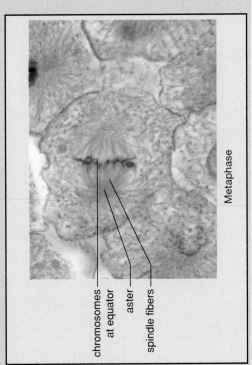

chromosomes at equator

aster

spindle fibers

Metaphase

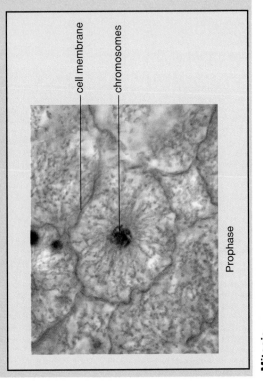

cell membrane

chromosomes

Prophase

Mitosis
Figure 7.5

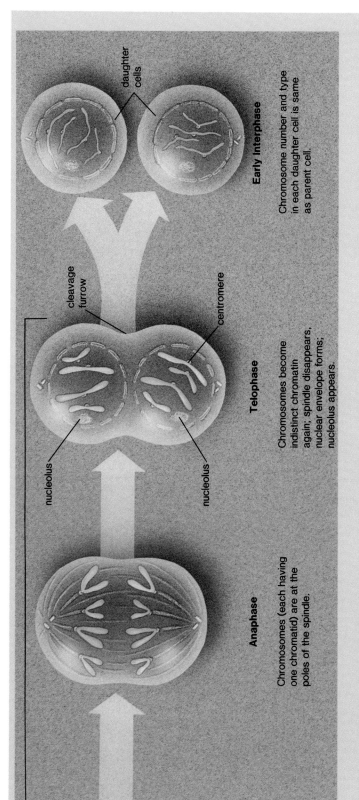

Anaphase

Chromosomes (each having one chromatid) are at the poles of the spindle.

Telophase

Chromosomes become indistinct chromatin again; spindle disappears, nuclear envelope forms; nucleolus appears.

nucleolus

nucleolus

cleavage furrow

centromere

daughter cells

Early Interphase

Chromosome number and type in each daughter cell is same as parent cell.

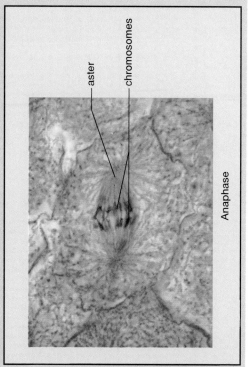

aster

chromosomes

Anaphase

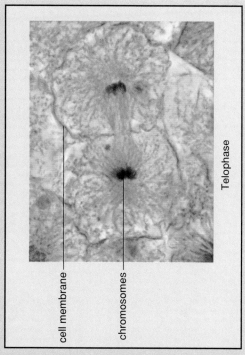

cell membrane

chromosomes

Telophase

Mitosis (cont'd)
Figure 7.5

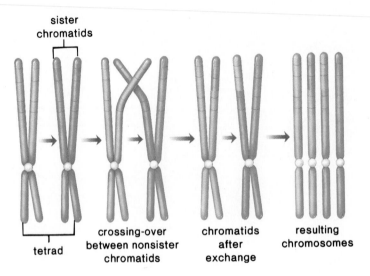

sister
chromatids

tetrad

crossing-over
between nonsister
chromatids

chromatids
after
exchange

resulting
chromosomes

Crossing-Over
Figure 7.10

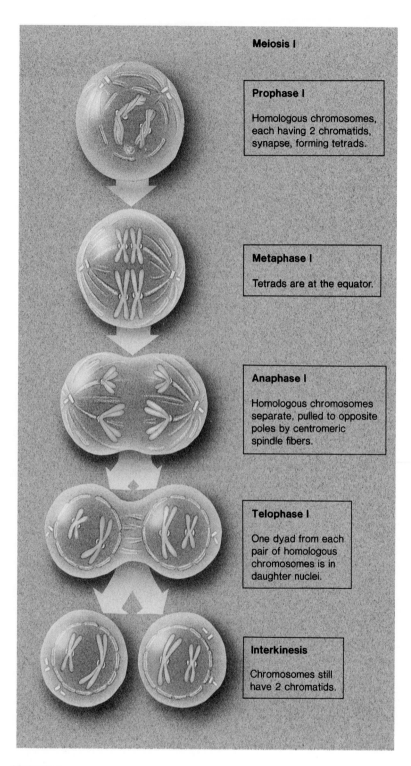

Meiosis I

Prophase I

Homologous chromosomes, each having 2 chromatids, synapse, forming tetrads.

Metaphase I

Tetrads are at the equator.

Anaphase I

Homologous chromosomes separate, pulled to opposite poles by centromeric spindle fibers.

Telophase I

One dyad from each pair of homologous chromosomes is in daughter nuclei.

Interkinesis

Chromosomes still have 2 chromatids.

Meiosis I
Figure 7.11

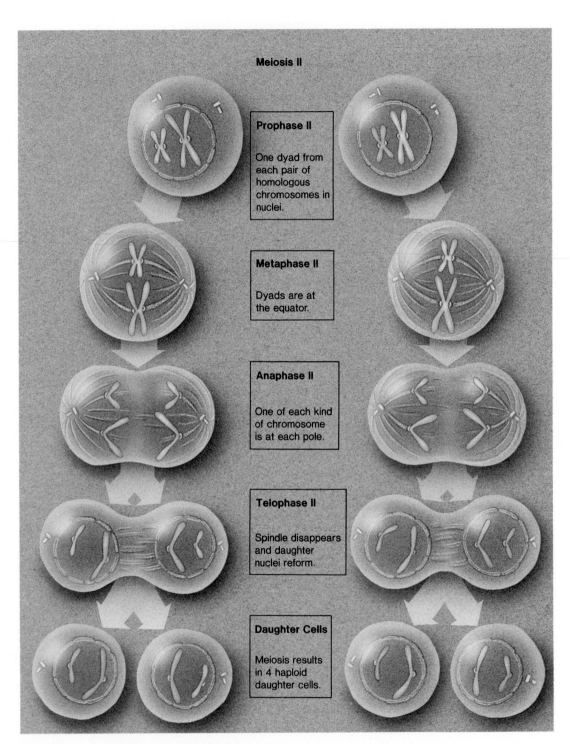

Meiosis II

Prophase II

One dyad from each pair of homologous chromosomes in nuclei.

Metaphase II

Dyads are at the equator.

Anaphase II

One of each kind of chromosome is at each pole.

Telophase II

Spindle disappears and daughter nuclei reform.

Daughter Cells

Meiosis results in 4 haploid daughter cells.

Meiosis II
Figure 7.12

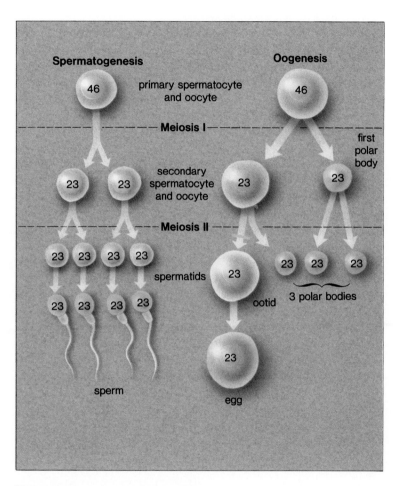

Spermatogenesis and Oogenesis
Figure 7.13

Meiosis

Mitosis

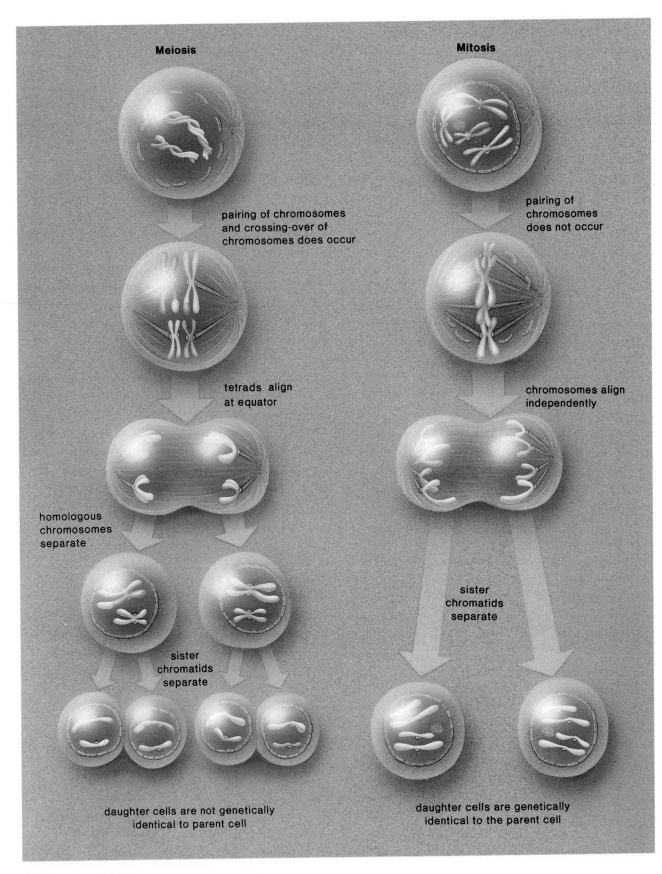

pairing of chromosomes
and crossing-over of
chromosomes does occur

pairing of
chromosomes
does not occur

tetrads align
at equator

chromosomes align
independently

homologous
chromosomes
separate

sister
chromatids
separate

sister
chromatids
separate

daughter cells are not genetically
identical to parent cell

daughter cells are genetically
identical to the parent cell

Mitosis vs. Meiosis
Figure 7.14

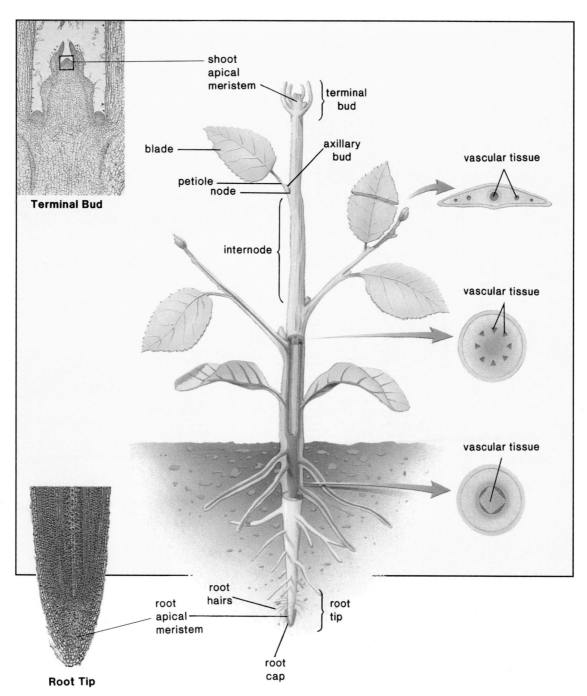

Terminal Bud

shoot
apical
meristem

terminal
bud

blade

axillary
bud

petiole

node

internode

vascular tissue

vascular tissue

vascular tissue

Root Tip

root
hairs

root
apical
meristem

root
tip

root
cap

Plant Organs
Figure 8.1

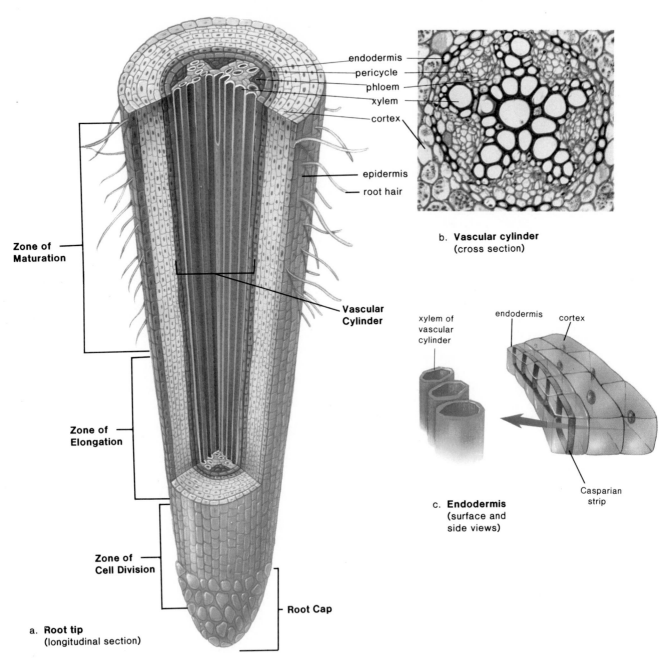

endodermis
pericycle
phloem
xylem
cortex

epidermis

root hair

Zone of
Maturation

Vascular
Cylinder

b. **Vascular cylinder**
(cross section)

xylem of
vascular
cylinder

endodermis   cortex

Casparian
strip

c. **Endodermis**
(surface and
side views)

Zone of
Elongation

Zone of
Cell Division

Root Cap

a. **Root tip**
(longitudinal section)

Root Anatomy
Figure 8.3

Monocots

one cotyledon in seed

vascular bundles scattered in stem

leaf veins form a parallel pattern

flower parts in threes and multiples of three

root xylem and phloem occur in a ring

Dicots

two cotyledons in seed

vascular bundles in a distinct ring

leaf veins form a net pattern

flower parts in fours or fives and multiples of four or five

root phloem occurs between arms of xylem

Monocot vs. Dicot
Figure 8.4

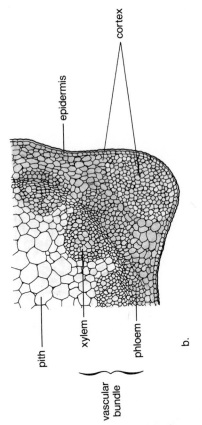

epidermis

cortex

pith

xylem

phloem

vascular bundle

b.

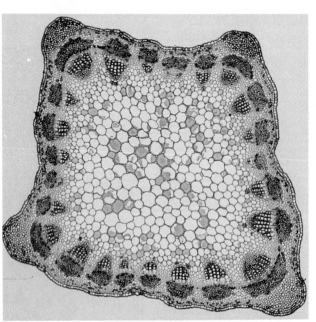

Herbaceous Dicot System
Figure 8.7

44

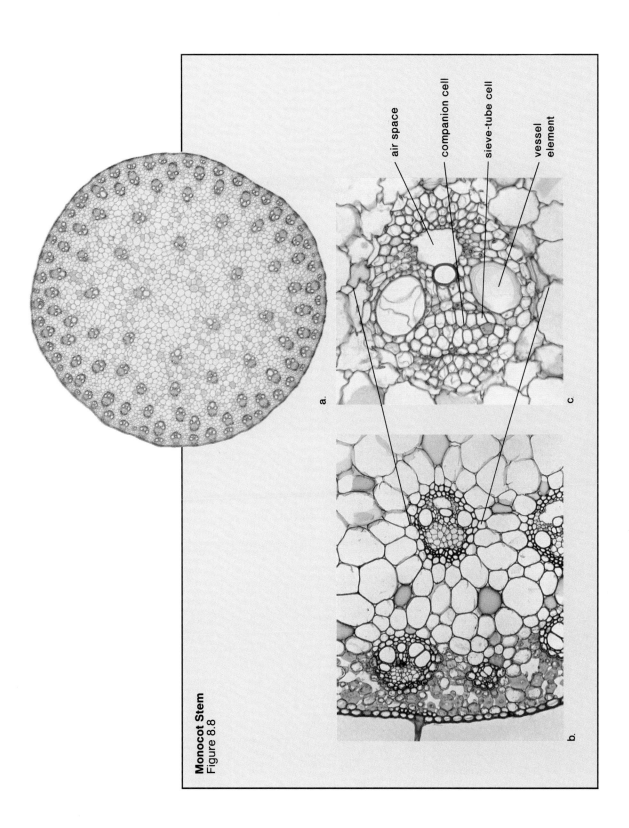

Monocot Stem
Figure 8.8

air space

companion cell

sieve-tube cell

vessel element

a.

b.

c.

45

Woody Stem
Figure 8.10

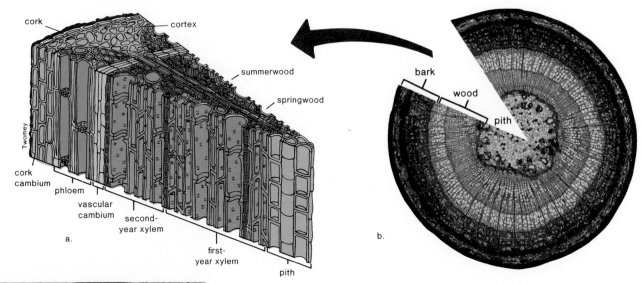

cork   cortex

summerwood

springwood

Twomey

cork cambium

phloem

vascular cambium

second-year xylem

first-year xylem

pith

a.

bark

wood

pith

b.

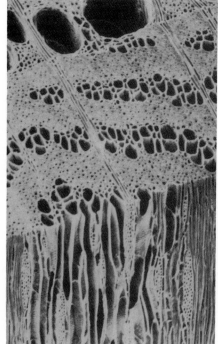

Leaf Anatomy
Figure 8.12

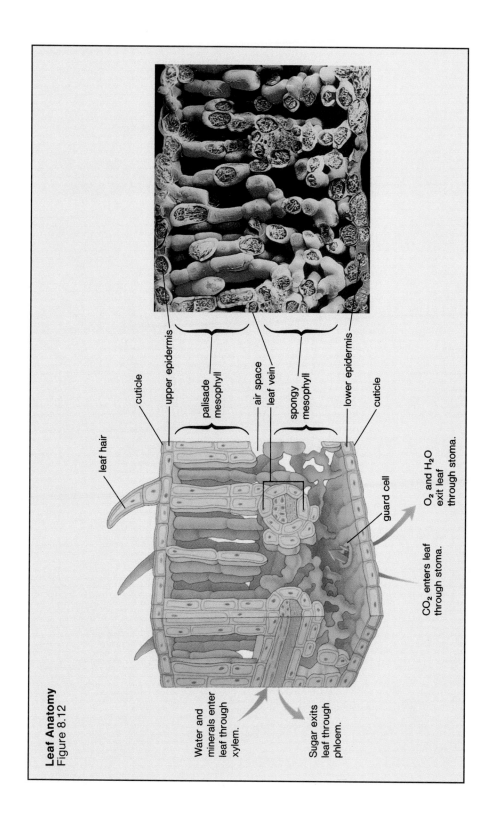

leaf hair

cuticle

upper epidermis

palisade mesophyll

air space

leaf vein

spongy mesophyll

lower epidermis

cuticle

guard cell

Water and minerals enter leaf through xylem.

Sugar exits leaf through phloem.

CO_2 enters leaf through stoma.

O_2 and H_2O exit leaf through stoma.

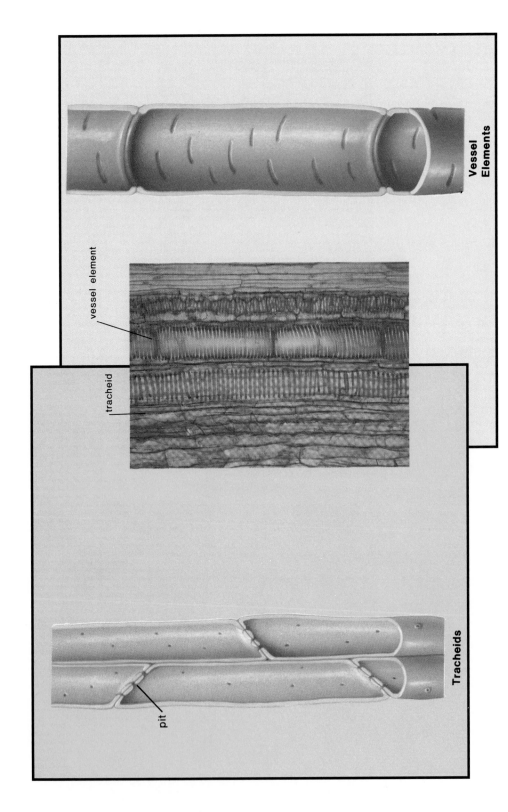

Vessel Elements

vessel element

tracheid

Tracheids

pit

Xylem Structure
Figure 9.1

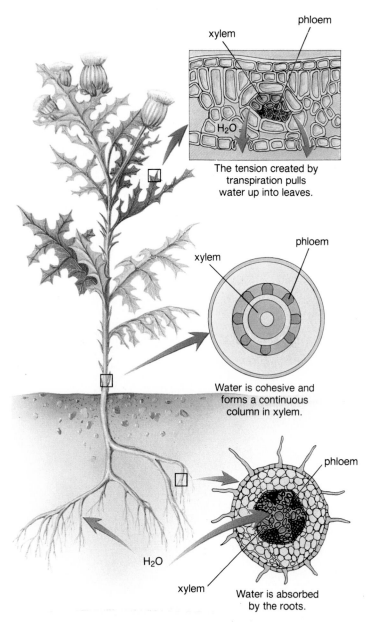

xylem

phloem

H_2O

The tension created by
transpiration pulls
water up into leaves.

xylem

phloem

Water is cohesive and
forms a continuous
column in xylem.

phloem

H_2O

xylem

Water is absorbed
by the roots.

Cohesion-Tension Theory of Water Transport
Figure 9.2

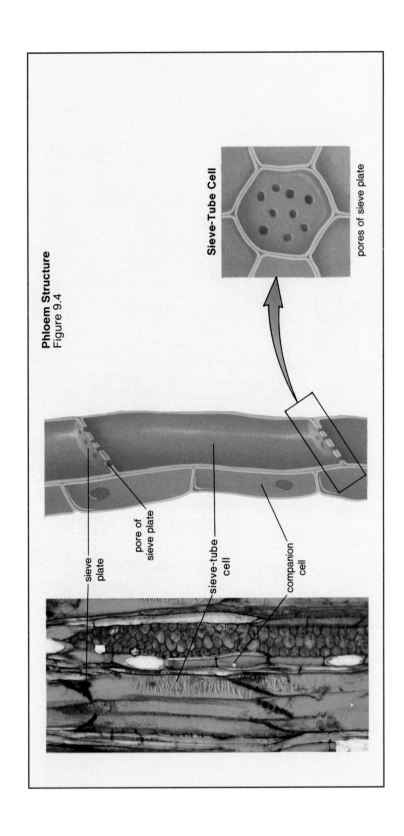

Phloem Structure
Figure 9.4

Sieve-Tube Cell

pores of sieve plate

sieve plate

pore of sieve plate

sieve-tube cell

companion cell

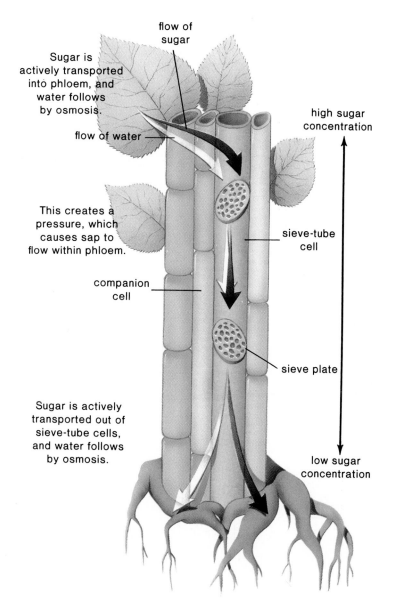

flow of
sugar

Sugar is
actively transported
into phloem, and
water follows
by osmosis.

flow of water

This creates a
pressure, which
causes sap to
flow within phloem.

companion
cell

Sugar is actively
transported out of
sieve-tube cells,
and water follows
by osmosis.

high sugar
concentration

sieve-tube
cell

sieve plate

low sugar
concentration

Pressure-Flow Theory of Organic Nutrient Transport
Figure 9.5

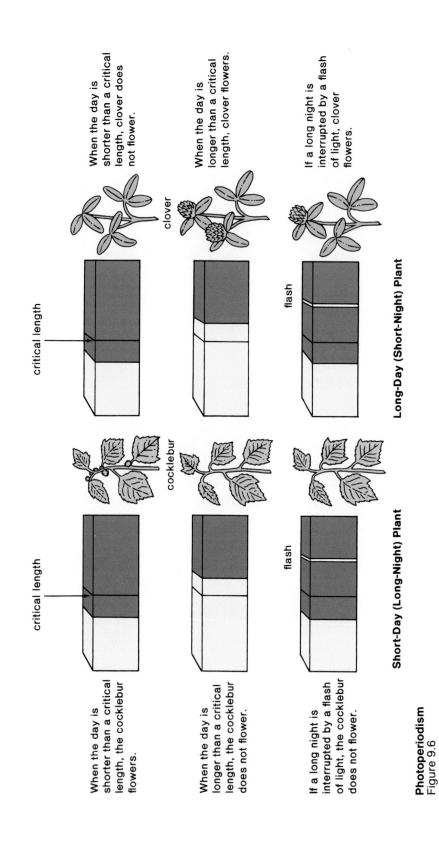

When the day is shorter than a critical length, the cocklebur flowers.

When the day is longer than a critical length, the cocklebur does not flower.

If a long night is interrupted by a flash of light, the cocklebur does not flower.

cocklebur

critical length

flash

Short-Day (Long-Night) Plant

When the day is shorter than a critical length, clover does not flower.

When the day is longer than a critical length, clover flowers.

If a long night is interrupted by a flash of light, clover flowers.

clover

critical length

flash

Long-Day (Short-Night) Plant

Photoperiodism
Figure 9.6

52

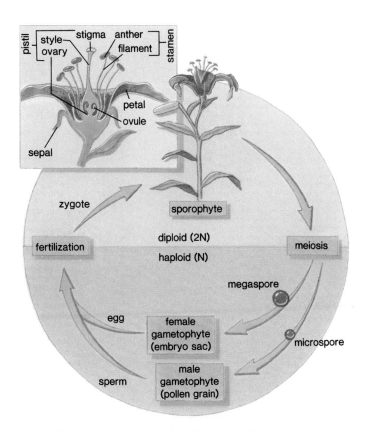

Alternation of Generations in a Flowering Plant
Figure 9.8

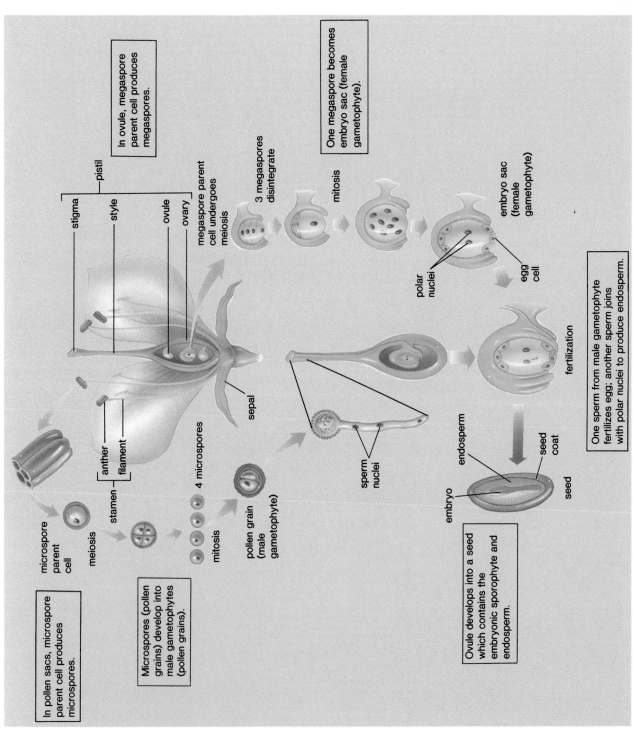

In pollen sacs, microspore parent cell produces microspores.

Microspores (pollen grains) develop into male gametophytes (pollen grains).

In ovule, megaspore parent cell produces megaspores.

One megaspore becomes embryo sac (female gametophyte).

Ovule develops into a seed which contains the embryonic sporophyte and endosperm.

One sperm from male gametophyte fertilizes egg; another sperm joins with polar nuclei to produce endosperm.

pistil

stigma

style

ovule

ovary

anther

filament

stamen

sepal

microspore parent cell

meiosis

4 microspores

mitosis

pollen grain (male gametophyte)

megaspore parent cell undergoes meiosis

3 megaspores disintegrate

mitosis

embryo sac (female gametophyte)

polar nuclei

egg cell

sperm nuclei

fertilization

embryo

endosperm

seed coat

seed

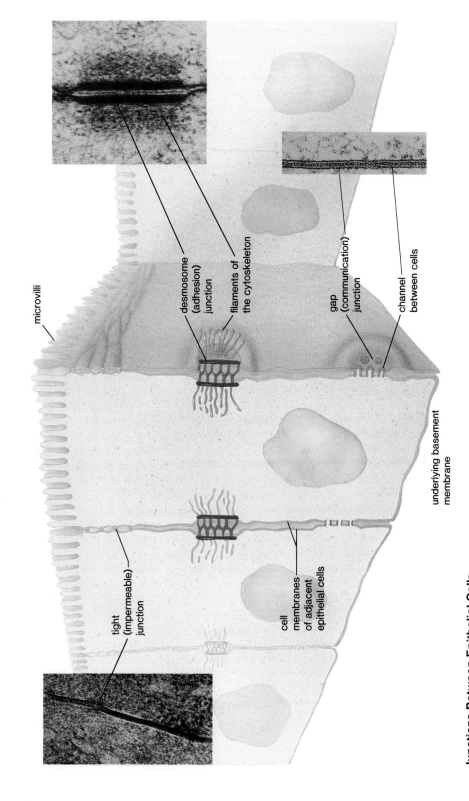

microvilli

desmosome (adhesion) junction

filaments of the cytoskeleton

gap (communication) junction

channel between cells

tight (impermeable) junction

cell membranes of adjacent epithelial cells

underlying basement membrane

Junctions Between Epithelial Cells
Figure 10.2

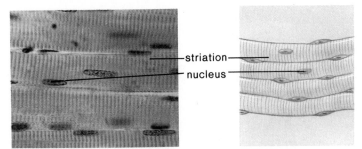

Skeletal muscle has striated cells with multiple nuclei.

a.

Occurrence: Attached to skeleton
Function: Voluntary movement

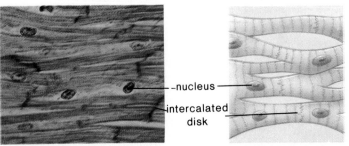

Smooth muscle has spindle-shaped cells, each with a single nucleus.

b.

Occurrence: Walls of internal organs
Function: Movement of substances in lumens of body

Cardiac muscle has branching striated cells, each with a single nucleus.

c.

Occurrence: Wall of heart
Function: Pumping of blood

Skin Anatomy
Figure 10.7

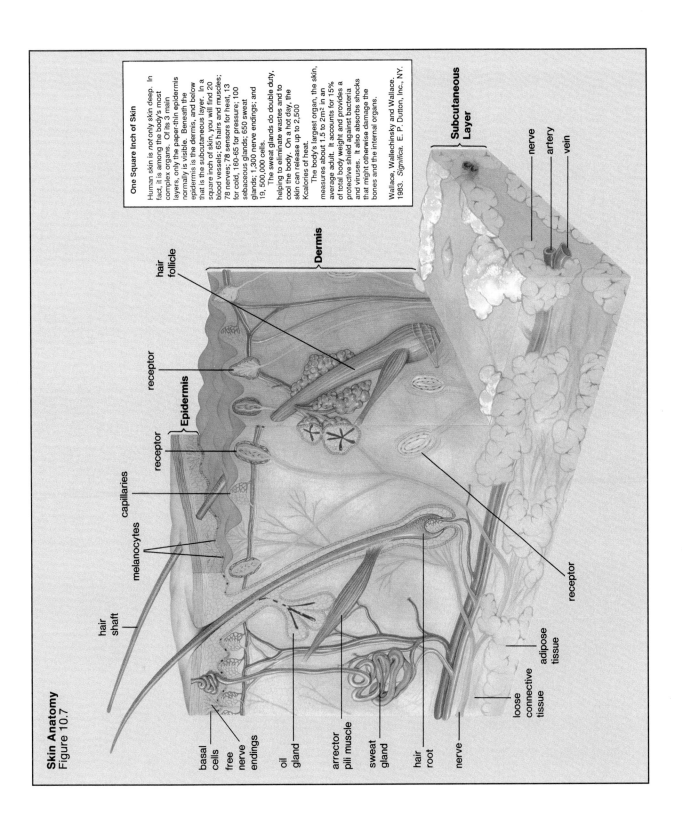

One Square Inch of Skin

Human skin is *not* only skin deep. In fact, it is among the body's most complex organs. Of its 3 main layers, only the paper-thin epidermis normally is visible. Beneath the epidermis is the dermis, and below that is the subcutaneous layer. In a square inch of skin, you will find 20 blood vessels; 65 hairs and muscles; 78 nerves; 78 sensors for heat, 13 for cold, 160-65 for pressure; 100 sebaceous glands; 650 sweat glands; 1,300 nerve endings; and 19, 500,000 cells.

The sweat glands do double duty, helping to eliminate wastes and to cool the body. On a hot day, the skin can release up to 2,500 Kcalories of heat.

The body's largest organ, the skin, measures about 1.5 to 2m^2 in an average adult. It accounts for 15% of total body weight and provides a protective shield against bacteria and viruses. It also absorbs shocks that might otherwise damage the bones and the internal organs.

Wallace, Wallechinsky and Wallace. 1983. *Significa.* E. P. Dutton, Inc., NY.

hair follicle

receptor

Epidermis

receptor

capillaries

melanocytes

hair shaft

Dermis

Subcutaneous Layer

nerve

artery

vein

receptor

basal cells

free nerve endings

oil gland

arrector pili muscle

sweat gland

hair root

nerve

adipose tissue

loose connective tissue

Body Cavities
Figure 10.9

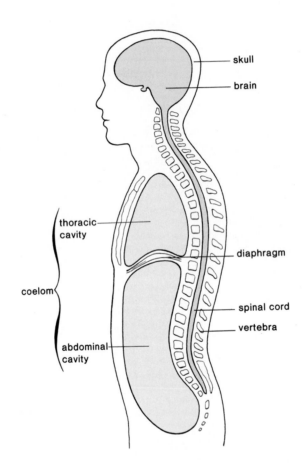

skull

brain

thoracic cavity

diaphragm

coelom

spinal cord

vertebra

abdominal cavity

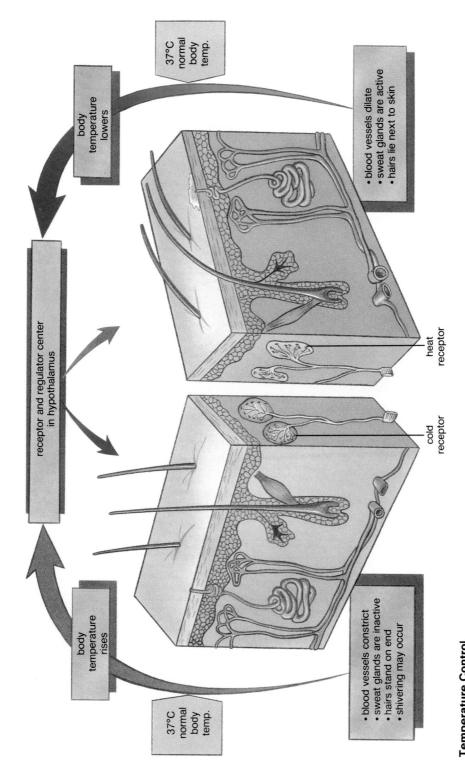

37°C
normal
body
temp.

body
temperature
lowers

· blood vessels dilate
· sweat glands are active
· hairs lie next to skin

heat
receptor

receptor and regulator center
in hypothalamus

cold
receptor

body
temperature
rises

37°C
normal
body
temp.

· blood vessels constrict
· sweat glands are inactive
· hairs stand on end
· shivering may occur

Temperature Control
Figure 10.12

Human Digestive System
Figure 11.1

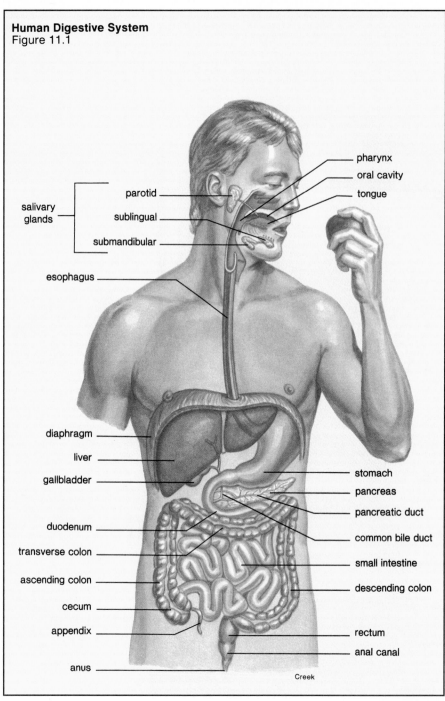

salivary glands
- parotid
- sublingual
- submandibular

pharynx
oral cavity
tongue

esophagus

diaphragm
liver
gallbladder

stomach
pancreas
pancreatic duct
common bile duct

duodenum
transverse colon
ascending colon
cecum
appendix
anus

small intestine
descending colon

rectum
anal canal

Creek

Swallowing
Figure 11.4

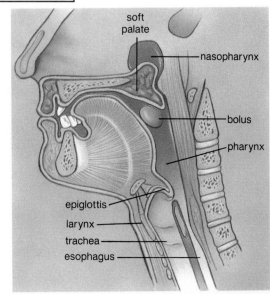

soft palate
nasopharynx
bolus
pharynx
epiglottis
larynx
trachea
esophagus

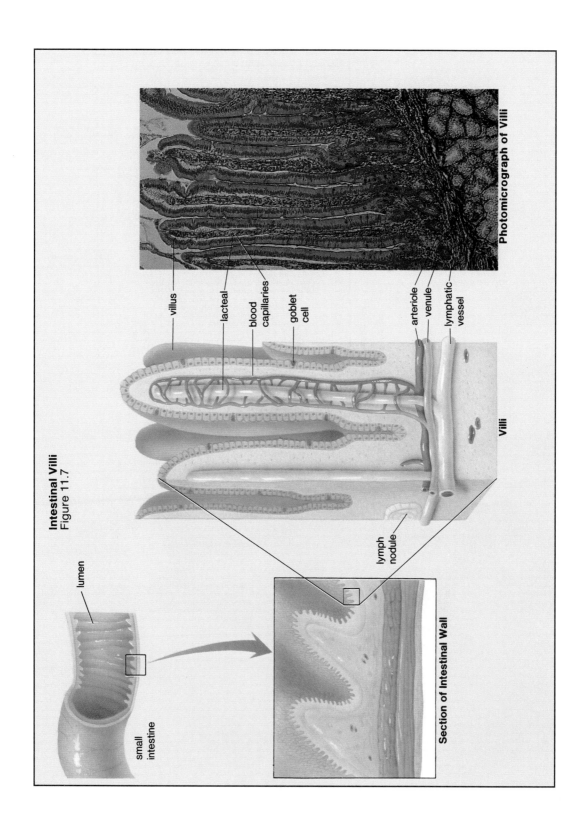

Intestinal Villi
Figure 11.7

lumen

small
intestine

Section of Intestinal Wall

lymph
nodule

villus

lacteal

blood
capillaries

goblet
cell

arteriole

venule

lymphatic
vessel

Villi

Photomicrograph of Villi

61

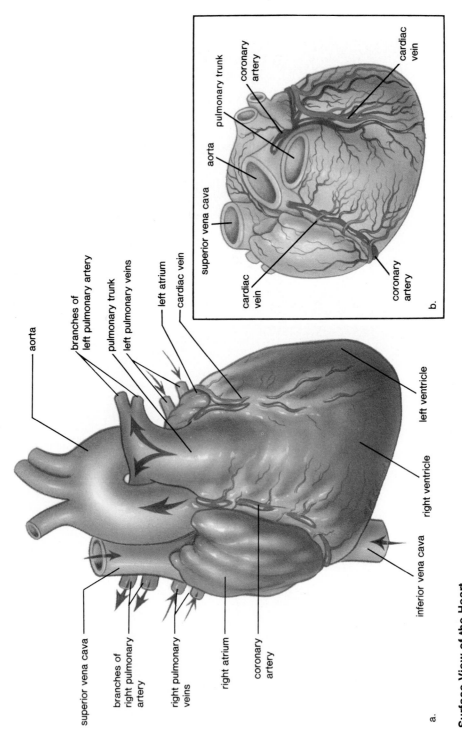

Surface View of the Heart
Figure 12.2

superior vena cava

branches of
right pulmonary
artery

right pulmonary
veins

right atrium

coronary
artery

inferior vena cava

right ventricle

left ventricle

a.

aorta

branches of
left pulmonary artery

pulmonary trunk

left pulmonary veins

left atrium

cardiac vein

superior vena cava

aorta

pulmonary trunk

coronary
artery

cardiac
vein

cardiac
vein

coronary
artery

b.

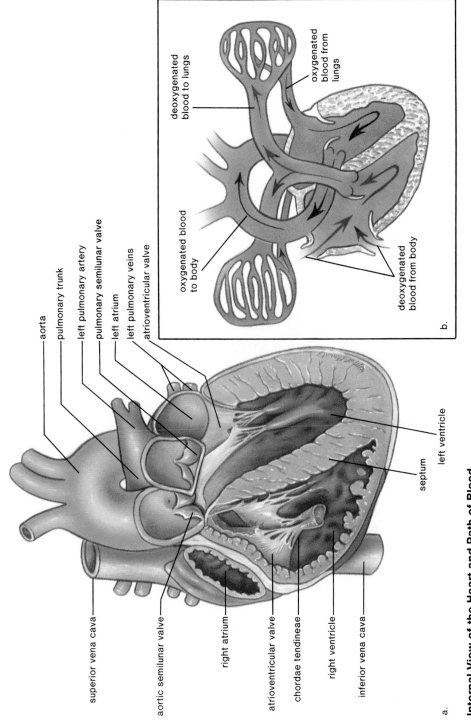

deoxygenated blood to lungs

oxygenated blood from lungs

oxygenated blood to body

deoxygenated blood from body

b.

aorta

pulmonary trunk

left pulmonary artery

pulmonary semilunar valve

left atrium

left pulmonary veins

atrioventricular valve

superior vena cava

aortic semilunar valve

right atrium

atrioventricular valve

chordae tendineae

right ventricle

inferior vena cava

left ventricle

septum

a.

Internal View of the Heart and Path of Blood
Figure 12.3

Cardiac Cycle
Figure 12.4

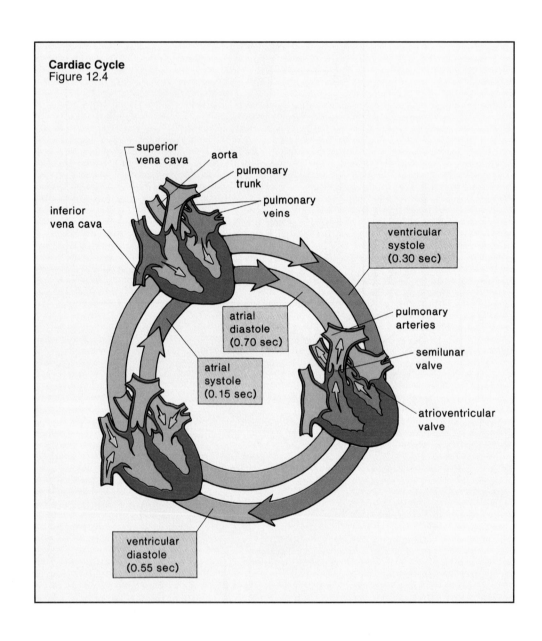

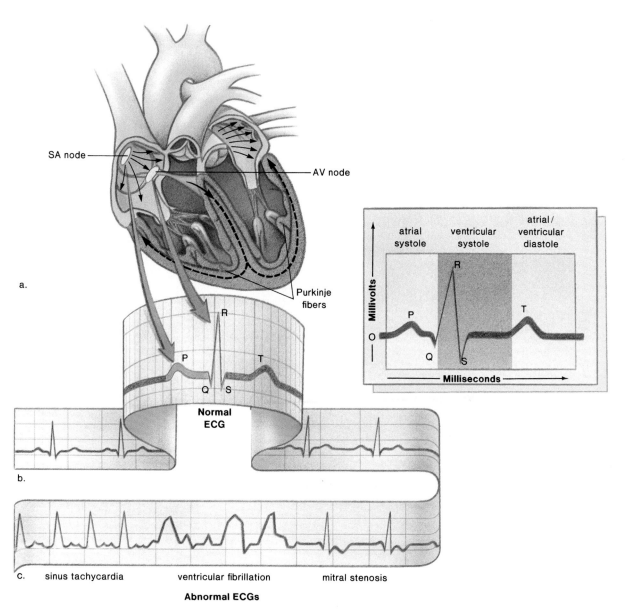

a.

SA node

AV node

Purkinje fibers

R

P

T

Q   S

Normal ECG

b.

atrial systole

ventricular systole

atrial / ventricular diastole

Millivolts

O

P

R

Q

S

T

Milliseconds

c.   sinus tachycardia   ventricular fibrillation   mitral stenosis

Abnormal ECGs

Electrical Conduction in the Heart
Figure 12.5

Velocity and Blood Pressure Related to Total Cross-Sectional Area of Blood Vessels
Figure 12.7

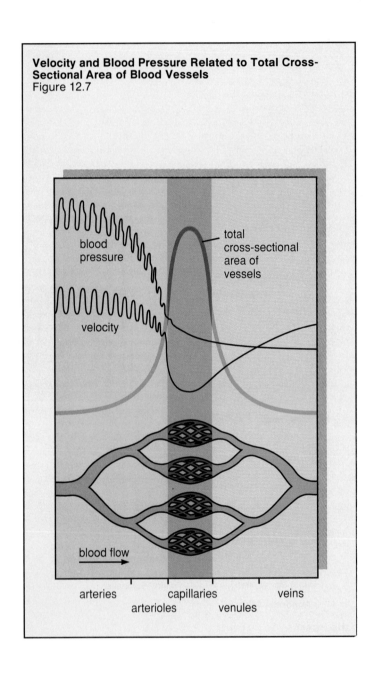

blood pressure

total cross-sectional area of vessels

velocity

blood flow

arteries

arterioles

capillaries

venules

veins

Path of Blood in the Body
Figure 12.9

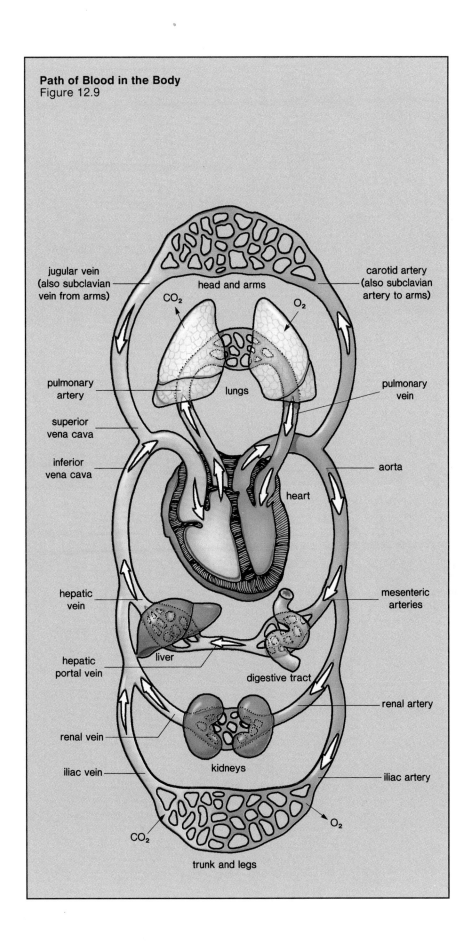

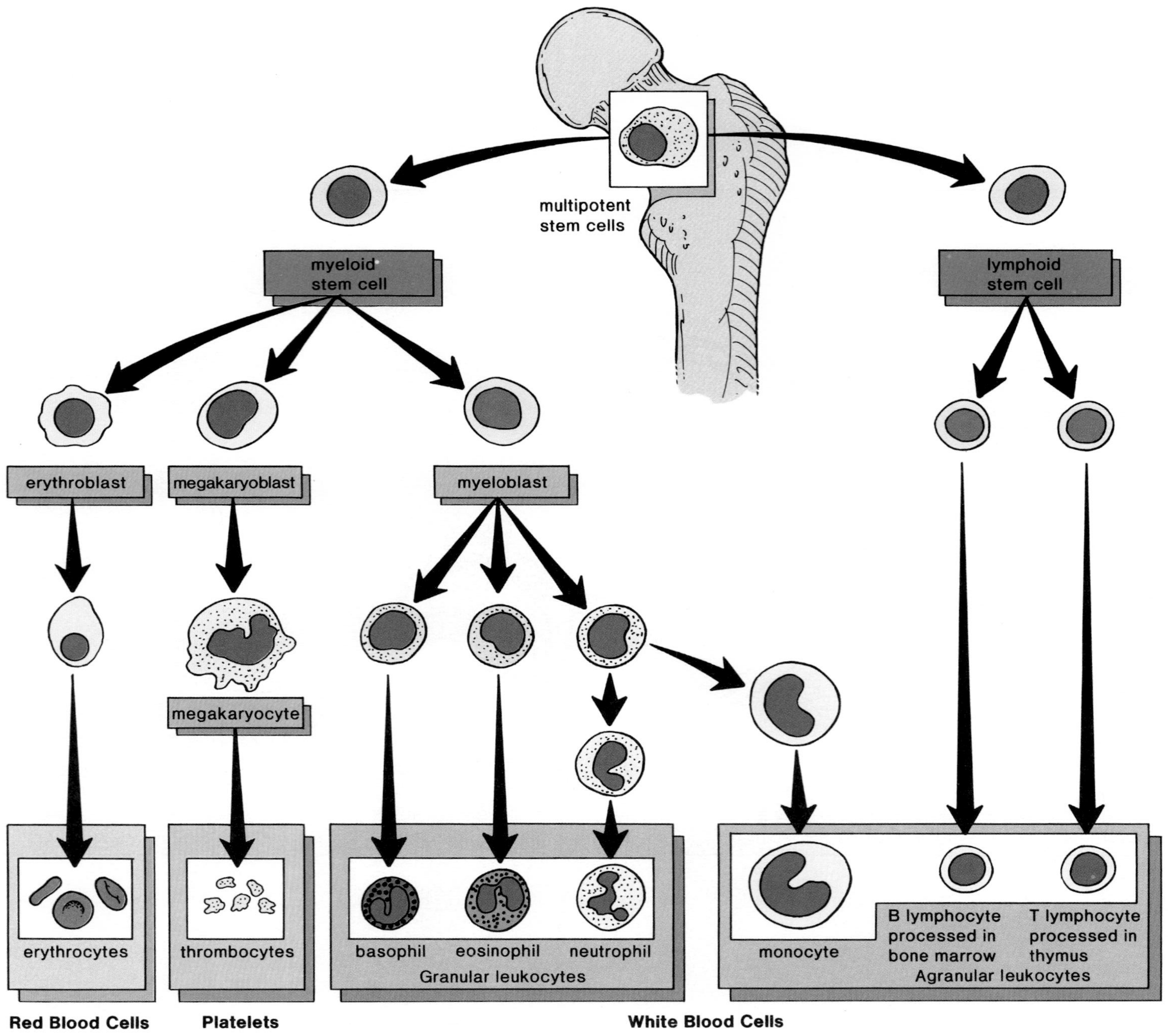

Blood Cell Formation
Figure 12.13

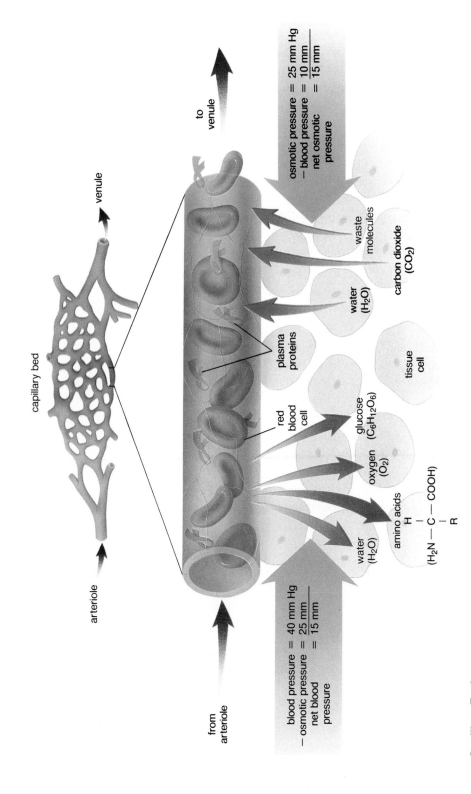

arteriole

capillary bed

venule

from
arteriole

to
venule

blood pressure = 40 mm Hg
− osmotic pressure = 25 mm
net blood = 15 mm
pressure

osmotic pressure = 25 mm Hg
− blood pressure = 10 mm
net osmotic = 15 mm
pressure

red
blood
cell

plasma
proteins

tissue
cell

waste
molecules

carbon dioxide
(CO_2)

water
(H_2O)

glucose
($C_6H_{12}O_6$)

oxygen
(O_2)

amino acids

$$H$$
$$(H_2N - C - COOH)$$
$$R$$

water
(H_2O)

Capillary Exchange
Figure 12.15

Lymphatic System
Figure 13.1

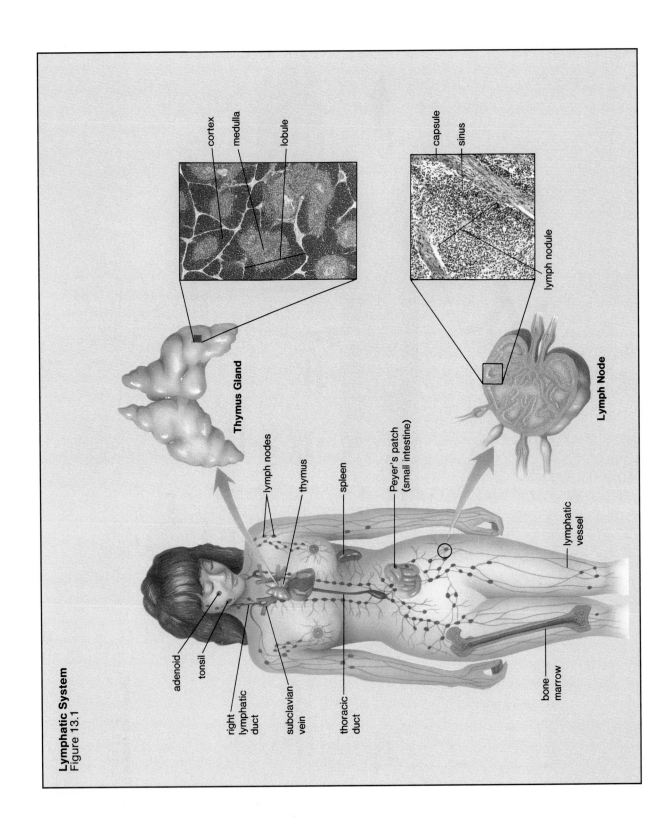

cortex

medulla

lobule

capsule

sinus

lymph nodule

Thymus Gland

Lymph Node

lymph nodes

thymus

spleen

Peyer's patch
(small intestine)

lymphatic
vessel

adenoid

tonsil

right
lymphatic
duct

subclavian
vein

thoracic
duct

bone
marrow

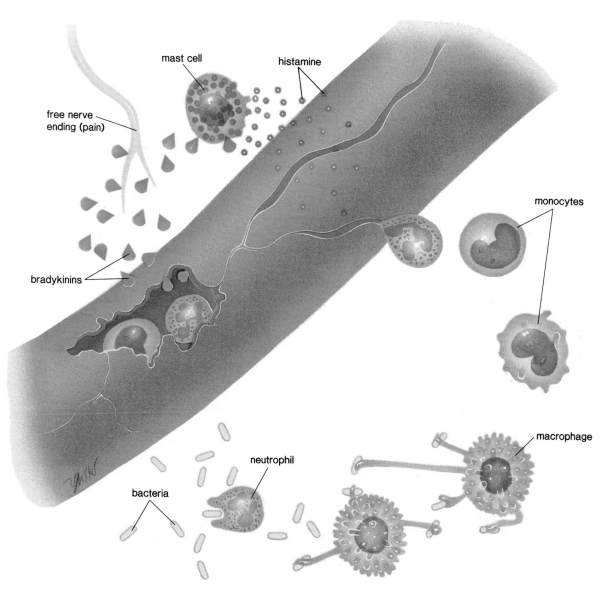

Inflammatory Reaction
Figure 13.3

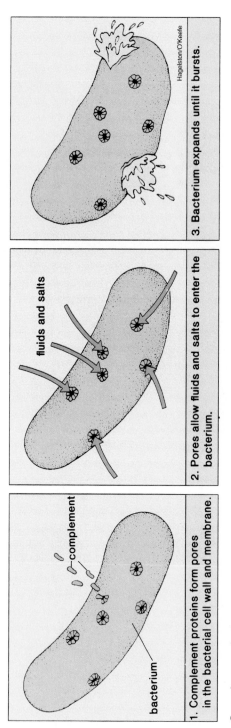

1. Complement proteins form pores in the bacterial cell wall and membrane.

complement

bacterium

2. Pores allow fluids and salts to enter the bacterium.

fluids and salts

3. Bacterium expands until it bursts.

Hagelston/O'Keefe

Complement Action
Figure 13.4

Clonal Selection Theory
Figure 13.5

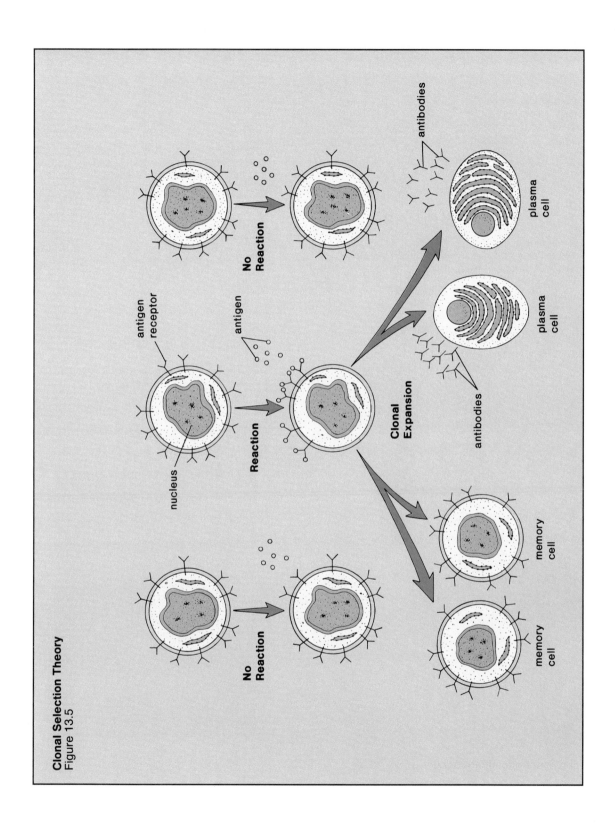

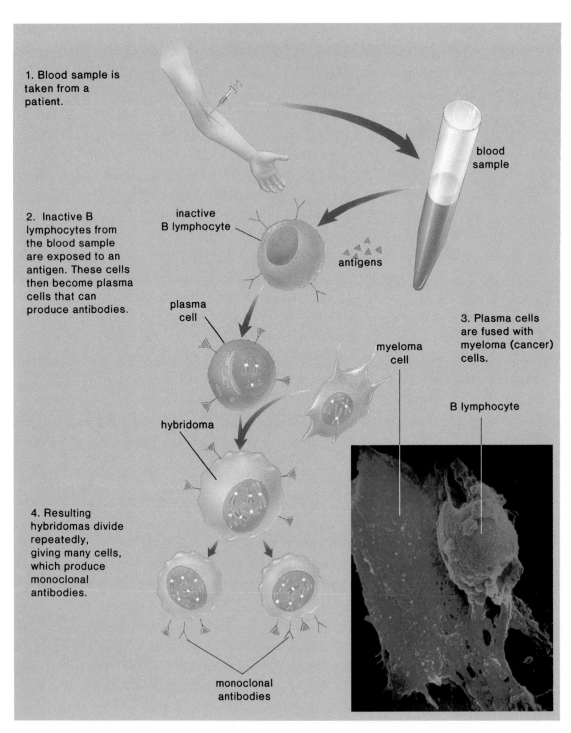

1. Blood sample is taken from a patient.

blood sample

2. Inactive B lymphocytes from the blood sample are exposed to an antigen. These cells then become plasma cells that can produce antibodies.

inactive B lymphocyte

antigens

plasma cell

3. Plasma cells are fused with myeloma (cancer) cells.

myeloma cell

B lymphocyte

hybridoma

4. Resulting hybridomas divide repeatedly, giving many cells, which produce monoclonal antibodies.

monoclonal antibodies

Monoclonal Antibody Production
Figure 13.12

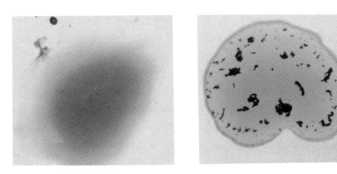

a.

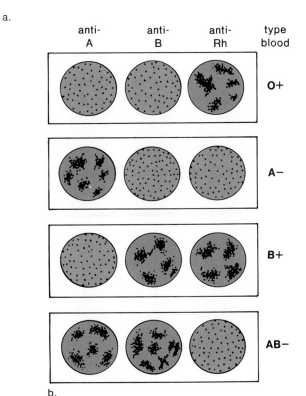

b.

Blood Typing
Figure 13.13

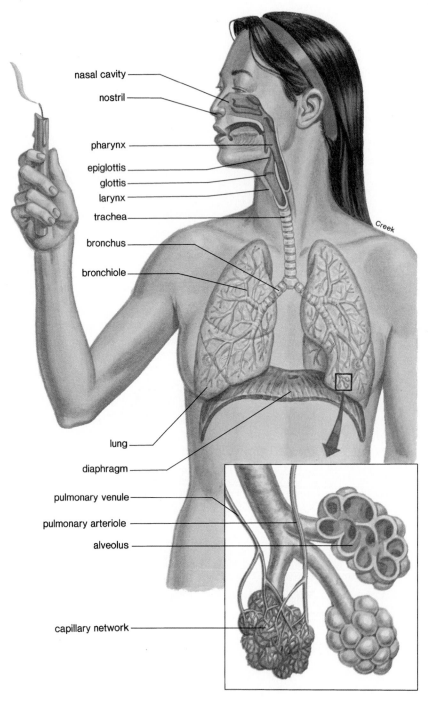

nasal cavity

nostril

pharynx

epiglottis

glottis

larynx

trachea

bronchus

bronchiole

Creek

lung

diaphragm

pulmonary venule

pulmonary arteriole

alveolus

capillary network

Respiratory System
Figure 14.2

Nervous Control of Breathing
Figure 14.6

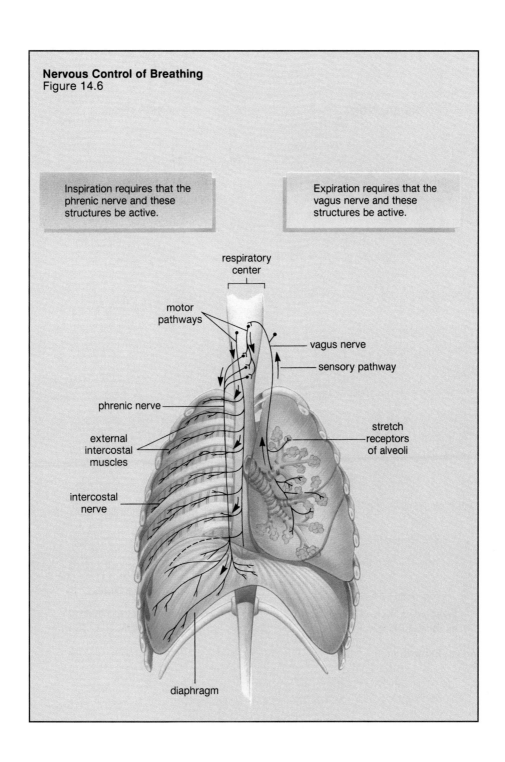

Inspiration requires that the phrenic nerve and these structures be active.

Expiration requires that the vagus nerve and these structures be active.

respiratory center

motor pathways

vagus nerve

sensory pathway

phrenic nerve

external intercostal muscles

stretch receptors of alveoli

intercostal nerve

diaphragm

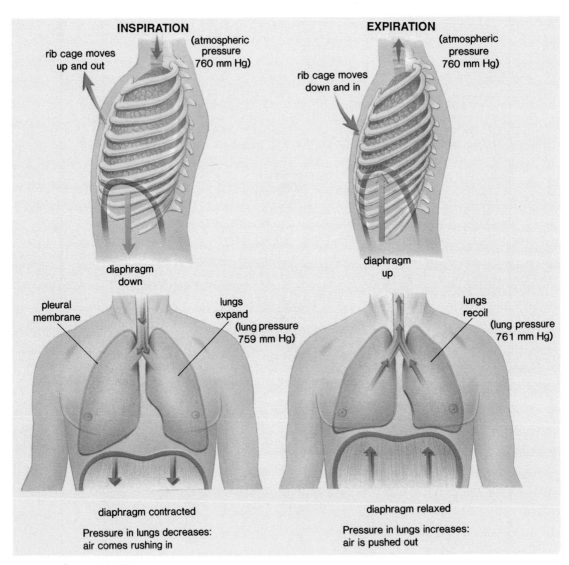

Inspiration vs. Expiration
Figure 14.7

Vital Capacity
Figure 14.8

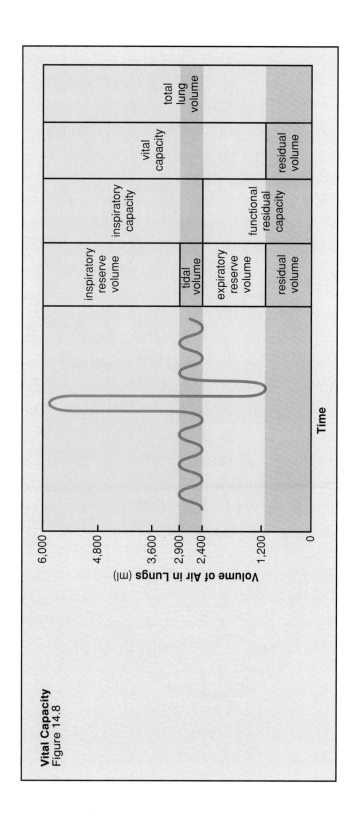

External vs. Internal Respiration
Figure 14.10

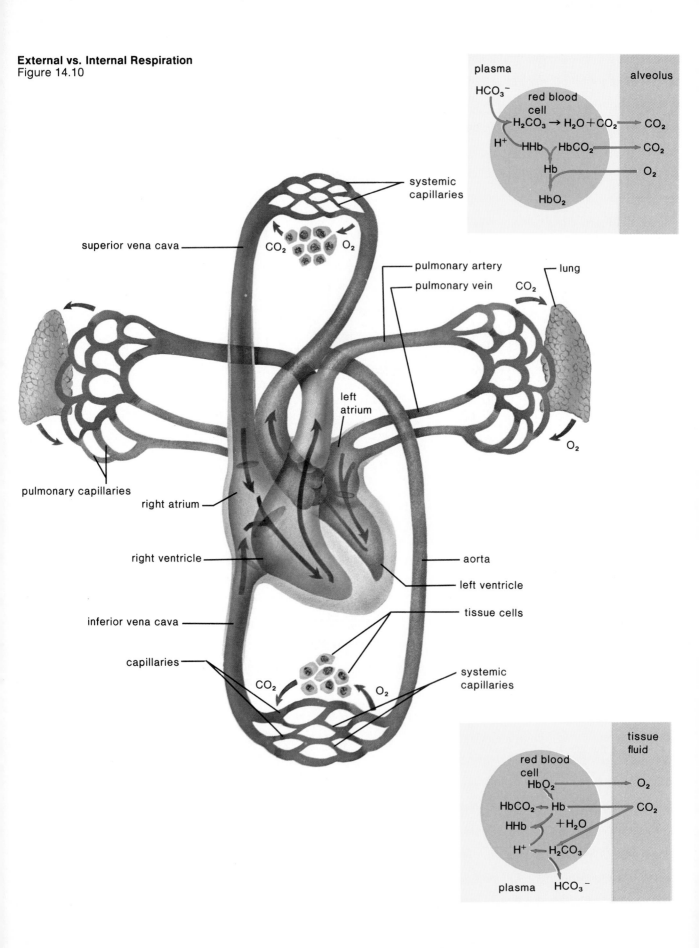

plasma

alveolus

HCO_3^-

red blood cell

$H_2CO_3 \rightarrow H_2O + CO_2$ → CO_2

H^+ HHb $HbCO_2$ → CO_2

Hb → O_2

HbO_2

systemic capillaries

superior vena cava

CO_2 O_2

pulmonary artery

pulmonary vein

lung

CO_2

left atrium

O_2

pulmonary capillaries

right atrium

right ventricle

aorta

left ventricle

tissue cells

inferior vena cava

capillaries

CO_2 O_2

systemic capillaries

tissue fluid

red blood cell

HbO_2 → O_2

$HbCO_2 \leftarrow$ Hb → CO_2

HHb $+H_2O$

$H^+ \leftarrow H_2CO_3$

plasma HCO_3^-

Organs of Excretion
Figure 15.1

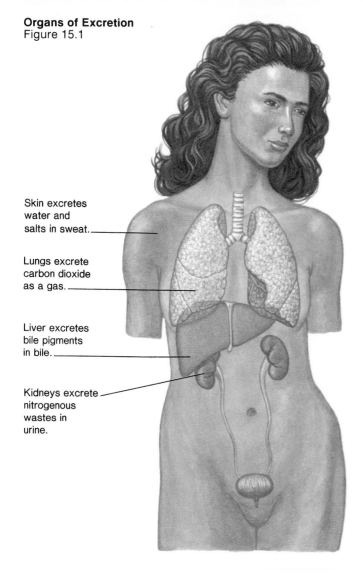

Skin excretes water and salts in sweat.

Lungs excrete carbon dioxide as a gas.

Liver excretes bile pigments in bile.

Kidneys excrete nitrogenous wastes in urine.

Urinary System
Figure 15.5

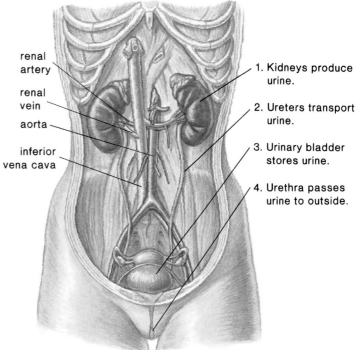

renal artery

renal vein

aorta

inferior vena cava

1. Kidneys produce urine.

2. Ureters transport urine.

3. Urinary bladder stores urine.

4. Urethra passes urine to outside.

Gross Anatomy of the Kidney
Figure 15.6

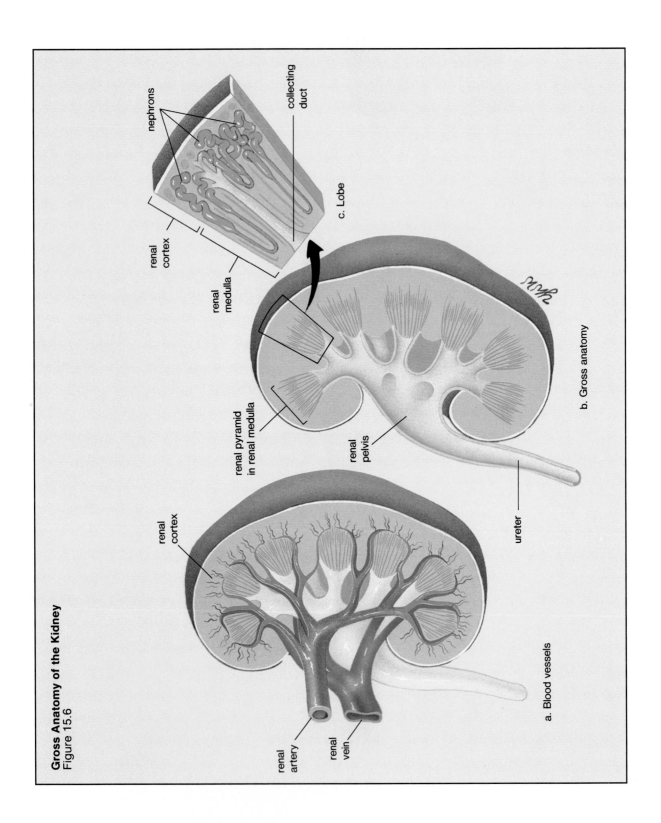

nephrons

collecting
duct

renal
cortex

renal
medulla

c. Lobe

renal pyramid
in renal medulla

renal
pelvis

b. Gross anatomy

ureter

renal
cortex

renal
artery

renal
vein

a. Blood vessels

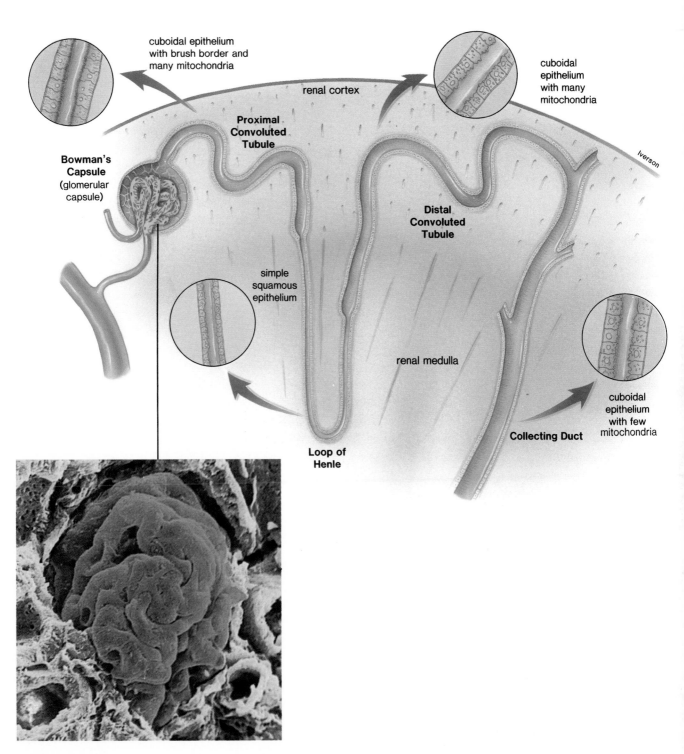

cuboidal epithelium
with brush border and
many mitochondria

renal cortex

cuboidal
epithelium
with many
mitochondria

Iverson

**Proximal
Convoluted
Tubule**

**Bowman's
Capsule**
(glomerular
capsule)

**Distal
Convoluted
Tubule**

simple
squamous
epithelium

renal medulla

**Loop of
Henle**

cuboidal
epithelium
with few
mitochondria

Collecting Duct

Nephron Anatomy
Figure 15.7

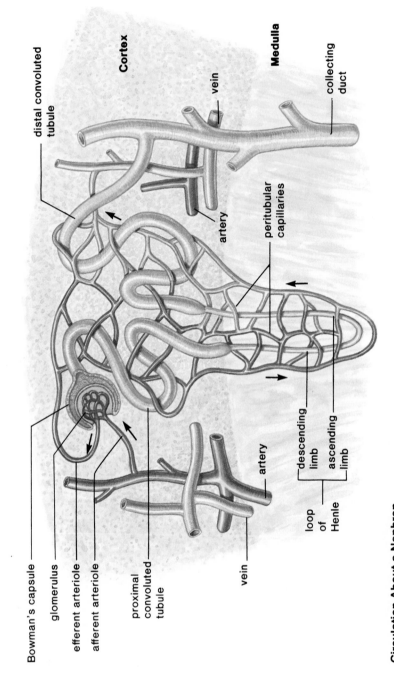

Circulation About a Nephron
Figure 15.8

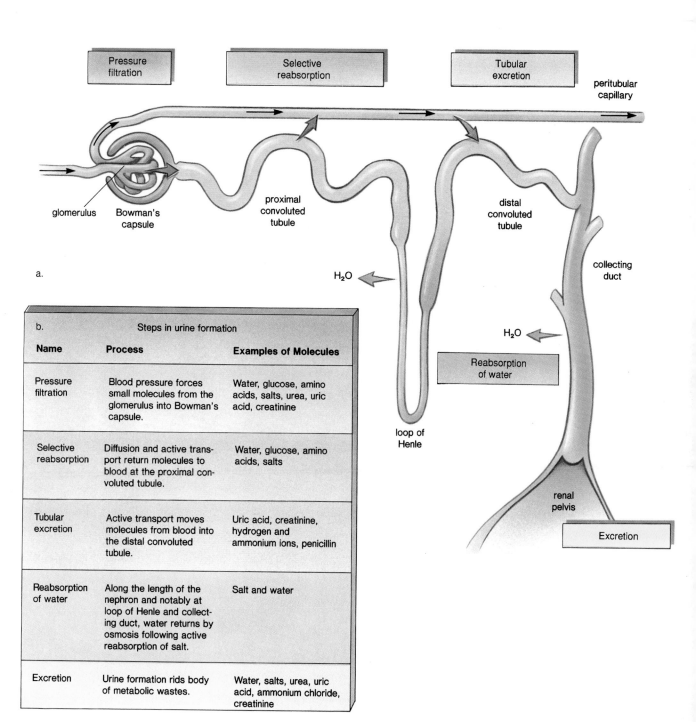

Pressure filtration

Selective reabsorption

Tubular excretion

peritubular capillary

glomerulus   Bowman's capsule

proximal convoluted tubule

distal convoluted tubule

collecting duct

a.

H$_2$O

H$_2$O

Reabsorption of water

loop of Henle

renal pelvis

Excretion

b.   Steps in urine formation

Name	Process	Examples of Molecules
Pressure filtration	Blood pressure forces small molecules from the glomerulus into Bowman's capsule.	Water, glucose, amino acids, salts, urea, uric acid, creatinine
Selective reabsorption	Diffusion and active transport return molecules to blood at the proximal convoluted tubule.	Water, glucose, amino acids, salts
Tubular excretion	Active transport moves molecules from blood into the distal convoluted tubule.	Uric acid, creatinine, hydrogen and ammonium ions, penicillin
Reabsorption of water	Along the length of the nephron and notably at loop of Henle and collecting duct, water returns by osmosis following active reabsorption of salt.	Salt and water
Excretion	Urine formation rids body of metabolic wastes.	Water, salts, urea, uric acid, ammonium chloride, creatinine

Steps in Urine Formation
Figure 15.9

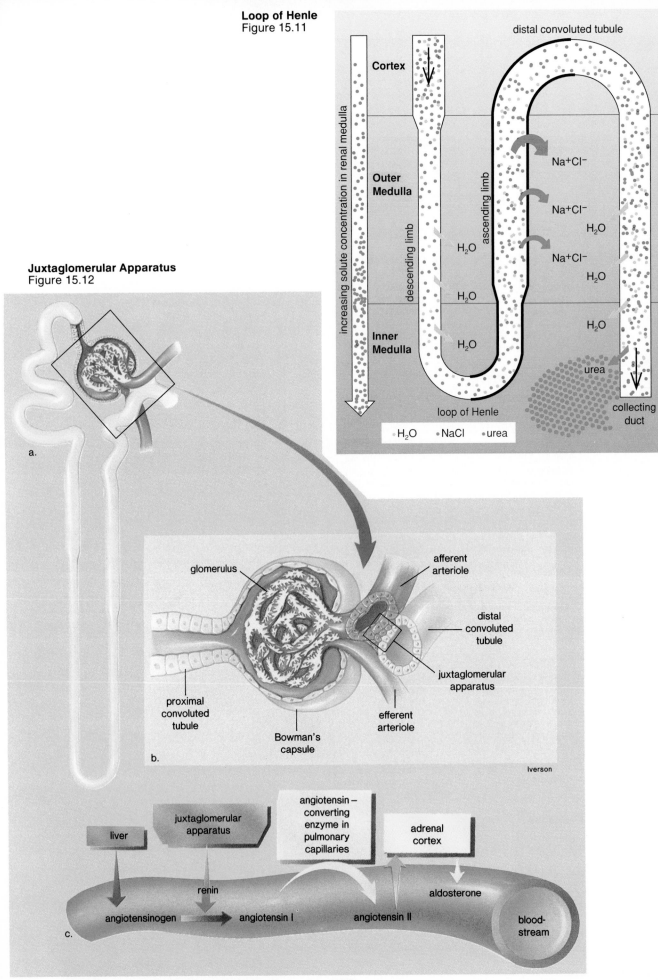

Loop of Henle
Figure 15.11

Cortex

Outer
Medulla

Inner
Medulla

increasing solute concentration in renal medulla

distal convoluted tubule

descending limb

ascending limb

Na^+Cl^-

Na^+Cl^-

H_2O

Na^+Cl^-

H_2O

H_2O

H_2O

H_2O

H_2O

urea

collecting
duct

loop of Henle

○ H_2O ● NaCl   ● urea

Juxtaglomerular Apparatus
Figure 15.12

a.

glomerulus

afferent
arteriole

distal
convoluted
tubule

juxtaglomerular
apparatus

proximal
convoluted
tubule

Bowman's
capsule

efferent
arteriole

b.

Iverson

liver

juxtaglomerular
apparatus

angiotensin—
converting
enzyme in
pulmonary
capillaries

adrenal
cortex

renin

aldosterone

blood-
stream

angiotensinogen

angiotensin I

angiotensin II

c.

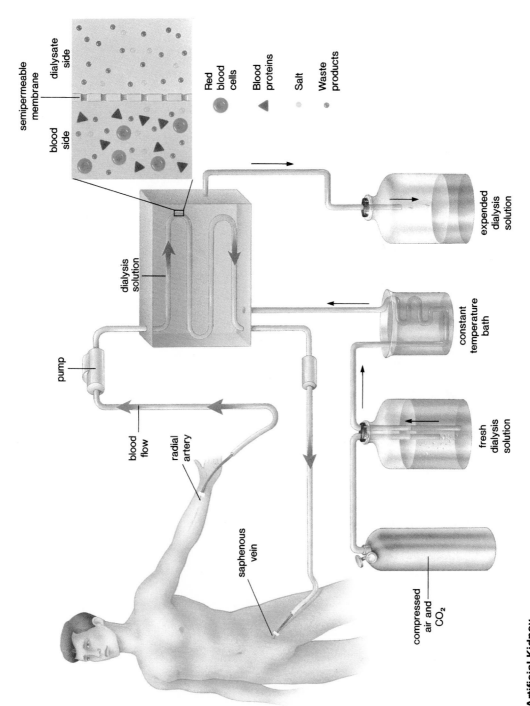

semipermeable membrane

dialysate side

blood side

Red blood cells

Blood proteins

Salt

Waste products

dialysis solution

expended dialysis solution

pump

blood flow

radial artery

saphenous vein

constant temperature bath

fresh dialysis solution

compressed air and CO_2

Artificial Kidney
Figure 15.13

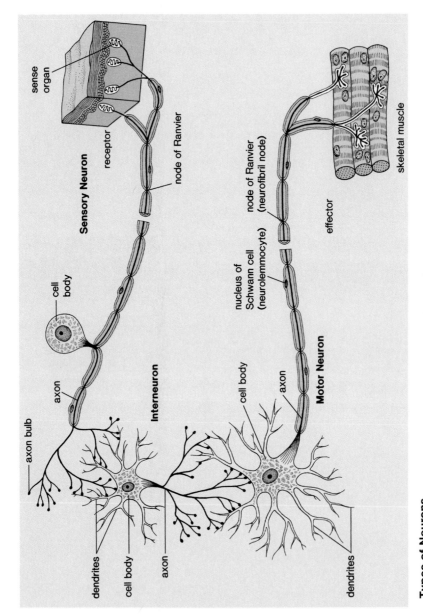

Types of Neurons
Figure 16.2

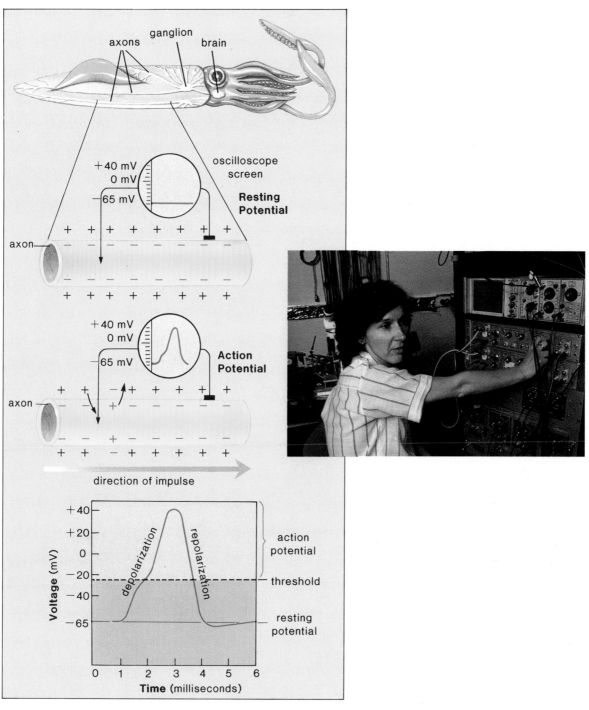

Nerve Impulse
Figure 16.4

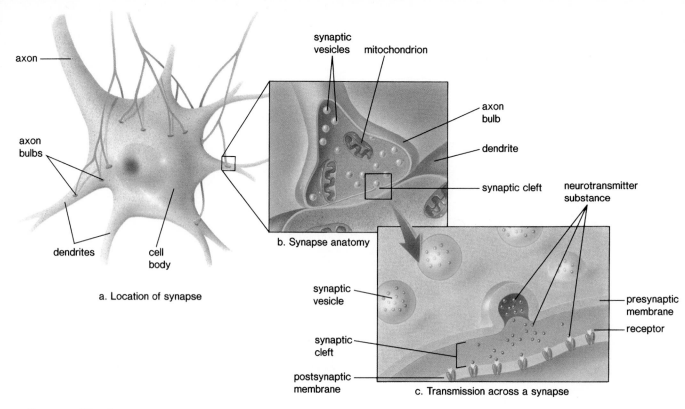

Synapse Structure
Figure 16.7

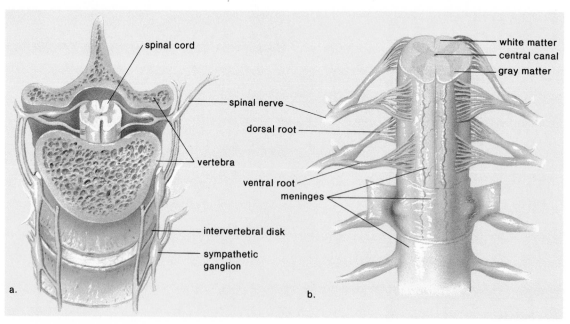

Spinal Cord Anatomy
Figure 16.10

Reflex Arc
Figure 16.11

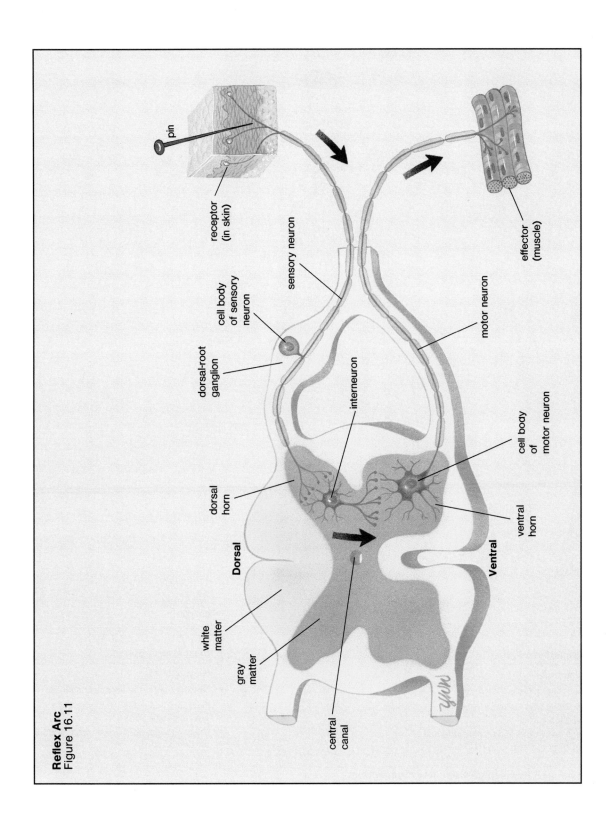

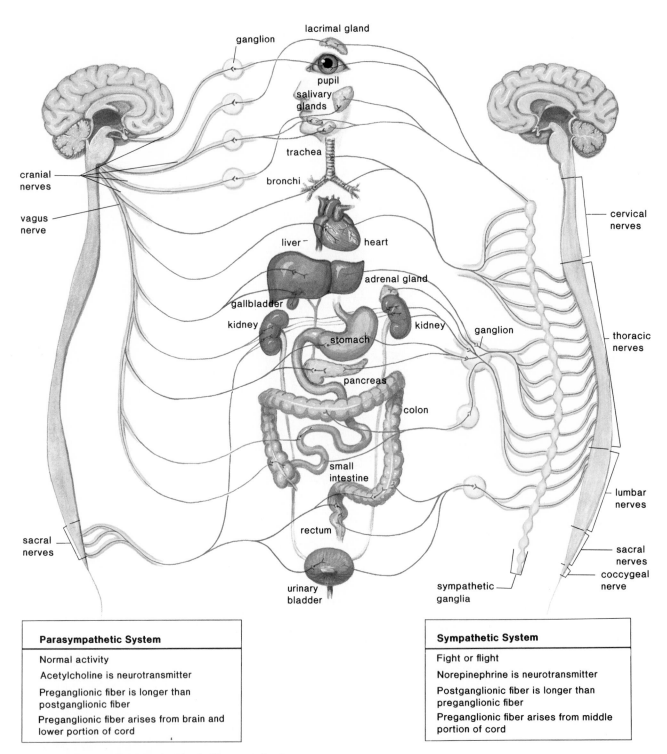

Parasympathetic System

Normal activity

Acetylcholine is neurotransmitter

Preganglionic fiber is longer than postganglionic fiber

Preganglionic fiber arises from brain and lower portion of cord

Sympathetic System

Fight or flight

Norepinephrine is neurotransmitter

Postganglionic fiber is longer than preganglionic fiber

Preganglionic fiber arises from middle portion of cord

Sympathetic and Parasympathetic Nervous System
Figure 16.12

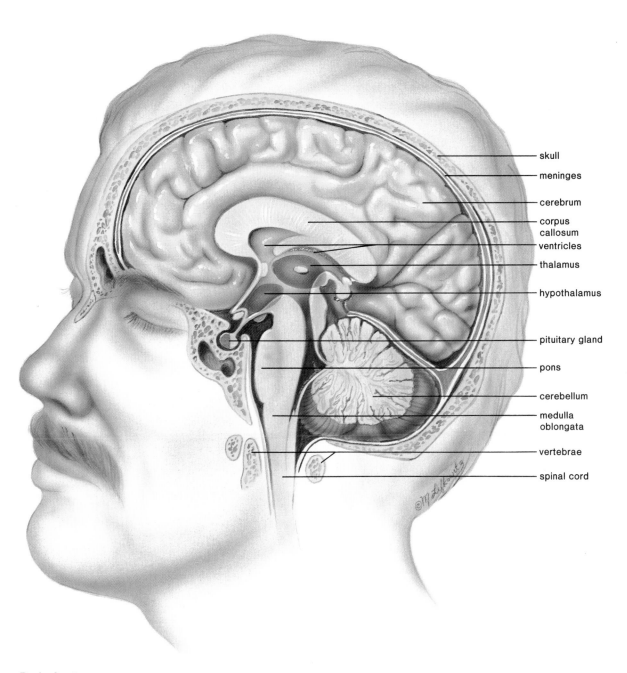

skull

meninges

cerebrum

corpus
callosum

ventricles

thalamus

hypothalamus

pituitary gland

pons

cerebellum

medulla
oblongata

vertebrae

spinal cord

Brain Anatomy
Figure 16.13

Lobes of the Brain
Figure 16.16

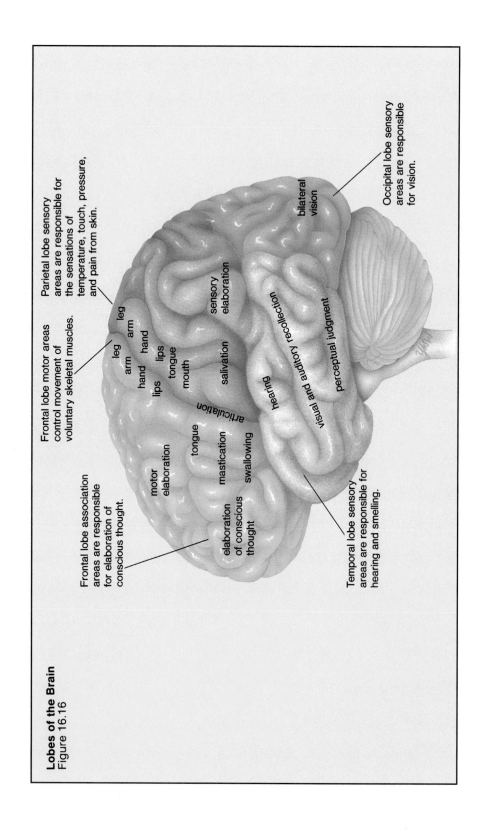

Frontal lobe association
areas are responsible
for elaboration of
conscious thought.

Frontal lobe motor areas
control movement of
voluntary skeletal muscles.

Parietal lobe sensory
areas are responsible for
the sensations of
temperature, touch, pressure,
and pain from skin.

Occipital lobe sensory
areas are responsible
for vision.

Temporal lobe sensory
areas are responsible for
hearing and smelling.

elaboration
of conscious
thought

motor
elaborration

tongue
mastication
swallowing

articulation

leg
leg
arm
arm
hand
hand
lips
lips
tongue
mouth

sensory
elaboration

salivation

hearing

visual and auditory recollection

perceptual judgment

bilateral
vision

Musculoskeletal System
Figure 17.1

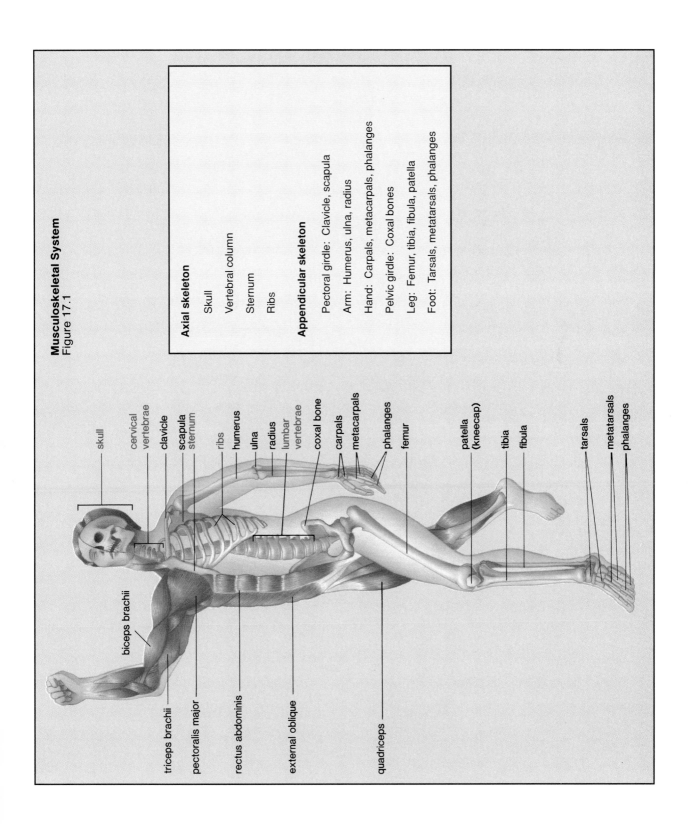

Axial skeleton

Skull

Vertebral column

Sternum

Ribs

Appendicular skeleton

Pectoral girdle: Clavicle, scapula

Arm: Humerus, ulna, radius

Hand: Carpals, metacarpals, phalanges

Pelvic girdle: Coxal bones

Leg: Femur, tibia, fibula, patella

Foot: Tarsals, metatarsals, phalanges

skull

cervical
vertebrae

clavicle

scapula
sternum

ribs

humerus

ulna

radius

lumbar
vertebrae

coxal bone

carpals

metacarpals

phalanges

femur

patella
(kneecap)

tibia

fibula

tarsals

metatarsals

phalanges

biceps brachii

triceps brachii

pectoralis major

rectus abdominis

external oblique

quadriceps

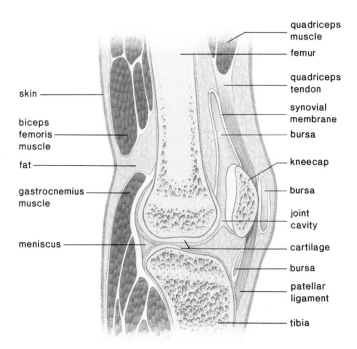

quadriceps
muscle

femur

skin

quadriceps
tendon

biceps
femoris
muscle

synovial
membrane

bursa

fat

kneecap

gastrocnemius
muscle

bursa

joint
cavity

meniscus

cartilage

bursa

patellar
ligament

tibia

Knee Anatomy
Figure 17.5

Anatomy of a Long Bone
Figure 17.6

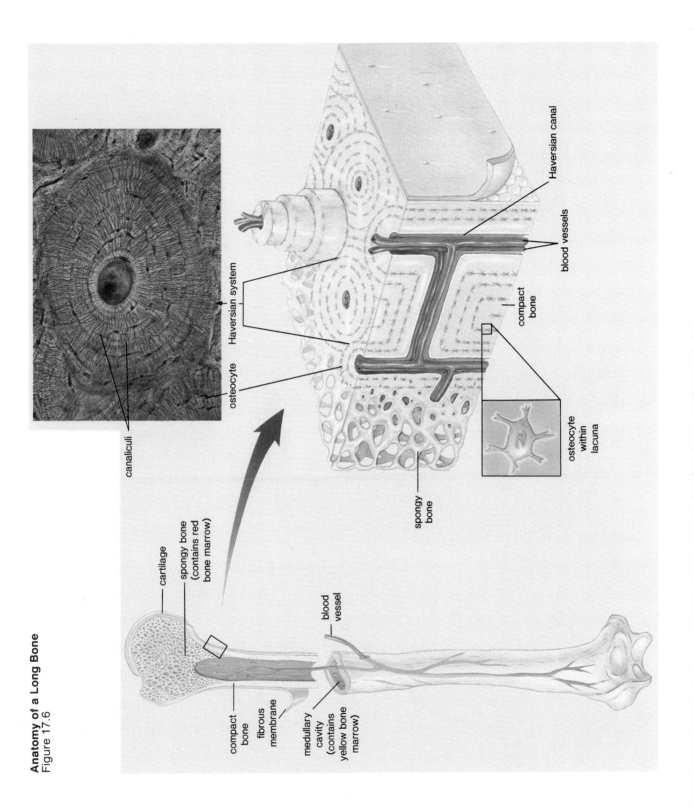

canaliculi

Haversian system

osteocyte

Haversian canal

blood vessels

compact bone

osteocyte within lacuna

spongy bone

cartilage

spongy bone (contains red bone marrow)

compact bone

fibrous membrane

medullary cavity (contains yellow bone marrow)

blood vessel

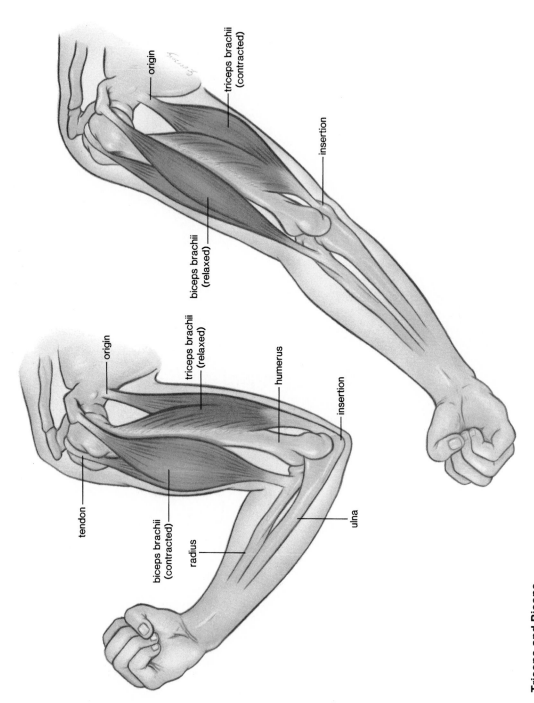

origin

triceps brachii
(contracted)

insertion

biceps brachii
(relaxed)

origin

triceps brachii
(relaxed)

humerus

insertion

tendon

biceps brachii
(contracted)

radius

ulna

Triceps and Biceps
Figure 17.7

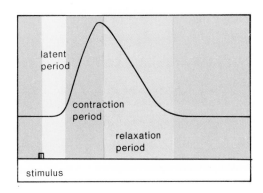

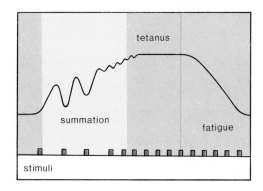

Physiology of Muscle Contraction
Figure 17.8

Anatomy and Function of Skeletal Muscle
Figure 17.9

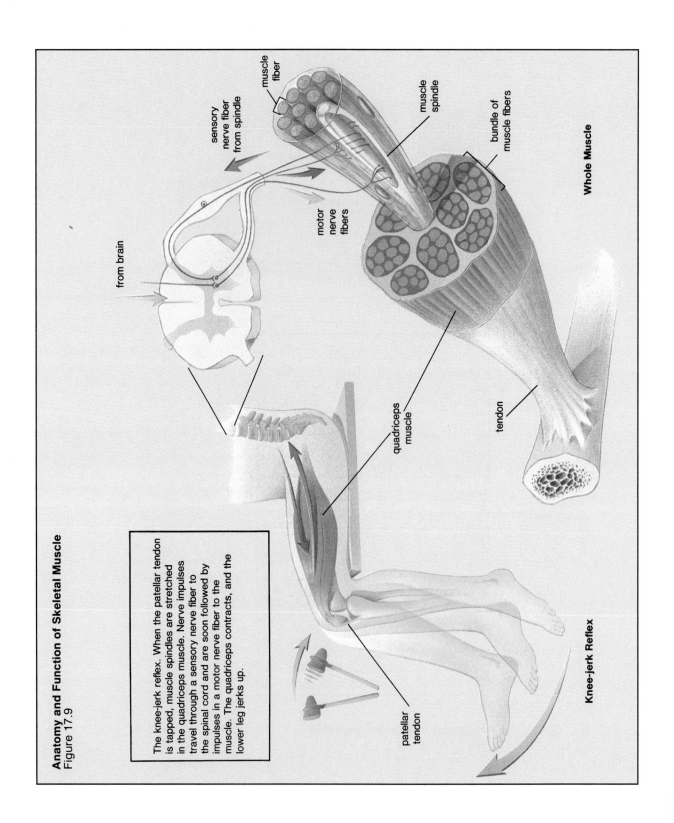

The knee-jerk reflex. When the patellar tendon is tapped, muscle spindles are stretched in the quadriceps muscle. Nerve impulses travel through a sensory nerve fiber to the spinal cord and are soon followed by impulses in a motor nerve fiber to the muscle. The quadriceps contracts, and the lower leg jerks up.

muscle fiber

sensory nerve fiber from spindle

muscle spindle

from brain

bundle of muscle fibers

motor nerve fibers

quadriceps muscle

tendon

patellar tendon

Whole Muscle

Knee-jerk Reflex

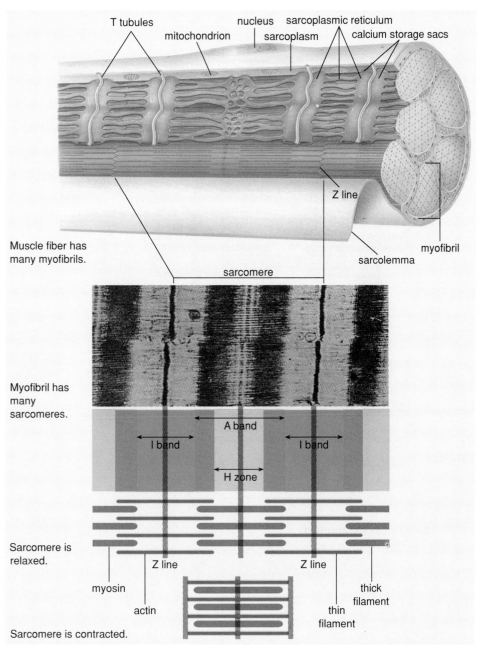

T tubules   mitochondrion   nucleus   sarcoplasm   sarcoplasmic reticulum   calcium storage sacs

Z line

Muscle fiber has
many myofibrils.

myofibril

sarcolemma

sarcomere

Myofibril has
many
sarcomeres.

A band

I band   I band

H zone

Sarcomere is
relaxed.

Z line   Z line

myosin

actin

thick
filament

thin
filament

Sarcomere is contracted.

Anatomy and Function of Muscle Fiber
Figure 17.10

a.

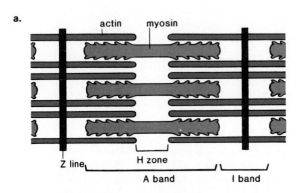

actin   myosin

Z line   H zone

A band   I band

b.

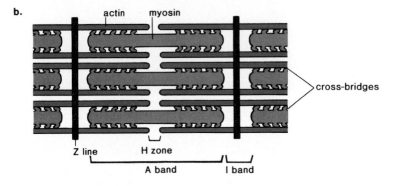

actin   myosin

cross-bridges

Z line   H zone

A band   I band

Sarcomere Contraction
Figure 17.11

Muscle Fiber Innervations
Figure 17.12

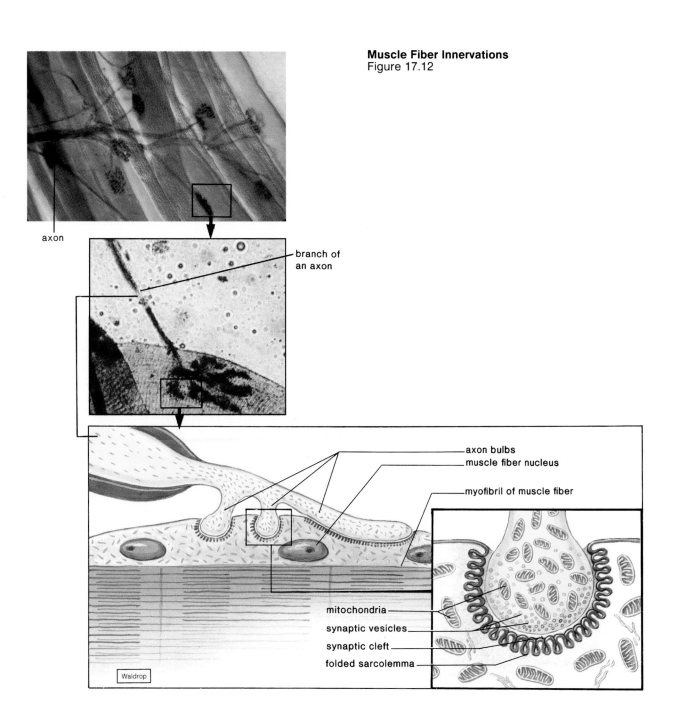

axon

branch of
an axon

axon bulbs
muscle fiber nucleus

myofibril of muscle fiber

mitochondria
synaptic vesicles
synaptic cleft
folded sarcolemma

Waldrop

103

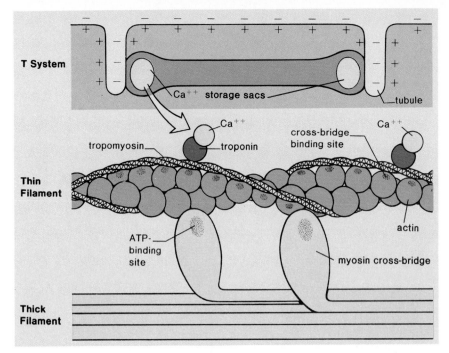

Role of Calcium in Muscle Contraction
Figure 17.13

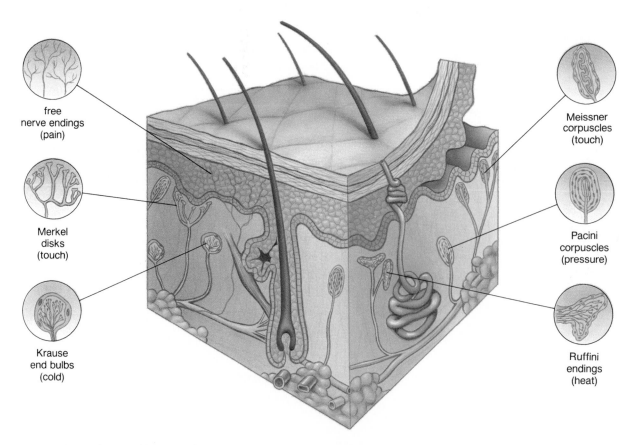

free
nerve endings
(pain)

Merkel
disks
(touch)

Krause
end bulbs
(cold)

Meissner
corpuscles
(touch)

Pacini
corpuscles
(pressure)

Ruffini
endings
(heat)

Receptors in Human Skin
Figure 18.2

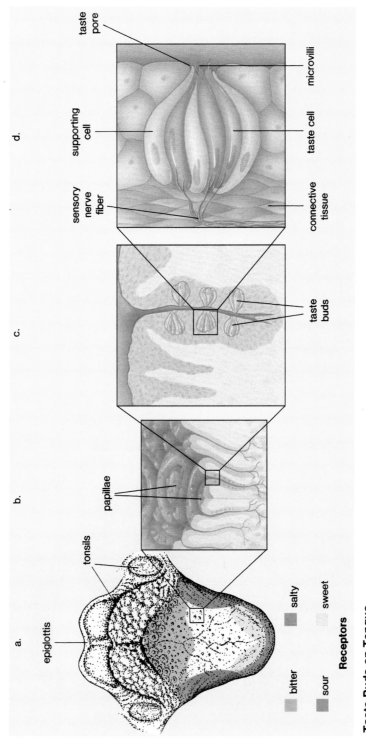

Taste Buds on Tongue
Figure 18.3

a.

epiglottis

tonsils

Receptors

bitter

sour

salty

sweet

b.

papillae

c.

taste buds

d.

taste pore

supporting cell

sensory nerve fiber

microvilli

taste cell

connective tissue

105

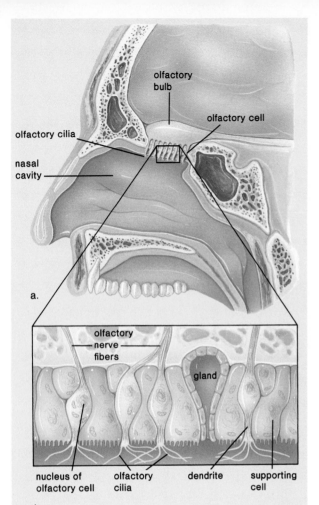

a.

olfactory bulb

olfactory cell

olfactory cilia

nasal cavity

olfactory nerve fibers

gland

nucleus of olfactory cell

olfactory cilia

dendrite

supporting cell

b.

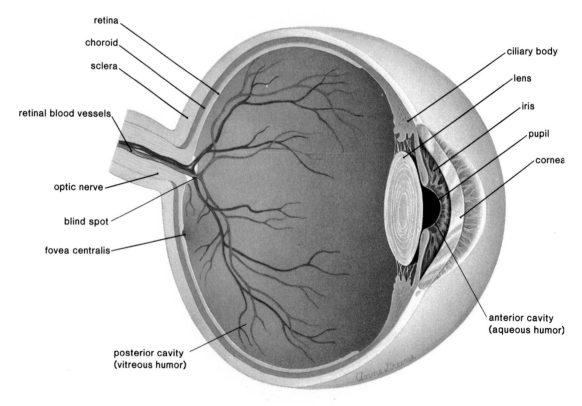

retina

choroid

sclera

retinal blood vessels

optic nerve

blind spot

fovea centralis

posterior cavity
(vitreous humor)

ciliary body

lens

iris

pupil

cornea

anterior cavity
(aqueous humor)

Eye Anatomy
Figure 18.5

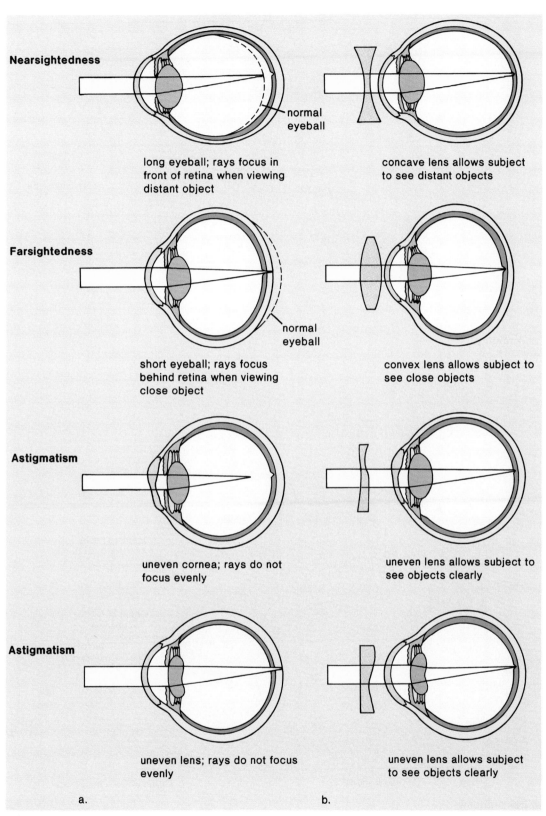

Nearsightedness

long eyeball; rays focus in front of retina when viewing distant object

normal eyeball

concave lens allows subject to see distant objects

Farsightedness

short eyeball; rays focus behind retina when viewing close object

normal eyeball

convex lens allows subject to see close objects

Astigmatism

uneven cornea; rays do not focus evenly

uneven lens allows subject to see objects clearly

Astigmatism

uneven lens; rays do not focus evenly

uneven lens allows subject to see objects clearly

a.

b.

Abnormalities of the Eye
Figure 18.11

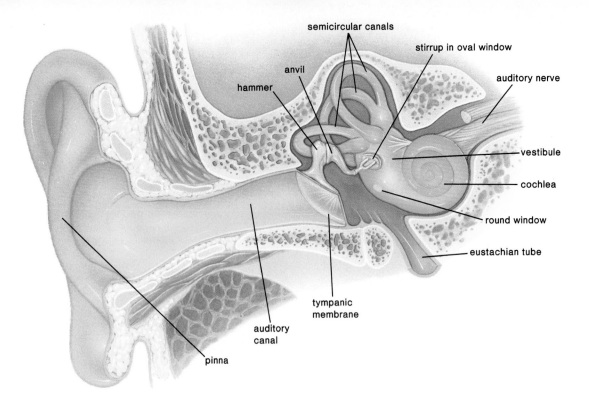

Ear Anatomy
Figure 18.12

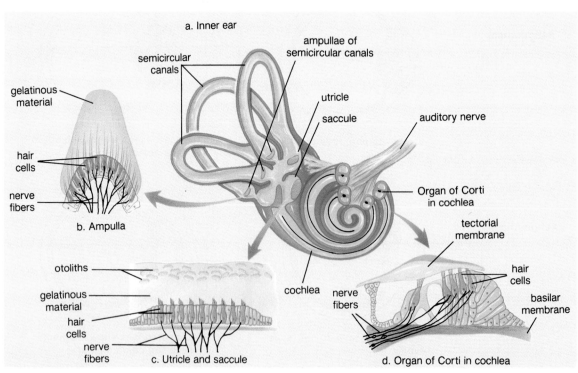

Inner Ear Anatomy
Figure 18.13

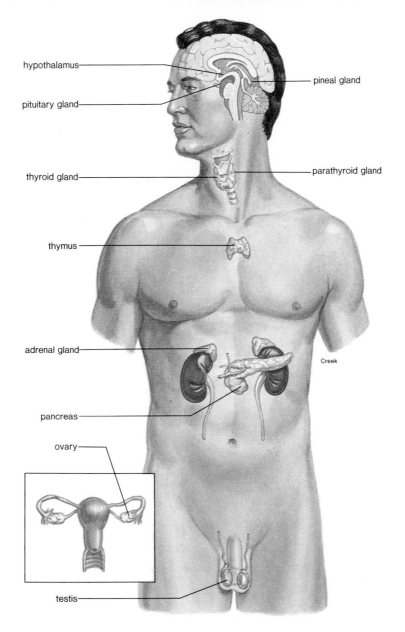

hypothalamus

pituitary gland

pineal gland

thyroid gland

parathyroid gland

thymus

adrenal gland

Creek

pancreas

ovary

testis

Endocrine Gland Location
Figure 19.1

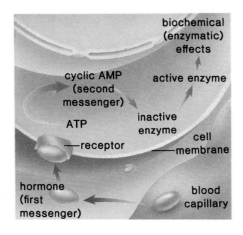

biochemical
(enzymatic)
effects

cyclic AMP
(second
messenger)

active enzyme

ATP

inactive
enzyme

receptor

cell
membrane

hormone
(first
messenger)

blood
capillary

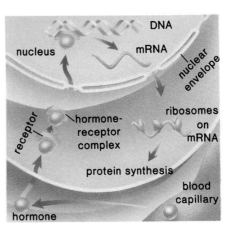

DNA

nucleus

mRNA

nuclear
envelope

receptor

hormone-
receptor
complex

ribosomes
on
mRNA

protein synthesis

blood
capillary

hormone

Hormonal Cellular Activity
Figure 19.2

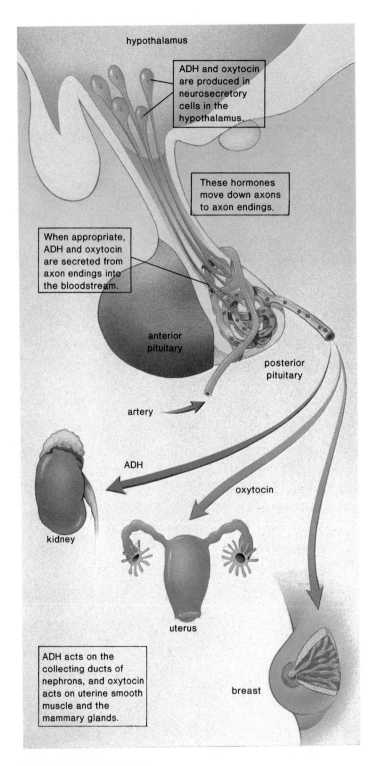

hypothalamus

ADH and oxytocin are produced in neurosecretory cells in the hypothalamus.

These hormones move down axons to axon endings.

When appropriate, ADH and oxytocin are secreted from axon endings into the bloodstream.

anterior pituitary

posterior pituitary

artery

ADH

oxytocin

kidney

uterus

breast

ADH acts on the collecting ducts of nephrons, and oxytocin acts on uterine smooth muscle and the mammary glands.

Action of Posterior Pituitary
Figure 19.3

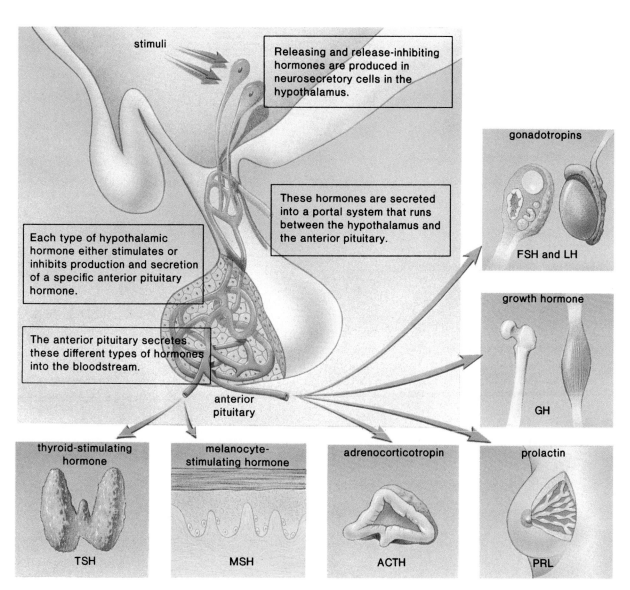

stimuli

Releasing and release-inhibiting hormones are produced in neurosecretory cells in the hypothalamus.

These hormones are secreted into a portal system that runs between the hypothalamus and the anterior pituitary.

Each type of hypothalamic hormone either stimulates or inhibits production and secretion of a specific anterior pituitary hormone.

The anterior pituitary secretes these different types of hormones into the bloodstream.

anterior pituitary

gonadotropins

FSH and LH

growth hormone

GH

thyroid-stimulating hormone

TSH

melanocyte-stimulating hormone

MSH

adrenocorticotropin

ACTH

prolactin

PRL

Action of Anterior Pituitary
Figure 19.5

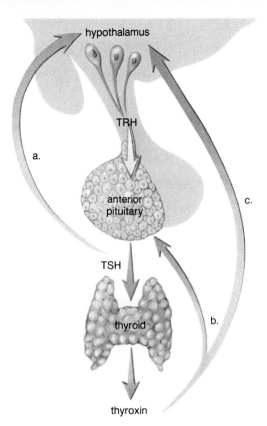

Feedback Control of Hormonal Secretion
Figure 19.8

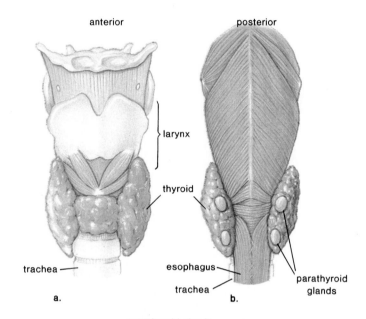

Action of Parathyroid Glands
Figure 19.13

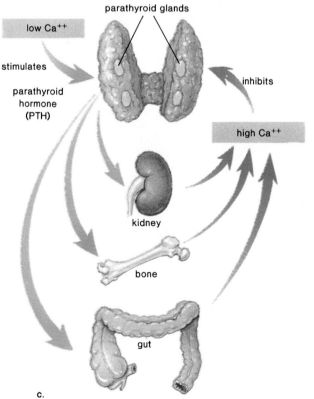

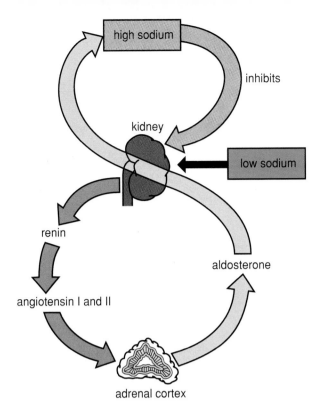

Renin-Angiotensin-Aldosterone System
Figure 19.14

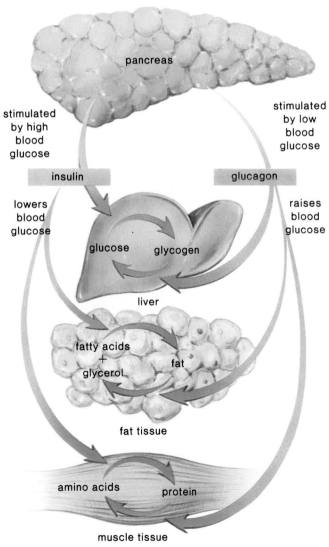

Action of Insulin and Glucagon
Figure 19.18

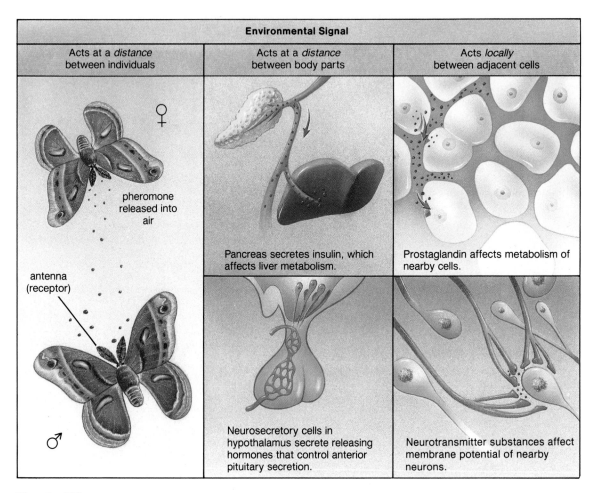

Environmental Signal		
Acts at a *distance* between individuals	Acts at a *distance* between body parts	Acts *locally* between adjacent cells
pheromone released into air antenna (receptor)	Pancreas secretes insulin, which affects liver metabolism. Neurosecretory cells in hypothalamus secrete releasing hormones that control anterior pituitary secretion.	Prostaglandin affects metabolism of nearby cells. Neurotransmitter substances affect membrane potential of nearby neurons.

Chemical Messengers
Figure 19.19

Male Anatomy
Figure 20.1

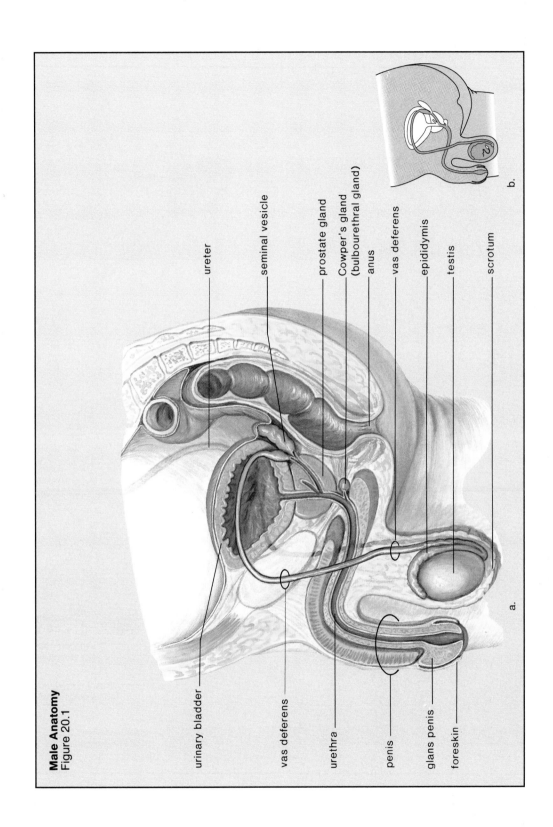

ureter

seminal vesicle

prostate gland

Cowper's gland
(bulbourethral gland)

anus

vas deferens

epididymis

testis

scrotum

urinary bladder

vas deferens

urethra

penis

glans penis

foreskin

a.

b.

Testis Anatomy
Figure 20.2

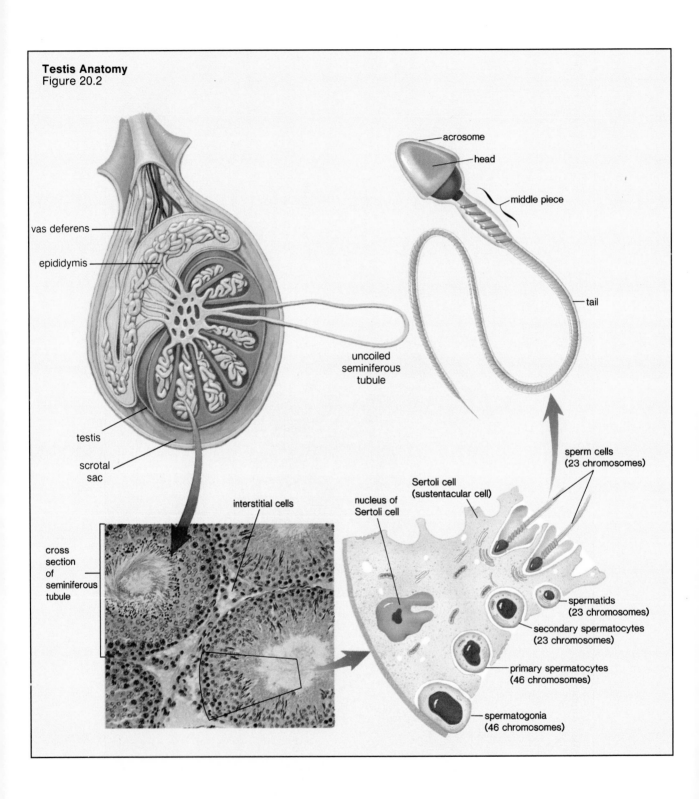

acrosome

head

middle piece

vas deferens

epididymis

tail

uncoiled
seminiferous
tubule

testis

scrotal
sac

sperm cells
(23 chromosomes)

interstitial cells

Sertoli cell
(sustentacular cell)

nucleus of
Sertoli cell

cross
section
of
seminiferous
tubule

spermatids
(23 chromosomes)

secondary spermatocytes
(23 chromosomes)

primary spermatocytes
(46 chromosomes)

spermatogonia
(46 chromosomes)

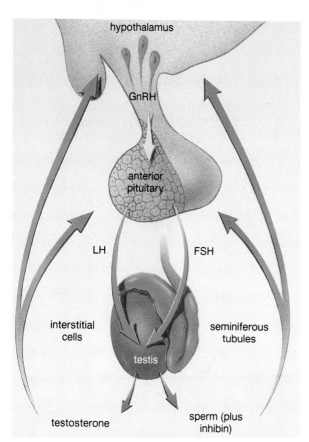

Hormonal Control in the Male
Figure 20.4

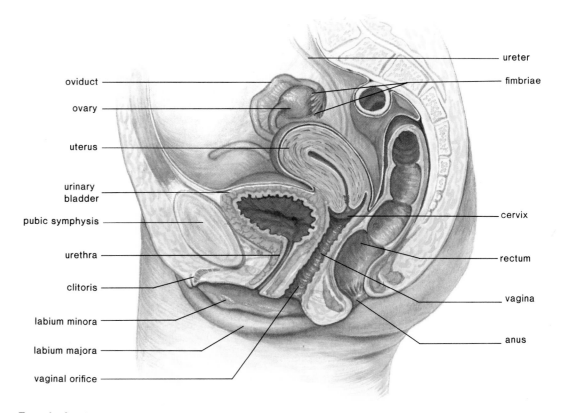

Female Anatomy
Figure 20.5

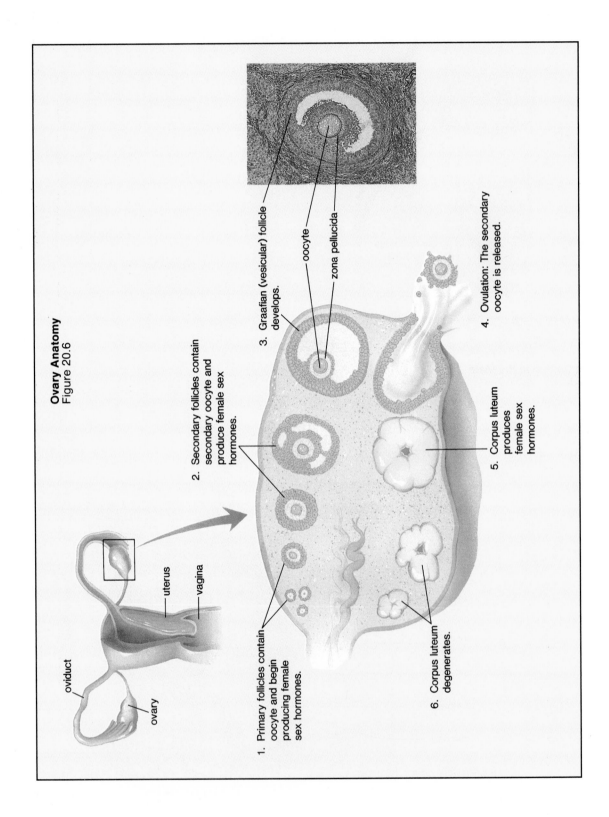

Ovary Anatomy
Figure 20.6

oviduct

ovary

uterus

vagina

oocyte

zona pellucida

3. Graafian (vesicular) follicle develops.

2. Secondary follicles contain secondary oocyte and produce female sex hormones.

4. Ovulation: The secondary oocyte is released.

5. Corpus luteum produces female sex hormones.

1. Primary follicles contain oocyte and begin producing female sex hormones.

6. Corpus luteum degenerates.

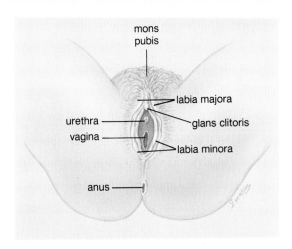

External Female Genitalia
Figure 20.8

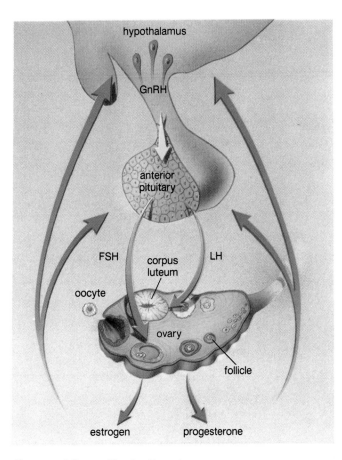

Hormonal Control in the Female
Figure 20.9

Ovarian and Uterine Cycle
Figure 20.10

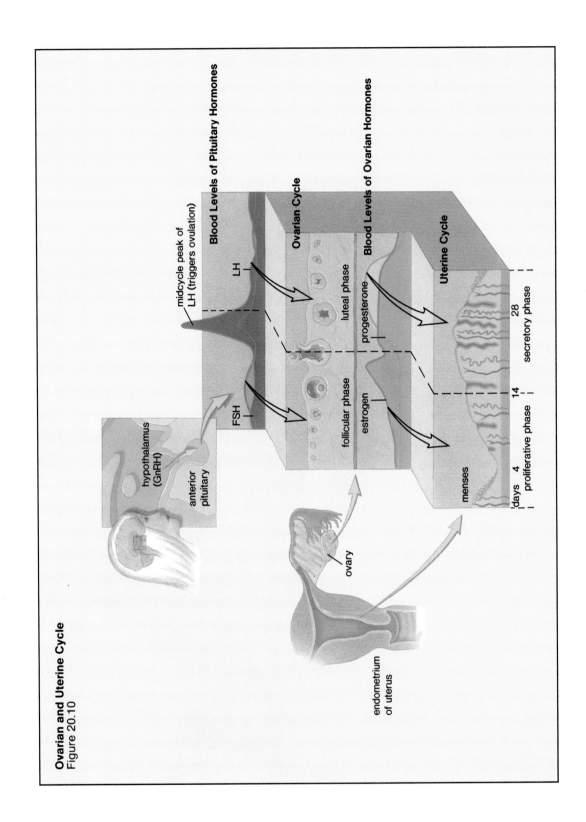

Lancelet vs. Human Development
Figure 21.1

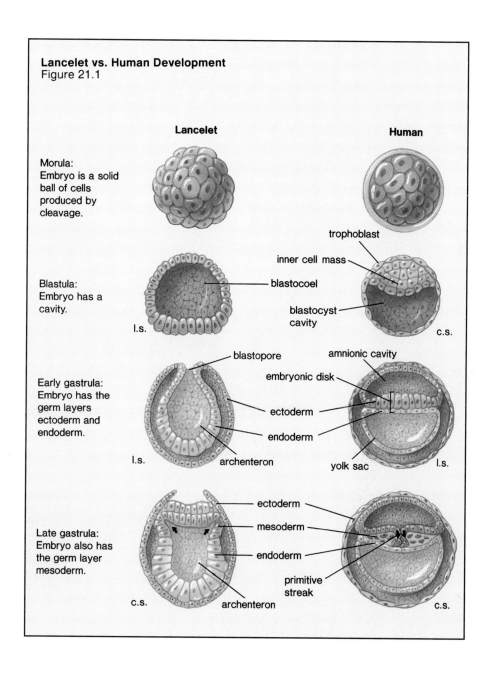

Lancelet   Human

Morula:
Embryo is a solid
ball of cells
produced by
cleavage.

trophoblast

inner cell mass

Blastula: blastocoel
Embryo has a
cavity.
                                                         blastocyst
                                                         cavity
l.s.   c.s.

blastopore   amnionic cavity

embryonic disk

Early gastrula:
Embryo has the
germ layers   ectoderm
ectoderm and
endoderm.   endoderm

l.s.   archenteron   yolk sac   l.s.

ectoderm

mesoderm

Late gastrula:
Embryo also has   endoderm
the germ layer
mesoderm.   primitive
                                                         streak
c.s.   archenteron   c.s.

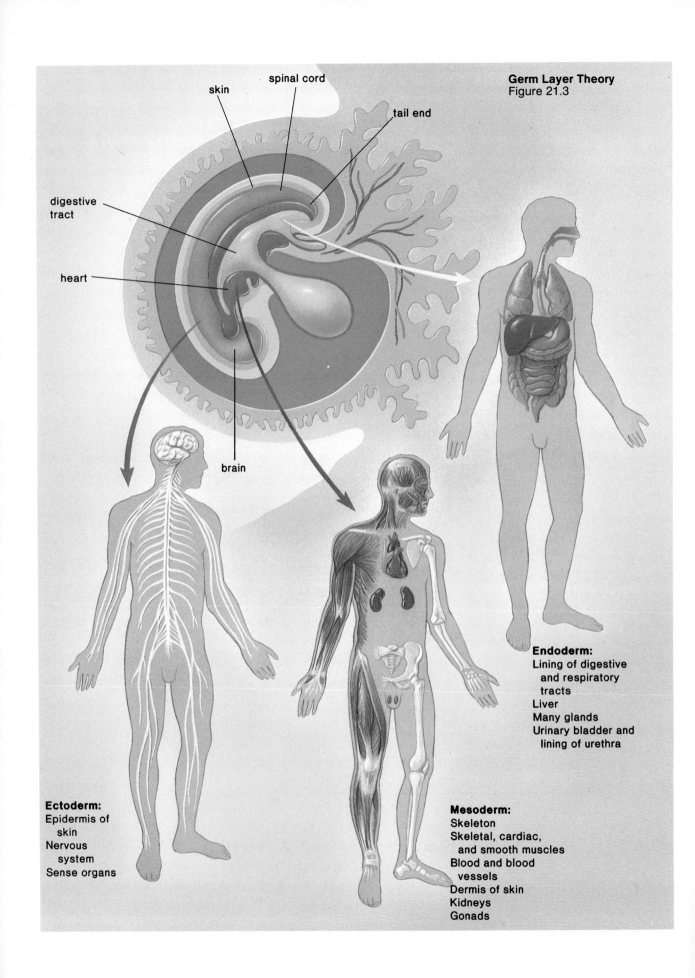

skin

spinal cord

tail end

digestive
tract

heart

brain

Ectoderm:
Epidermis of
  skin
Nervous
  system
Sense organs

Mesoderm:
Skeleton
Skeletal, cardiac,
  and smooth muscles
Blood and blood
  vessels
Dermis of skin
Kidneys
Gonads

Endoderm:
Lining of digestive
  and respiratory
  tracts
Liver
Many glands
Urinary bladder and
  lining of urethra

Ectoderm cells that lie above the presumptive notochord thicken to form a neural plate.

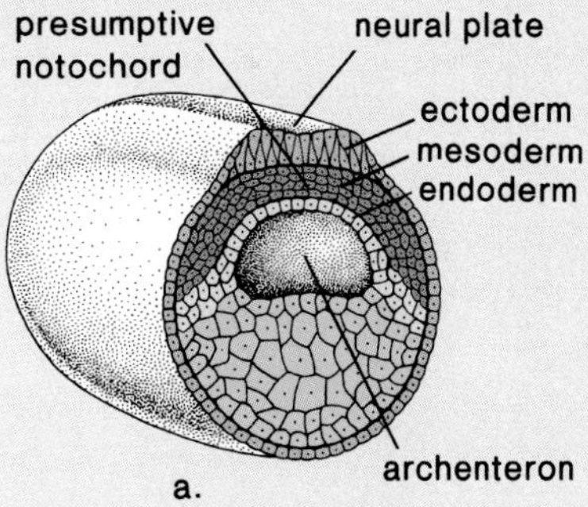

presumptive notochord

neural plate

ectoderm
mesoderm
endoderm

archenteron

a.

The neural groove and folds are noticeable as the neural tube begins to form.

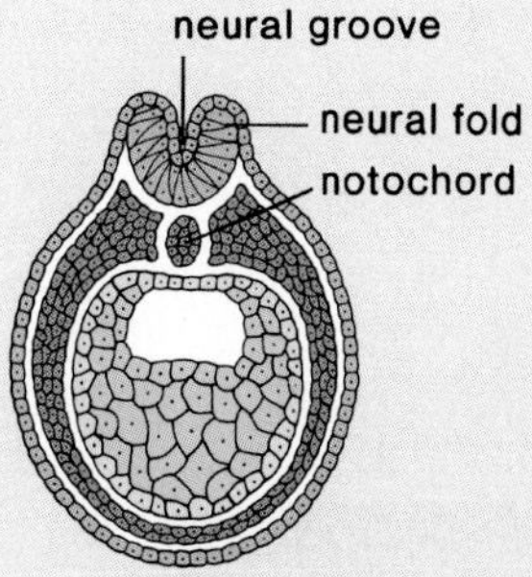

neural groove

neural fold
notochord

b.

Division of the mesoderm produces a coelom completely lined by mesoderm.

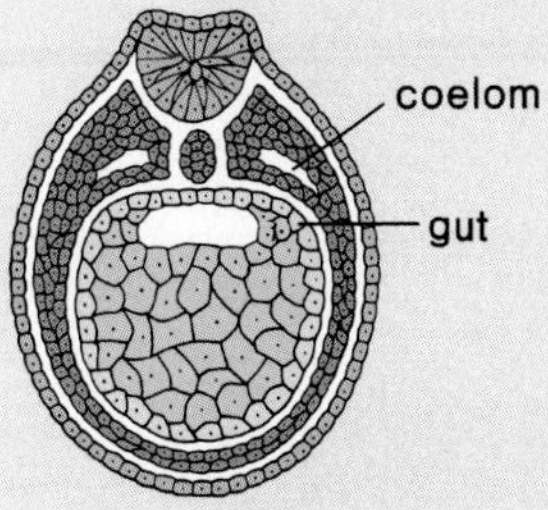

coelom

gut

c.

A neural tube and a coelom have now developed.

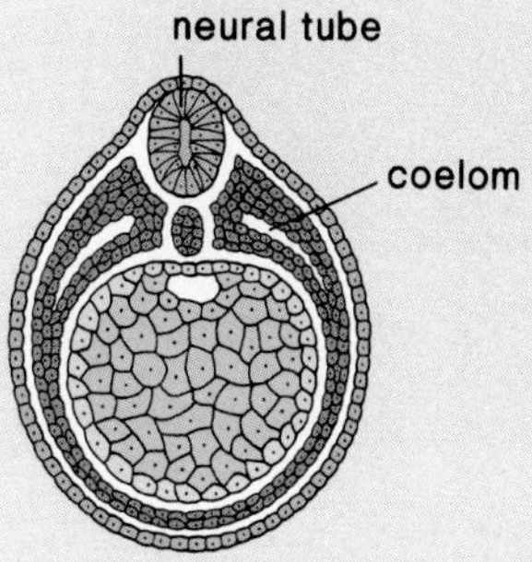

neural tube

coelom

d.

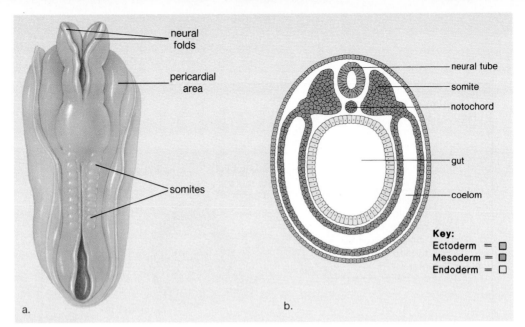

neural folds

pericardial area

somites

neural tube

somite

notochord

gut

coelom

Key:
Ectoderm =
Mesoderm =
Endoderm =

a.

b.

Vertebrate Cross Section
Figure 21.5

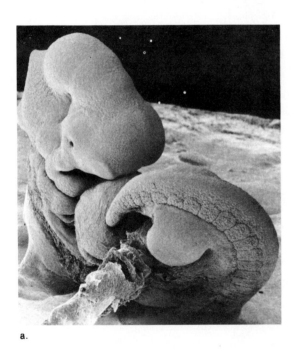

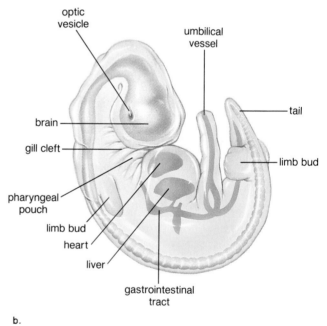

optic vesicle

umbilical vessel

brain

gill cleft

pharyngeal pouch

limb bud

heart

liver

gastrointestinal tract

tail

limb bud

a.

b.

Fifth-Week Embryo
Figure 21.6

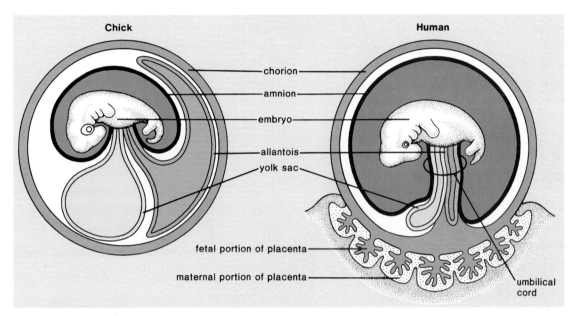

Extraembryonic Membranes
Figure 21.12

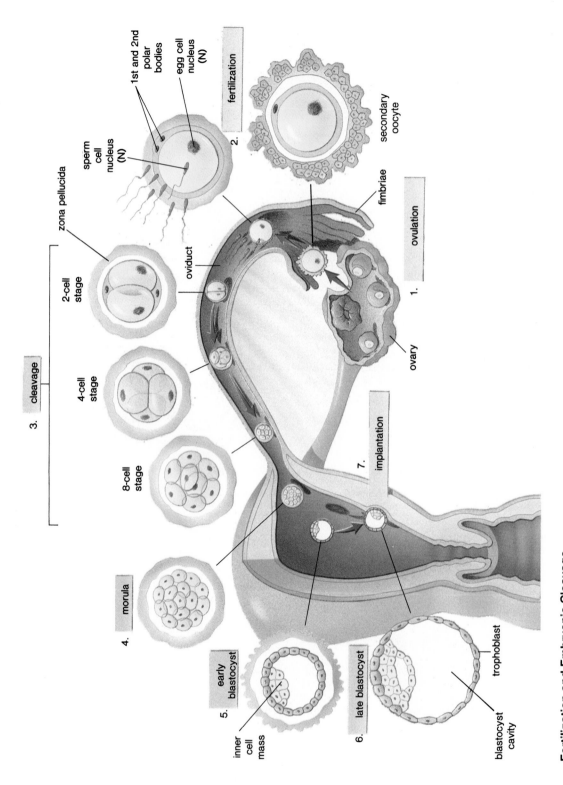

1st and 2nd polar bodies

egg cell nucleus (N)

sperm cell nucleus (N)

2. fertilization

secondary oocyte

zona pellucida

oviduct

fimbriae

1. ovulation

ovary

2-cell stage

4-cell stage

8-cell stage

3. cleavage

7. implantation

morula

4.

early blastocyst

5.

inner cell mass

late blastocyst

6.

trophoblast

blastocyst cavity

Fertilization and Embryonic Cleavage
Figure 21.13

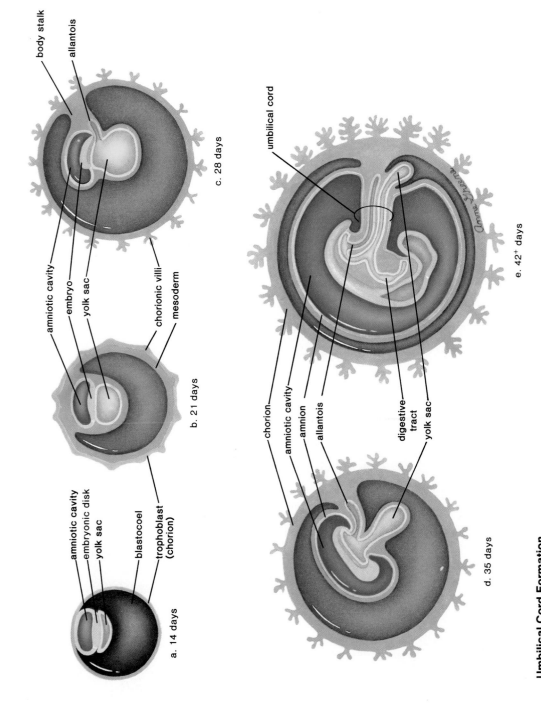

a. 14 days

- amniotic cavity
- embryonic disk
- yolk sac
- blastocoel
- trophoblast (chorion)

b. 21 days

- chorionic villi
- mesoderm

c. 28 days

- body stalk
- allantois
- amniotic cavity
- embryo
- yolk sac

d. 35 days

- chorion
- amniotic cavity
- amnion
- allantois

e. 42⁺ days

- umbilical cord
- digestive tract
- yolk sac

Umbilical Cord Formation
Figure 21.14

127

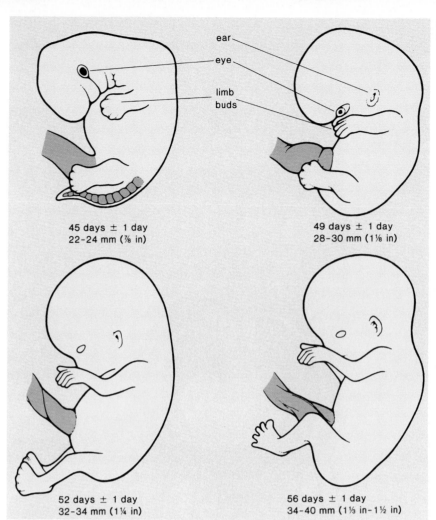

ear
eye
limb buds

45 days ± 1 day
22-24 mm (⅞ in)

49 days ± 1 day
28-30 mm (1⅛ in)

52 days ± 1 day
32-34 mm (1¼ in)

56 days ± 1 day
34-40 mm (1⅓ in-1½ in)

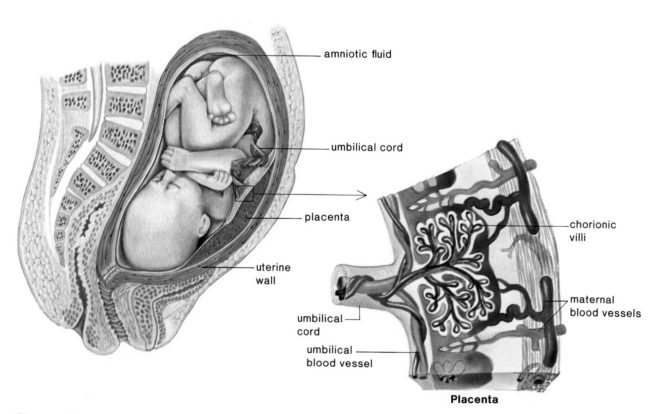

amniotic fluid

umbilical cord

placenta

uterine wall

chorionic villi

maternal blood vessels

umbilical cord

umbilical blood vessel

Placenta

Placental Structure
Figure 21.16

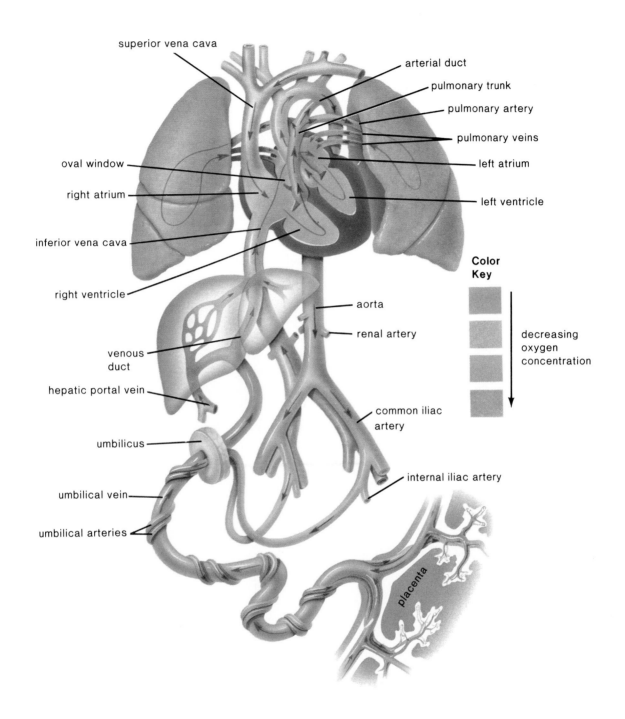

superior vena cava

arterial duct

pulmonary trunk

pulmonary artery

pulmonary veins

oval window

left atrium

right atrium

left ventricle

inferior vena cava

right ventricle

aorta

renal artery

venous
duct

hepatic portal vein

umbilicus

umbilical vein

umbilical arteries

common iliac
artery

internal iliac artery

placenta

Color
Key

decreasing
oxygen
concentration

Fetal Circulation
Figure 21.18

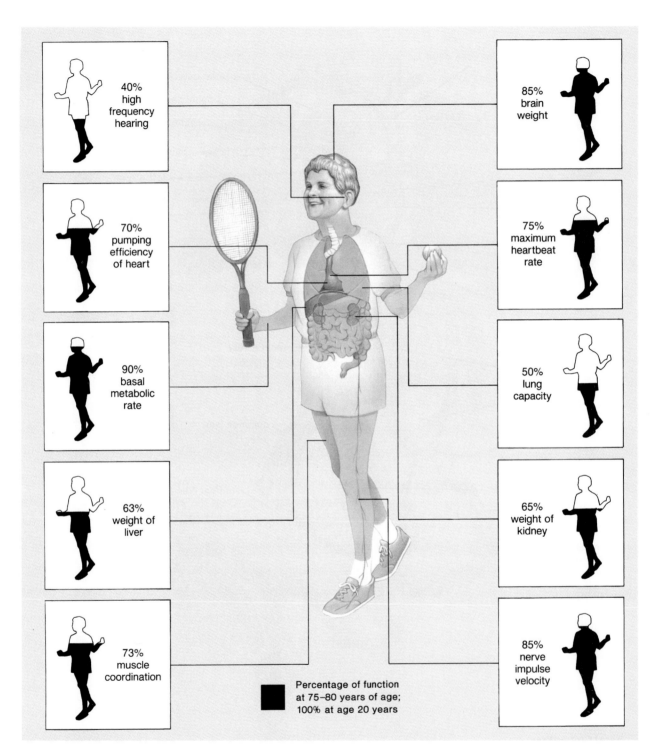

Eighty-Year-Old Person Compared to a Twenty-Year-Old Person
Figure 21.21

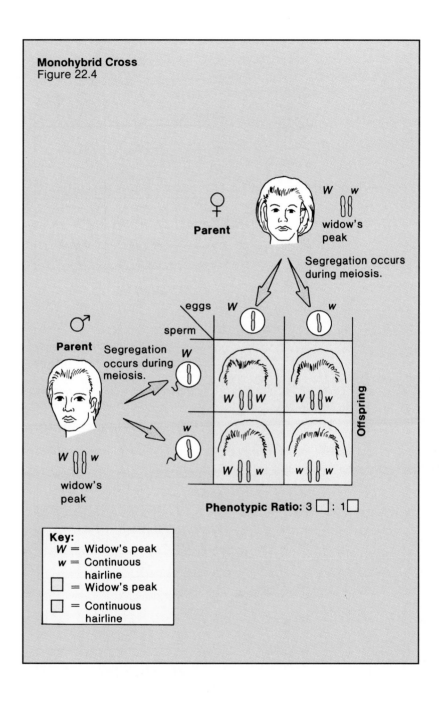

Monohybrid Cross
Figure 22.4

Parent ♀ — *W w* widow's peak

Segregation occurs during meiosis.

eggs — *W* — *w*

sperm

Parent ♂

Segregation occurs during meiosis. — *W*

W w
widow's peak — *w*

Offspring

W *W* | *W* *w*
W *w* | *w* *W*

Phenotypic Ratio: 3 ☐ : 1 ☐

Key:
W = Widow's peak
w = Continuous hairline
☐ = Widow's peak
☐ = Continuous hairline

One-Trait Testcross
Figure 22.5

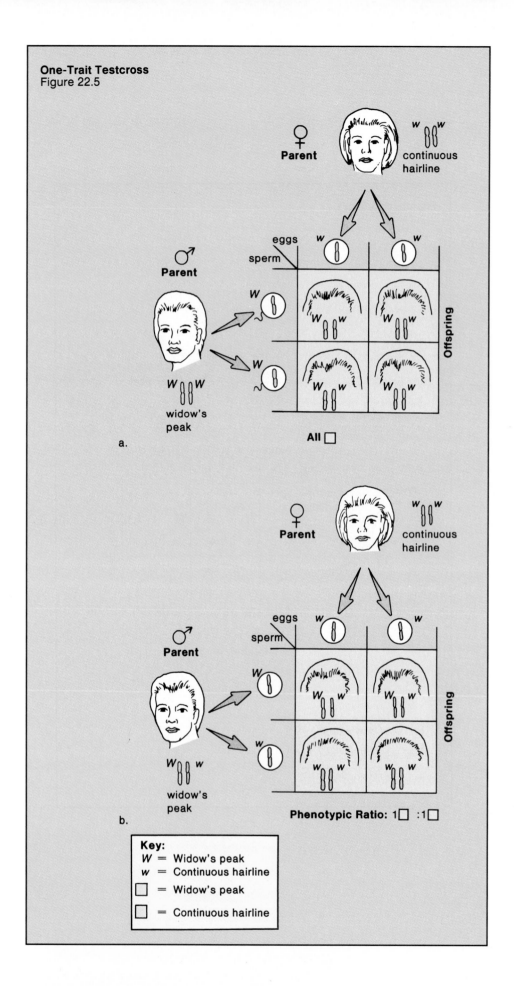

a.

All □

b. Phenotypic Ratio: 1□ :1□

Key:
W = Widow's peak
w = Continuous hairline
□ = Widow's peak
□ = Continuous hairline

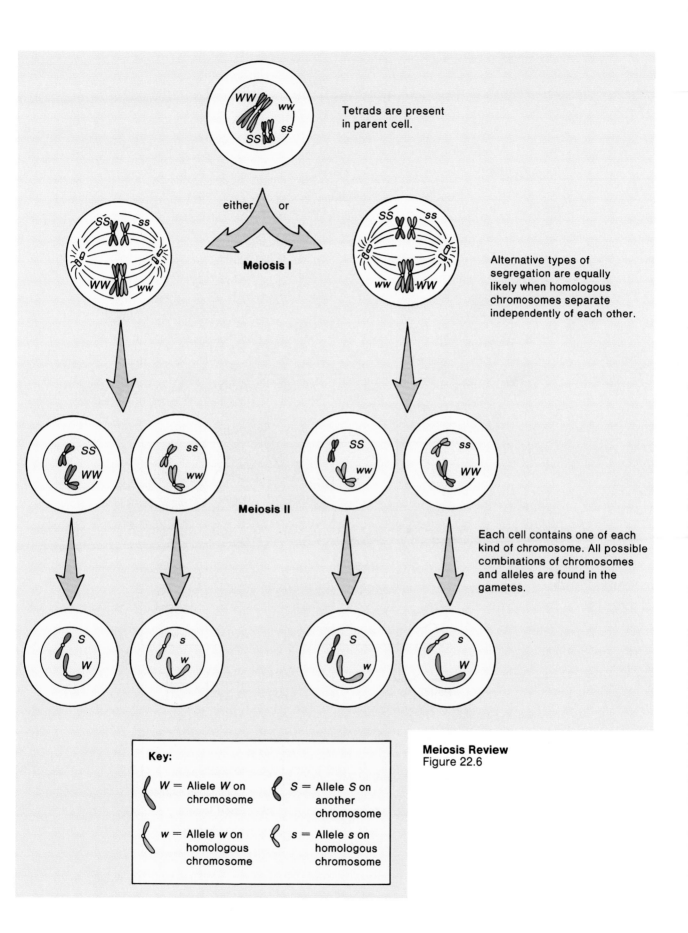

Tetrads are present in parent cell.

either or

Meiosis I

Alternative types of segregation are equally likely when homologous chromosomes separate independently of each other.

Meiosis II

Each cell contains one of each kind of chromosome. All possible combinations of chromosomes and alleles are found in the gametes.

Key:

W = Allele W on chromosome

w = Allele w on homologous chromosome

S = Allele S on another chromosome

s = Allele s on homologous chromosome

Meiosis Review
Figure 22.6

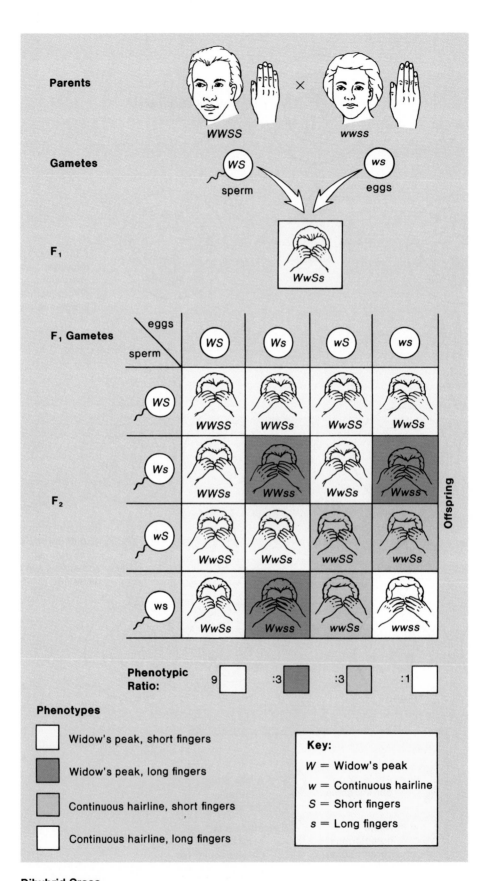

Parents

$WWSS$ × $wwss$

Gametes

WS sperm ws eggs

F₁

$WwSs$

F₁ Gametes

eggs / sperm

	WS	Ws	wS	ws
WS	$WWSS$	$WWSs$	$WwSS$	$WwSs$
Ws	$WWSs$	$WWss$	$WwSs$	$Wwss$
wS	$WwSS$	$WwSs$	$wwSS$	$wwSs$
ws	$WwSs$	$Wwss$	$wwSs$	$wwss$

F₂

Offspring

Phenotypic Ratio: 9 □ :3 ■ :3 ▨ :1 □

Phenotypes

□ Widow's peak, short fingers

■ Widow's peak, long fingers

▨ Continuous hairline, short fingers

□ Continuous hairline, long fingers

Key:
W = Widow's peak
w = Continuous hairline
S = Short fingers
s = Long fingers

Dihybrid Cross
Figure 22.7

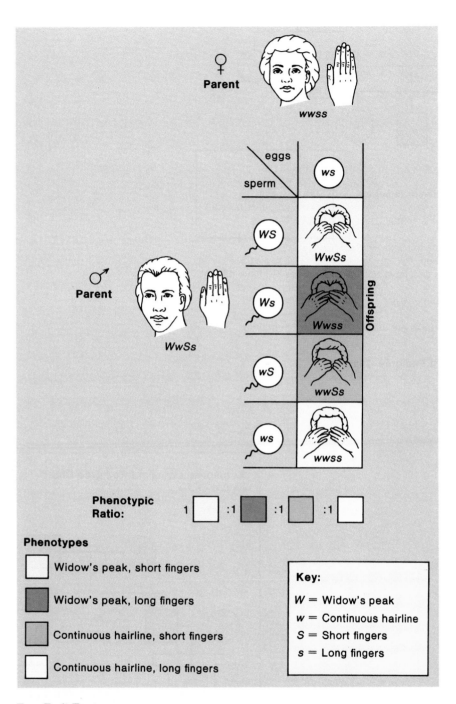

Two-Trait Testcross
Figure 22.8

135

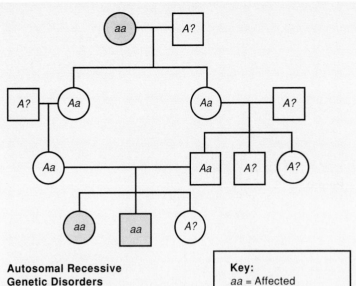

Autosomal Recessive Genetic Disorders

- Most affected children have normal parents.
- Heterozygotes have a normal phenotype.
- Two affected parents will always have affected children.
- Affected individuals who have noncarrier spouses will have normal children.
- Close relatives who marry are more likely to have affected children.
- Both males and females are affected with equal frequency.

Key:
aa = Affected
Aa = Carrier
(appears normal)
AA = Normal

Autosomal Recessive Pedigree Chart
Figure 22.9

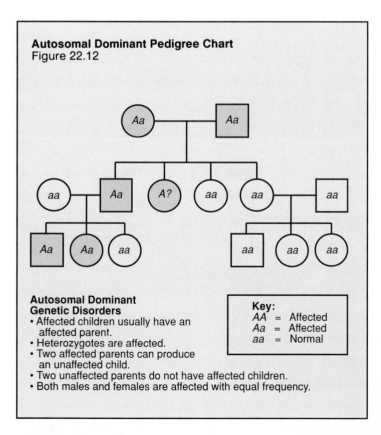

Autosomal Dominant Pedigree Chart
Figure 22.12

Autosomal Dominant Genetic Disorders

- Affected children usually have an affected parent.
- Heterozygotes are affected.
- Two affected parents can produce an unaffected child.
- Two unaffected parents do not have affected children.
- Both males and females are affected with equal frequency.

Key:
AA = Affected
Aa = Affected
aa = Normal

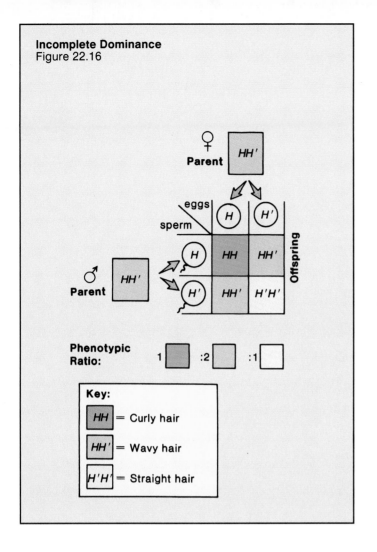

Incomplete Dominance
Figure 22.16

Phenotypic Ratio: 1 ▢ :2 ▢ :1 ▢

Key:
HH = Curly hair
HH' = Wavy hair
H'H' = Straight hair

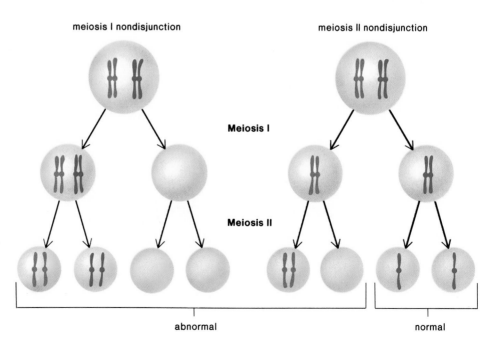

Nondisjunction of Autosomes During Oogenesis
Figure 23.1

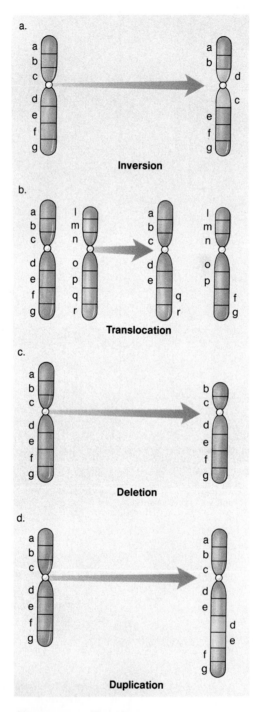

Chromosome Mutations
Figure 23.3

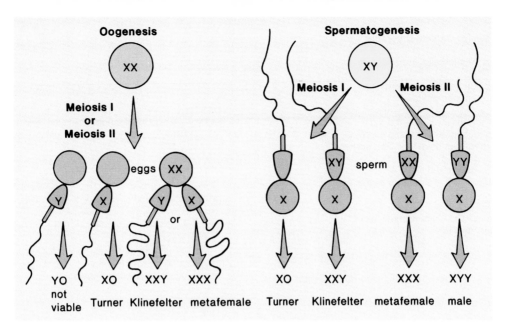

Nondisjunction of Sex Chromosomes During Oogenesis
Figure 23.7

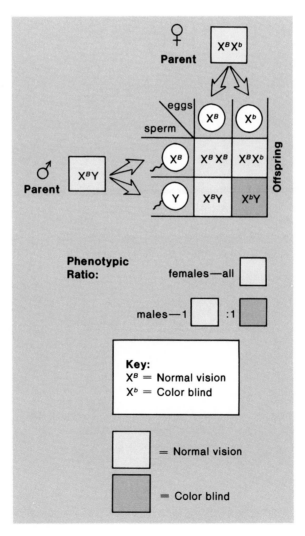

X-Linked Cross
Figure 23.9

X-linked Recessive Genetic Disorders

- More males than females are affected.

- An affected son can have parents who have the normal phenotype.

- In order for a female to have the characteristic, her father must also have it. Her mother must have it or be a carrier.

- The characteristic often skips a generation from the grandfather to the grandson.

- If a woman has the characteristic, all of her sons will have it.

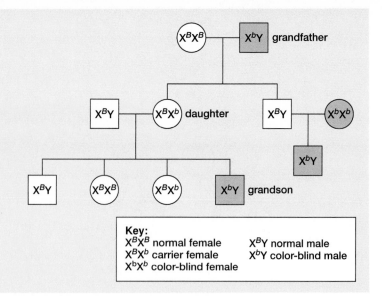

Key:
X^BX^B normal female X^BY normal male
X^BX^b carrier female X^bY color-blind male
X^bX^b color-blind female

X-Linked Recessive Pedigree Chart
Figure 23.10

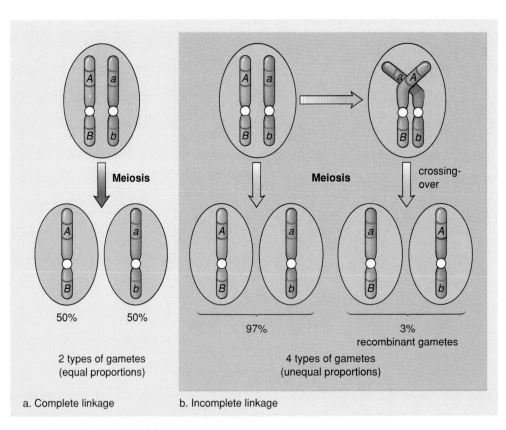

Linkage and Crossing-Over
Figure 23.13

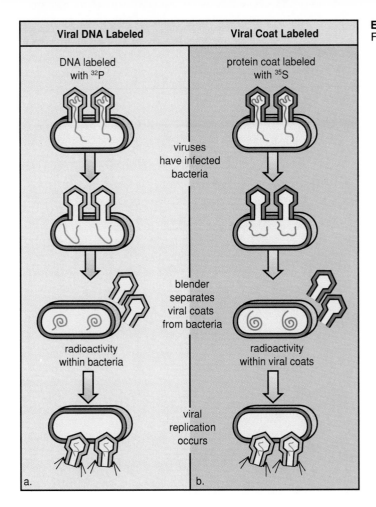

Viral DNA Labeled

DNA labeled with ^{32}P

Viral Coat Labeled

protein coat labeled with ^{35}S

viruses have infected bacteria

blender separates viral coats from bacteria

radioactivity within bacteria

radioactivity within viral coats

viral replication occurs

a.

b.

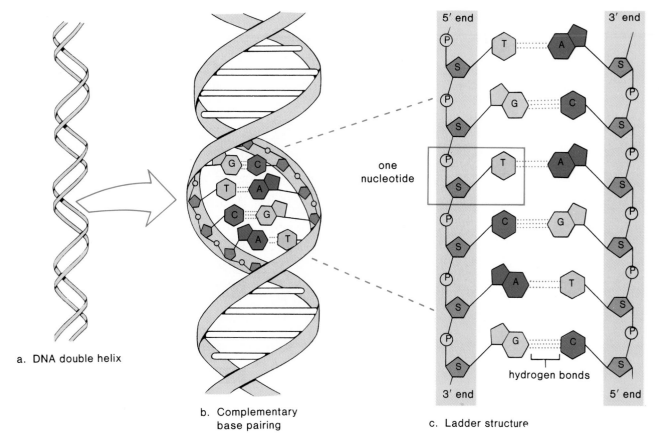

a. DNA double helix

b. Complementary base pairing

5' end

3' end

T ⋯ A

G ⋯ C

one nucleotide

T ⋯ A

C ⋯ G

A ⋯ T

G ⋯ C

hydrogen bonds

3' end

5' end

c. Ladder structure

DNA Flowchart
Figure 24.3

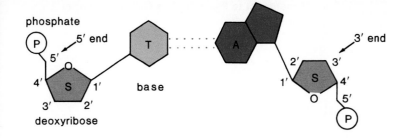

phosphate

5' end

base

deoxyribose

3' end

1. Thymine (T) is paired with adenine (A).

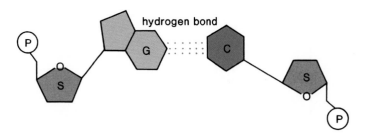

hydrogen bond

2. Guanine (G) is paired with cytosine (C).

DNA Structure
Figure 24.4

guanine

ribose

uracil

ribose

cytosine

ribose

adenine

ribose

RNA Structure
Figure 24.5

142

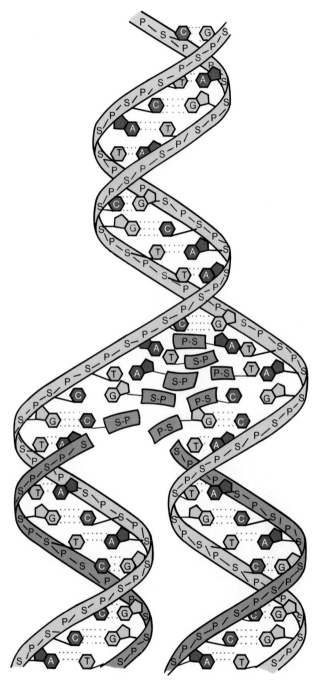

DNA Replication
Figure 24.6

Region of parental DNA helix. (Both backbones are light.)

Region of replication (simplified). Parental DNA is unwound and unzipped. New nucleotides are pairing with those in parental strands.

Region of completed replication. Each double helix is composed of an old parental strand (light) and a new daughter strand (dark). Notice that each double helix is exactly like the other and also like the original parental double helix.

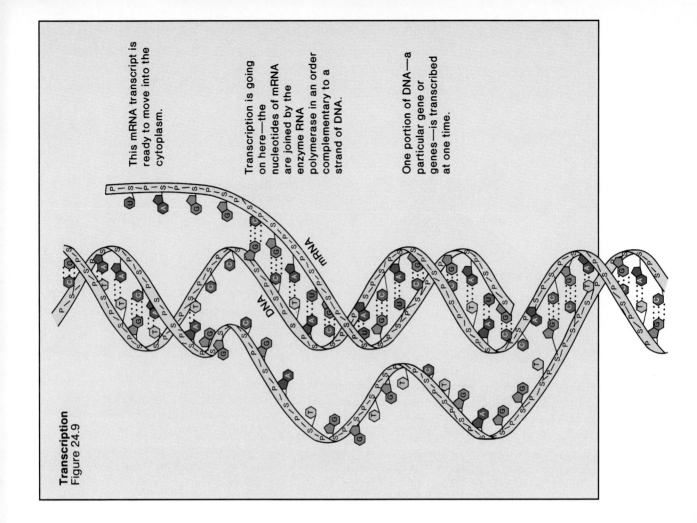

Transcription
Figure 24.9

This mRNA transcript is ready to move into the cytoplasm.

Transcription is going on here—the nucleotides of mRNA are joined by the enzyme RNA polymerase in an order complementary to a strand of DNA.

One portion of DNA—a particular gene or genes—is transcribed at one time.

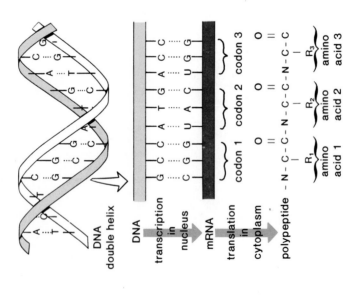

Protein Synthesis Overview
Figure 24.7

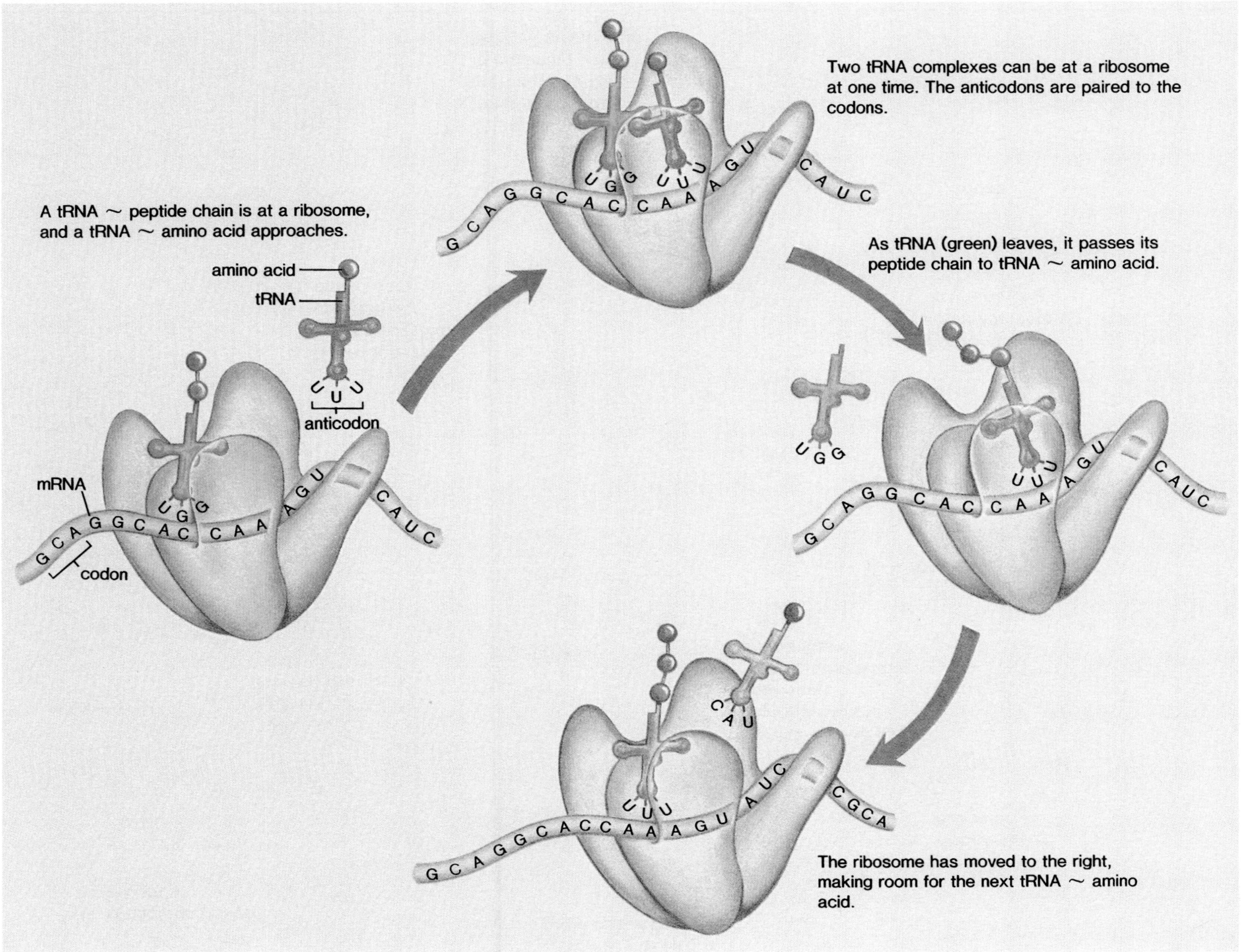

Two tRNA complexes can be at a ribosome at one time. The anticodons are paired to the codons.

As tRNA (green) leaves, it passes its peptide chain to tRNA ~ amino acid.

The ribosome has moved to the right, making room for the next tRNA ~ amino acid.

A tRNA ~ peptide chain is at a ribosome, and a tRNA ~ amino acid approaches.

amino acid

tRNA

anticodon

mRNA

codon

Translation
Figure 24.11

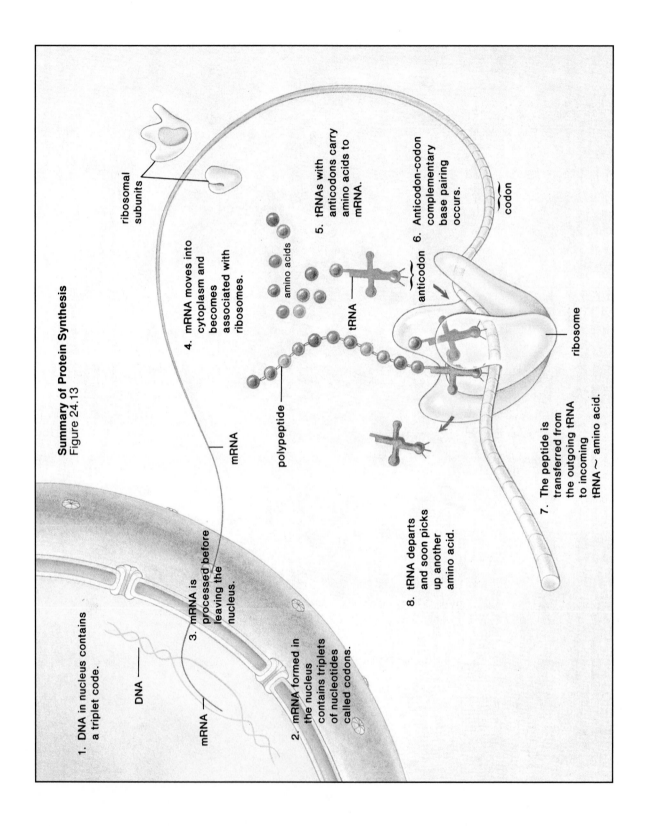

Summary of Protein Synthesis
Figure 24.13

1. DNA in nucleus contains a triplet code.

DNA

mRNA

2. mRNA formed in the nucleus contains triplets of nucleotides called codons.

3. mRNA is processed before leaving the nucleus.

mRNA

4. mRNA moves into cytoplasm and becomes associated with ribosomes.

ribosomal subunits

amino acids

5. tRNAs with anticodons carry amino acids to mRNA.

polypeptide

tRNA

anticodon

6. Anticodon-codon complementary base pairing occurs.

codon

ribosome

8. tRNA departs and soon picks up another amino acid.

7. The peptide is transferred from the outgoing tRNA to incoming tRNA ∼ amino acid.

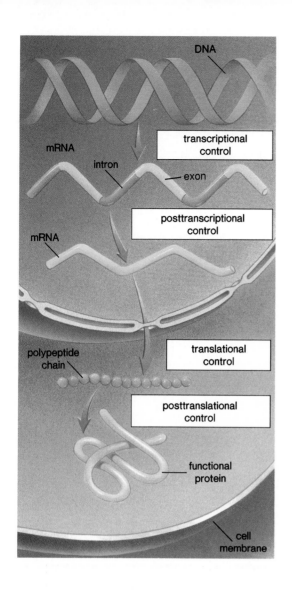

Levels of Control of Gene Expression
Figure 24.14

DNA

transcriptional
control

mRNA

intron

exon

posttranscriptional
control

mRNA

polypeptide
chain

translational
control

posttranslational
control

functional
protein

cell
membrane

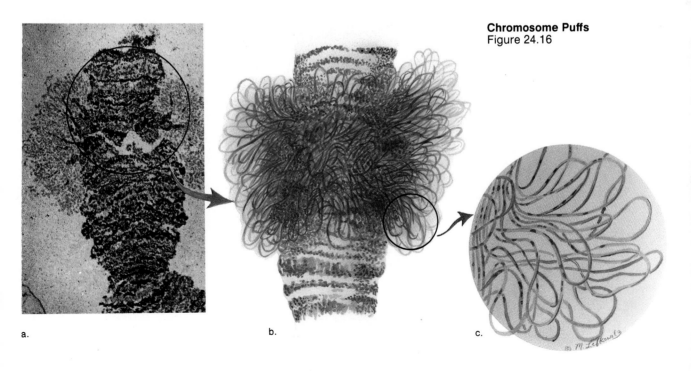

Chromosome Puffs
Figure 24.16

a.

b.

c.

147

Recombinant DNA Technology
Figure 25.3

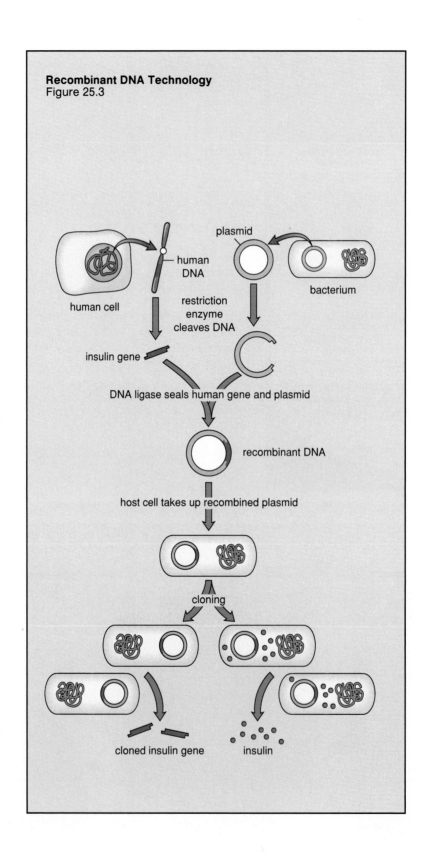

The primitive atmosphere contained gases, including water vapor, that escaped from volcanoes; as the water vapor cooled, some gases were washed into the oceans by rain.

The availability of energy from volcanic eruption and lightning allowed gases to form simple organic molecules.

Simple organic compounds could have joined to form proteins and nucleic acids, which became incorporated into membrane-bounded spheres. The spheres became the first cells, called protocells.

Eventually, various types of prokaryotes and then eukaryotes evolved. Some of the prokaryotes were oxygen-producing photosynthesizers. The presence of oxygen in the atmosphere was necessary for aerobic cellular respiration to evolve.

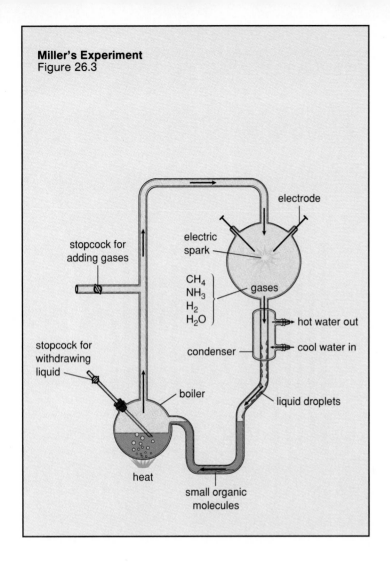

Miller's Experiment
Figure 26.3

electrode

electric
spark

CH_4
NH_3
H_2
H_2O

gases

stopcock for
adding gases

hot water out

cool water in

condenser

stopcock for
withdrawing
liquid

boiler

liquid droplets

heat

small organic
molecules

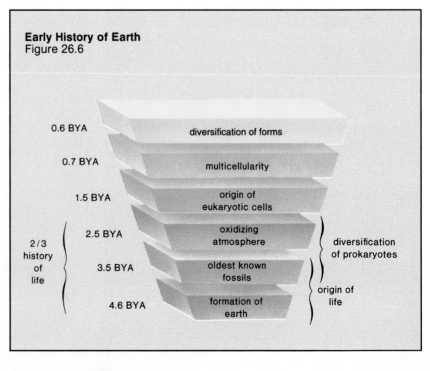

Early History of Earth
Figure 26.6

0.6 BYA — diversification of forms

0.7 BYA — multicellularity

1.5 BYA — origin of
eukaryotic cells

2.5 BYA — oxidizing
atmosphere

3.5 BYA — oldest known
fossils

4.6 BYA — formation of
earth

2/3
history
of
life

diversification
of prokaryotes

origin of
life

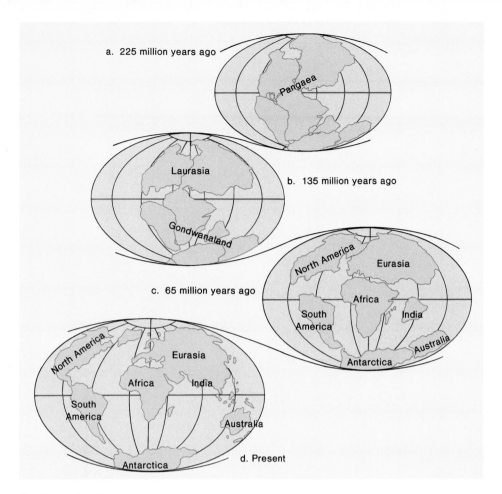

Continental Drift
Figure 27.2

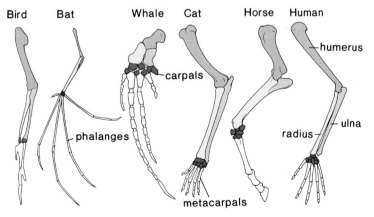

Homologous Structure
Figure 27.3

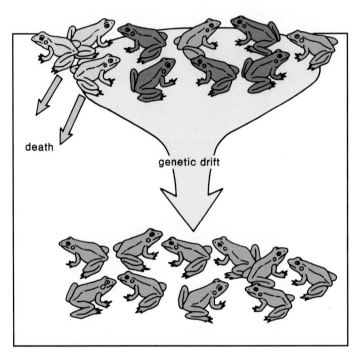

Genetic Drift
Figure 27.7

Early giraffes probably had short necks that they stretched to reach food.

Early giraffes probably had necks of various lengths.

Their offspring had longer necks that they stretched to reach food.

Natural selection due to competition led to survival of the longer-necked giraffes and their offspring.

Eventually, the continued stretching of the neck resulted in today's giraffe.

Eventually, only long-necked giraffes survived the competition.

a. Lamarck's theory

b. Darwin's theory

Lamarck's Theory vs. Darwin's Theory
Figure 27.A

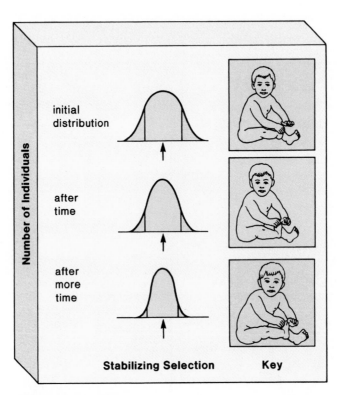

Stabilizing Selection
Figure 27.9

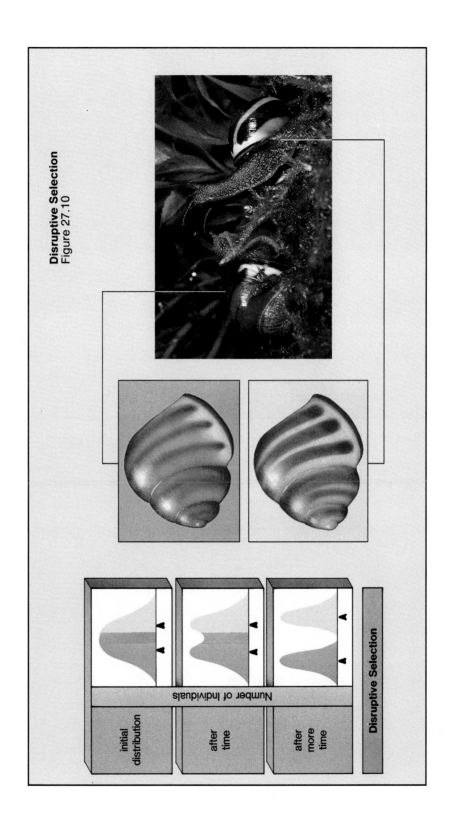

Disruptive Selection
Figure 27.10

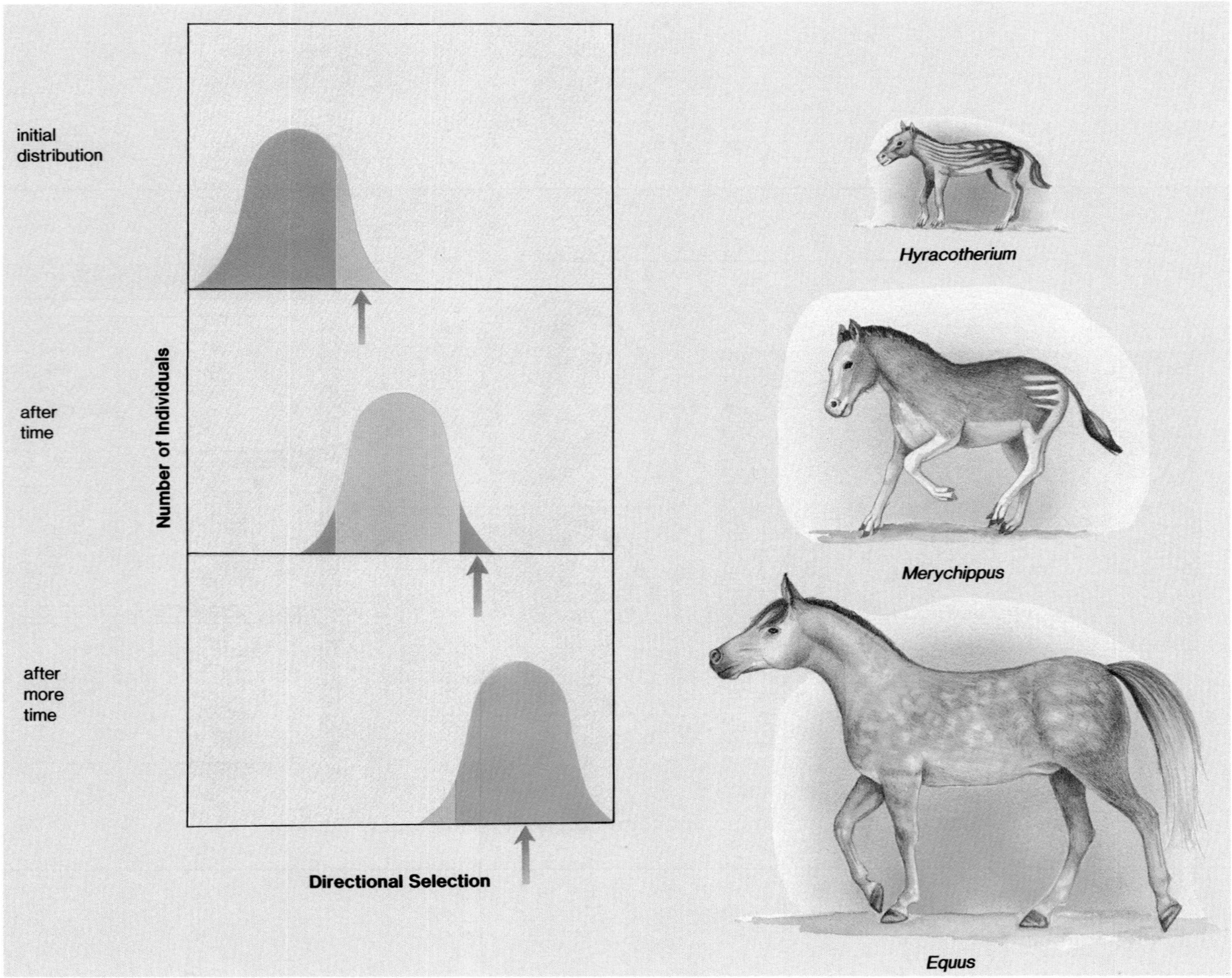

Number of Individuals

initial
distribution

after
time

after
more
time

Directional Selection

Hyracotherium

Merychippus

Equus

Directional Selection
Figure 27.11

156

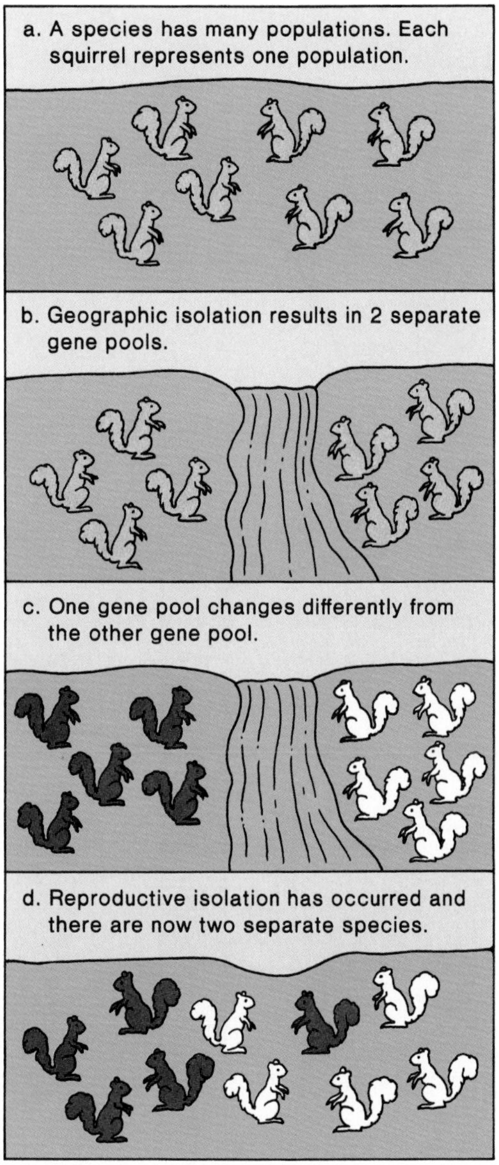

Speciation
Figure 27.12

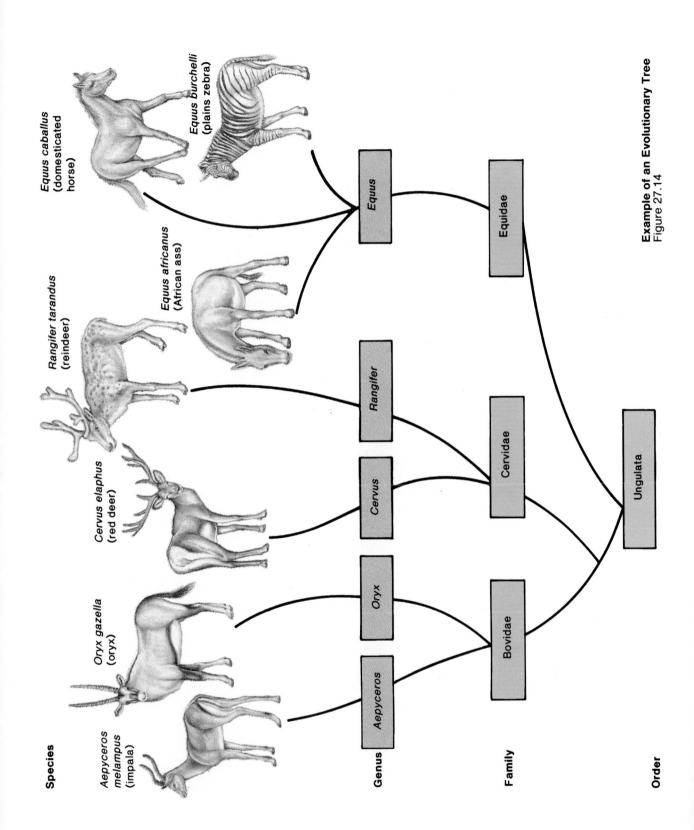

Species

Equus caballus (domesticated horse)

Equus burchelli (plains zebra)

Equus africanus (African ass)

Rangifer tarandus (reindeer)

Cervus elaphus (red deer)

Oryx gazella (oryx)

Aepyceros melampus (impala)

Genus

Equus

Rangifer

Cervus

Oryx

Aepyceros

Family

Equidae

Cervidae

Bovidae

Order

Ungulata

Example of an Evolutionary Tree
Figure 27.14

158

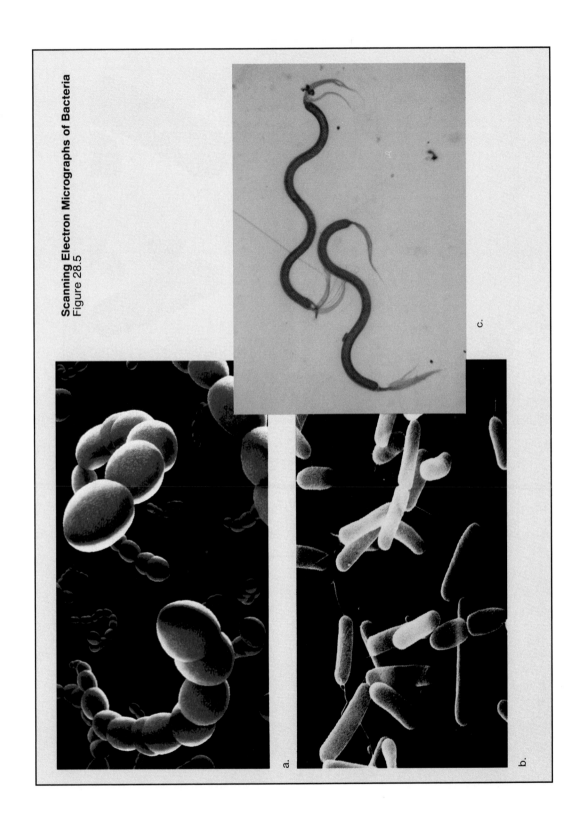

a.

b.

c.

Reproduction in Bacteria
Figure 28.6

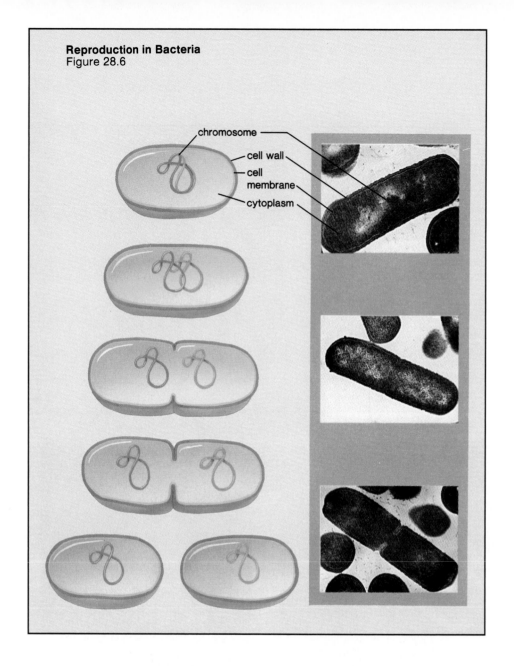

Amoeba proteus
Figure 28.10

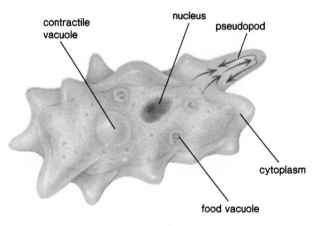

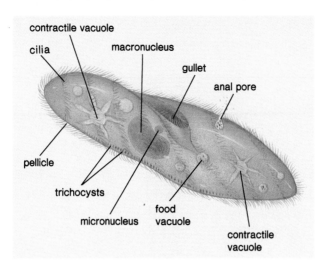

Paramecium caudatum
Figure 28.11

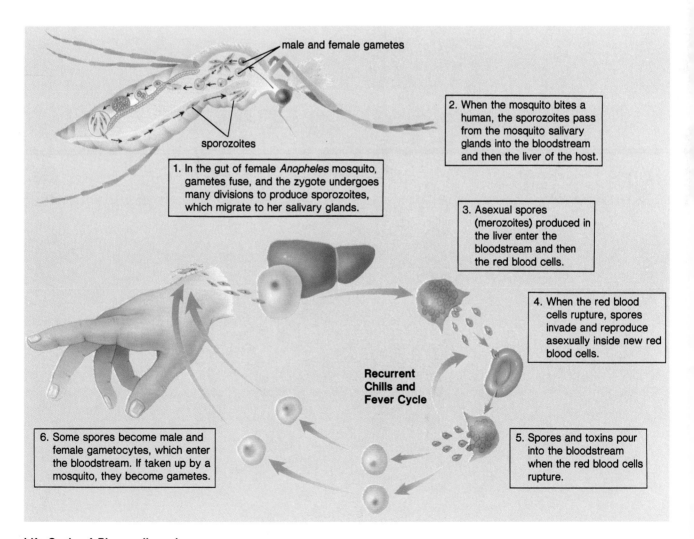

2. When the mosquito bites a human, the sporozoites pass from the mosquito salivary glands into the bloodstream and then the liver of the host.

1. In the gut of female *Anopheles* mosquito, gametes fuse, and the zygote undergoes many divisions to produce sporozoites, which migrate to her salivary glands.

3. Asexual spores (merozoites) produced in the liver enter the bloodstream and then the red blood cells.

4. When the red blood cells rupture, spores invade and reproduce asexually inside new red blood cells.

Recurrent Chills and Fever Cycle

5. Spores and toxins pour into the bloodstream when the red blood cells rupture.

6. Some spores become male and female gametocytes, which enter the bloodstream. If taken up by a mosquito, they become gametes.

Life Cycle of *Plasmodium vivax*
Figure 28.13

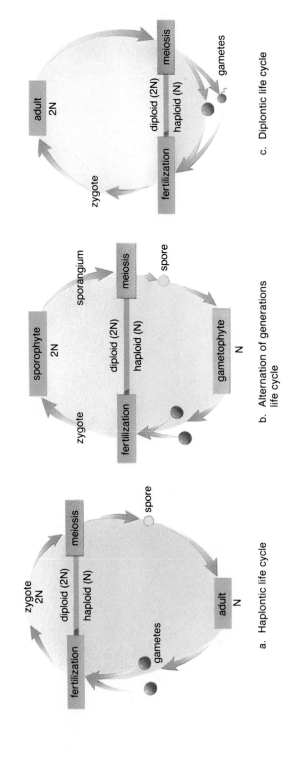

Life Cycles of Organisms
Figure 28.14

a. Haplontic life cycle

b. Alternation of generations
   life cycle

c. Diplontic life cycle

162

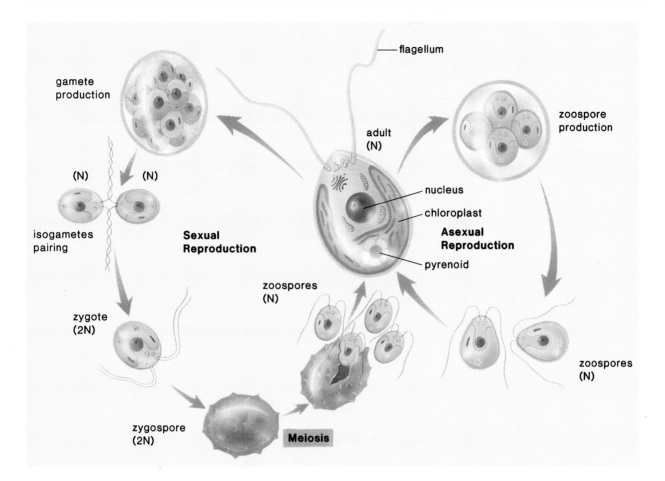

Chlamydomonas Structure and Life Cycle
Figure 28.15

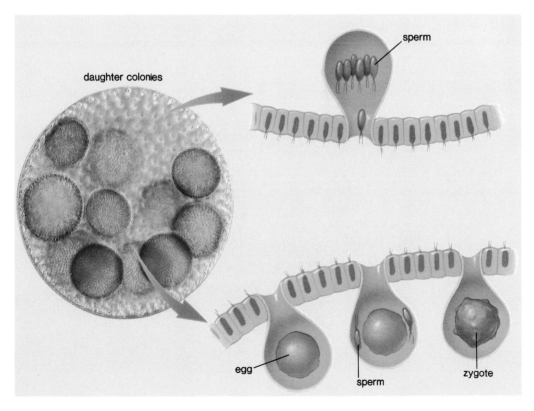

Volvox Structure and Sexual Reproduction
Figure 28.16

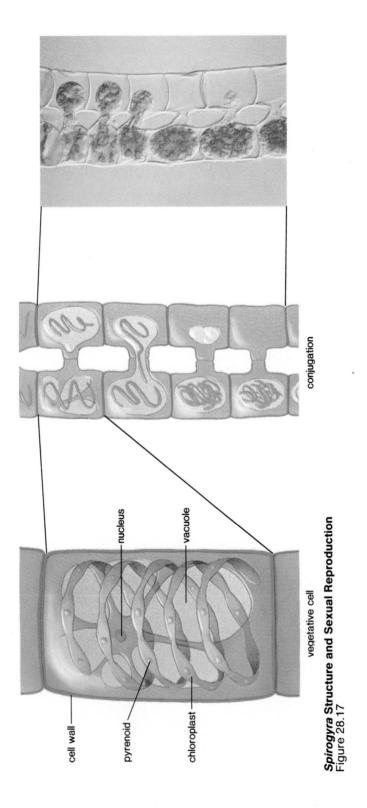

conjugation

vegetative cell

nucleus

vacuole

cell wall

pyrenoid

chloroplast

***Spirogyra* Structure and Sexual Reproduction**
Figure 28.17

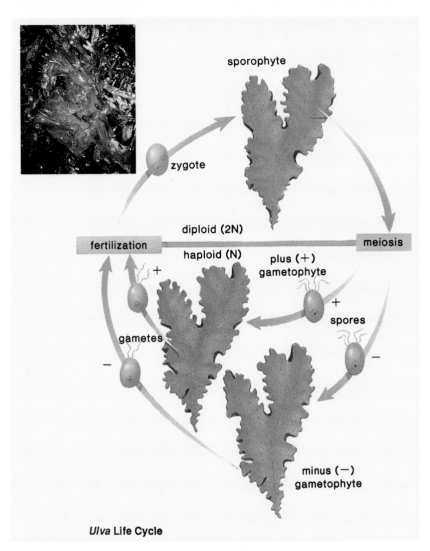

sporophyte

zygote

diploid (2N)

fertilization   meiosis

haploid (N)

plus (+)
gametophyte

+ spores

gametes

−

minus (−)
gametophyte

Ulva Life Cycle

***Ulva* Appearance and Life Cycle**
Figure 28.18

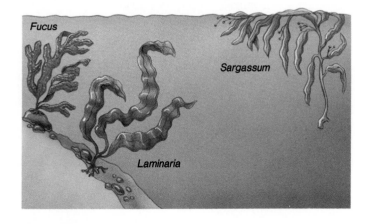

Fucus

Sargassum

Laminaria

Brown Algae
Figure 28.19

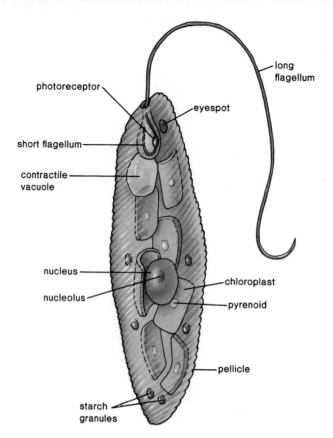

photoreceptor

long flagellum

eyespot

short flagellum

contractile vacuole

nucleus

nucleolus

chloroplast

pyrenoid

pellicle

starch granules

Euglena **Anatomy**
Figure 28.20

Micrographs of Dinoflagellate and Diatom
Figure 28.21

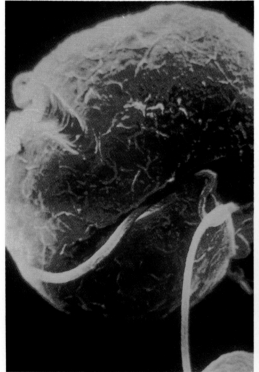

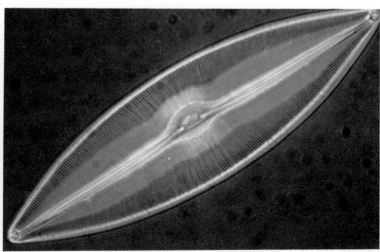

a.

b.

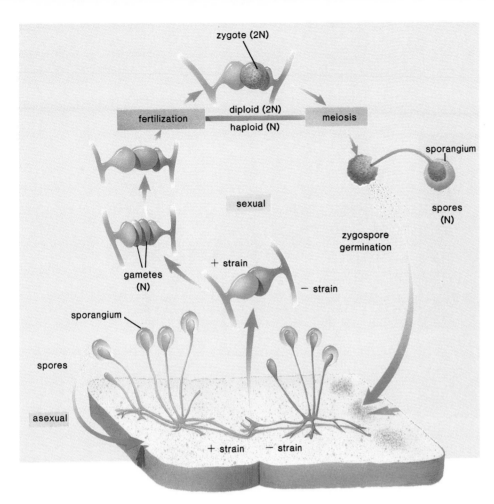

Life Cycle of *Rhizopus*
Figure 28.22

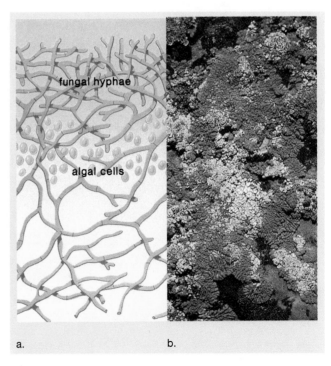

a.   b.

Lichen Structure
Figure 28.24

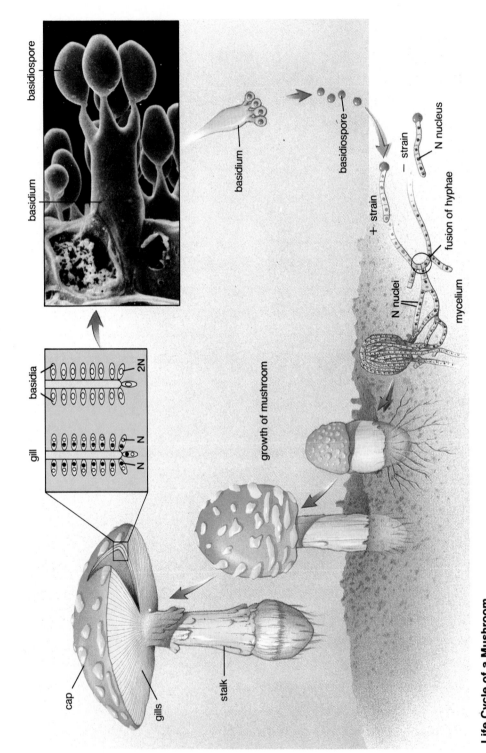

Life Cycle of a Mushroom
Figure 28.25

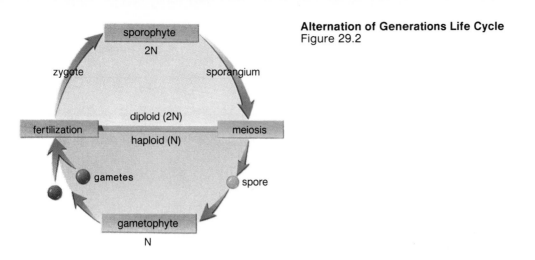

Alternation of Generations Life Cycle
Figure 29.2

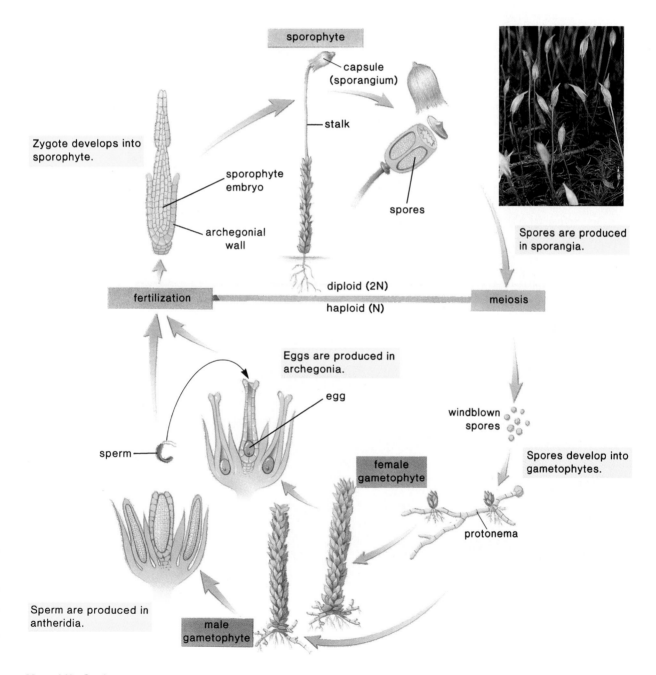

Zygote develops into
sporophyte.

sporophyte

capsule
(sporangium)

stalk

sporophyte
embryo

archegonial
wall

spores

Spores are produced
in sporangia.

diploid (2N)

haploid (N)

fertilization

meiosis

Eggs are produced in
archegonia.

egg

windblown
spores

Spores develop into
gametophytes.

sperm

female
gametophyte

protonema

Sperm are produced in
antheridia.

male
gametophyte

Moss Life Cycle
Figure 29.4

a.

b.

sporangium

c.

d.

Primitive Vascular Plants
Figure 29.5

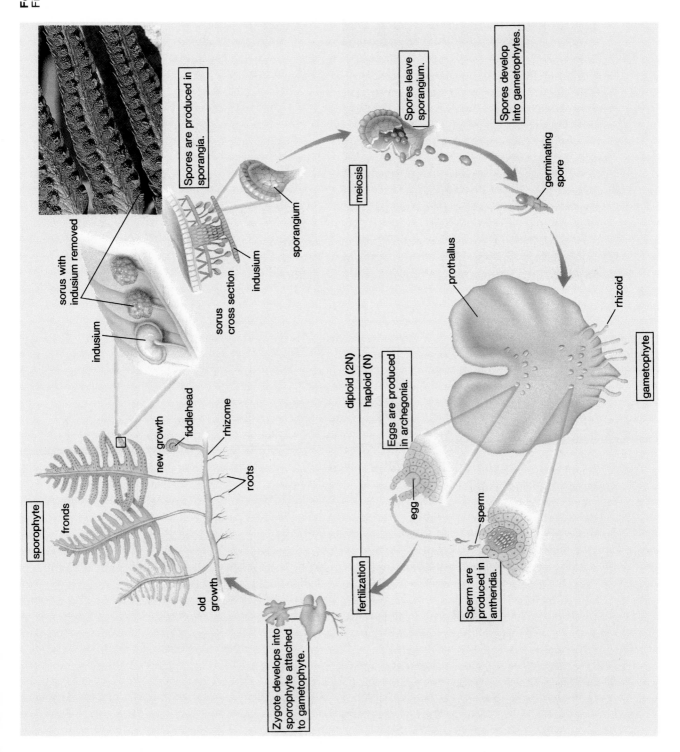

sorus with
indusium removed

indusium

sorus
cross section

indusium

sporangium

Spores are produced in sporangia.

Spores leave sporangium.

Spores develop into gametophytes.

germinating spore

meiosis

diploid (2N)

haploid (N)

prothallus

rhizoid

gametophyte

sporophyte

fronds

new growth

fiddlehead

rhizome

roots

old growth

Eggs are produced in archegonia.

egg

sperm

Sperm are produced in antheridia.

fertilization

Zygote develops into sporophyte attached to gametophyte.

a.

b.

Lesser Known Gymnosperms
Figure 29.10

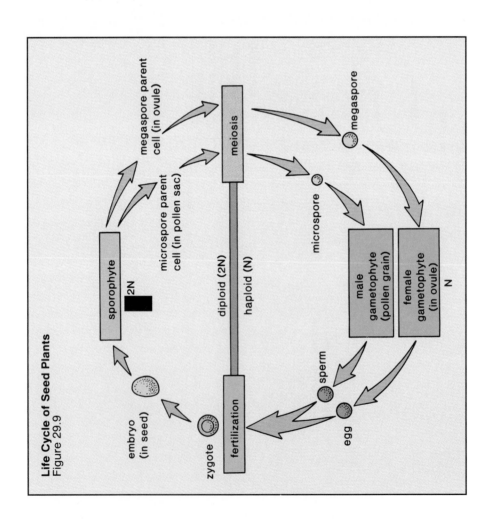

Life Cycle of Seed Plants
Figure 29.9

172

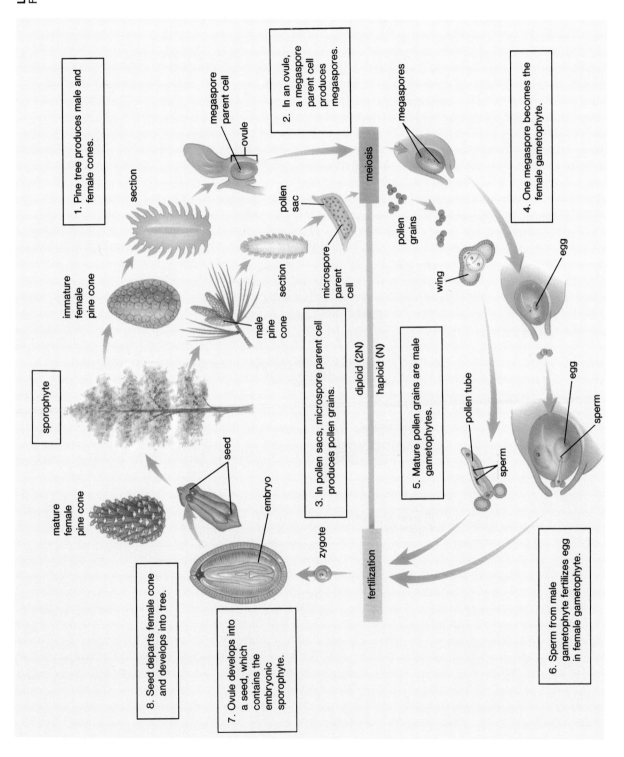

1. Pine tree produces male and female cones.

2. In an ovule, a megaspore parent cell produces megaspores.

3. In pollen sacs, microspore parent cell produces pollen grains.

4. One megaspore becomes the female gametophyte.

5. Mature pollen grains are male gametophytes.

6. Sperm from male gametophyte fertilizes egg in female gametophyte.

7. Ovule develops into a seed, which contains the embryonic sporophyte.

8. Seed departs female cone and develops into tree.

megaspore parent cell

ovule

megaspores

section

immature female pine cone

sporophyte

section

male pine cone

pollen sac

microspore parent cell

pollen grains

diploid (2N)

haploid (N)

wing

egg

meiosis

egg

sperm

pollen tube

sperm

mature female pine cone

seed

embryo

zygote

fertilization

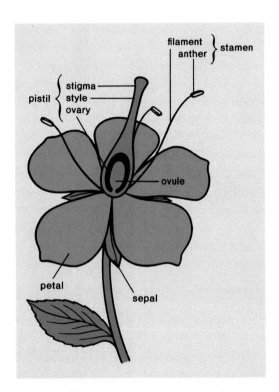

Flower Anatomy
Figure 29.14

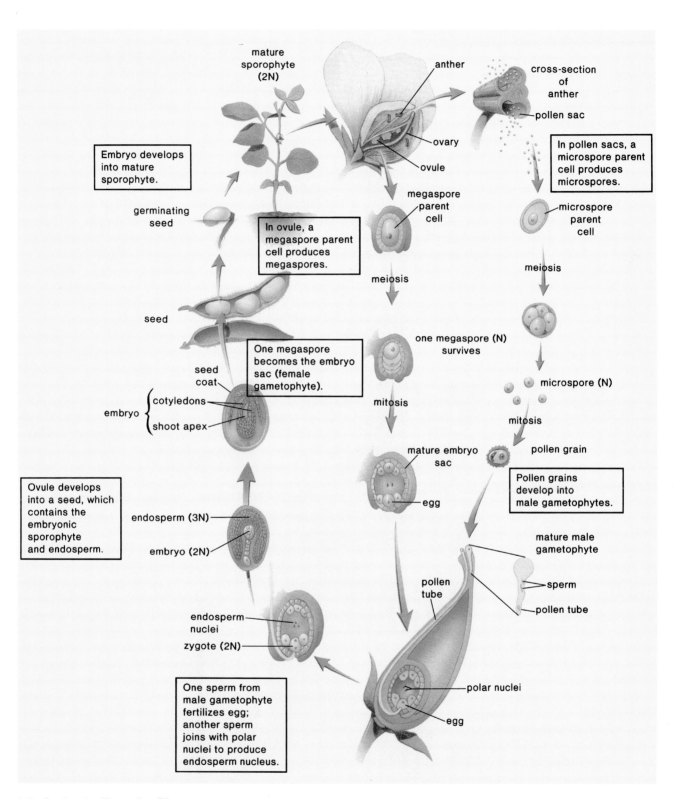

Life Cycle of a Flowering Plant
Figure 29.15

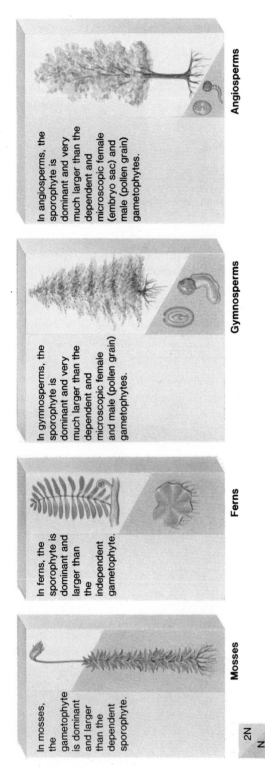

In mosses, the gametophyte is dominant and larger than the dependent sporophyte.

Mosses

In ferns, the sporophyte is dominant and larger than the independent gametophyte.

Ferns

In gymnosperms, the sporophyte is dominant and very much larger than the dependent and microscopic female and male (pollen grain) gametophytes.

Gymnosperms

In angiosperms, the sporophyte is dominant and very much larger than the dependent and microscopic female (embryo sac) and male (pollen grain) gametophytes.

Angiosperms

2N
N

Haploid/Diploid Generations Among Plants
Figure 29.17

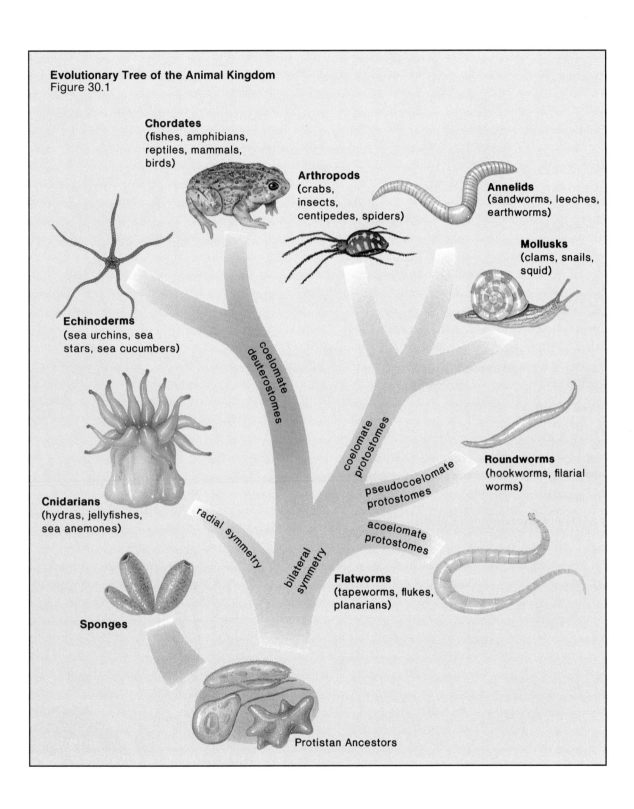

Evolutionary Tree of the Animal Kingdom
Figure 30.1

Chordates
(fishes, amphibians,
reptiles, mammals,
birds)

Arthropods
(crabs,
insects,
centipedes, spiders)

Annelids
(sandworms, leeches,
earthworms)

Mollusks
(clams, snails,
squid)

Echinoderms
(sea urchins, sea
stars, sea cucumbers)

coelomate
deuterostomes

coelomate
protostomes

pseudocoelomate
protostomes

Roundworms
(hookworms, filarial
worms)

Cnidarians
(hydras, jellyfishes,
sea anemones)

radial symmetry

acoelomate
protostomes

bilateral
symmetry

Flatworms
(tapeworms, flukes,
planarians)

Sponges

Protistan Ancestors

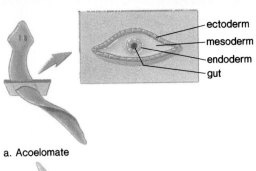

a. Acoelomate

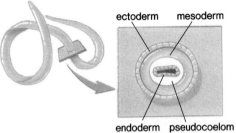

b. Pseudocoelomate

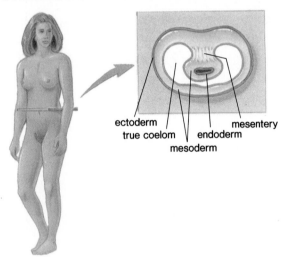

c. True coelomate

Comparison of Mesoderm Organization
Figure 30.2

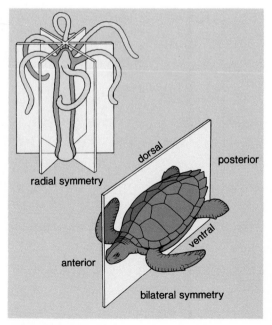

Types of Symmetry
Figure 30.3

Generalized Sponge Anatomy
Figure 30.5

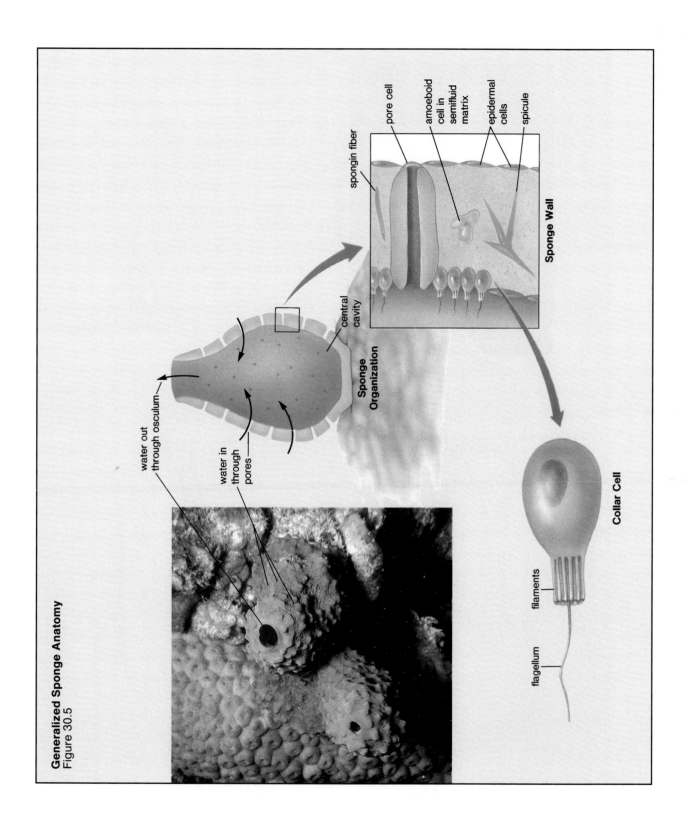

spongin fiber

pore cell

amoeboid cell in semifluid matrix

epidermal cells

spicule

Sponge Wall

central cavity

Sponge Organization

water out through osculum

water in through pores

filaments

flagellum

Collar Cell

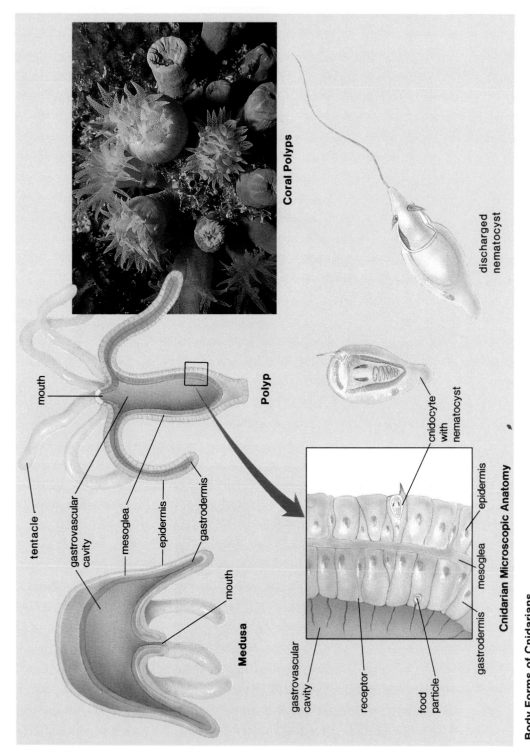

Coral Polyps

discharged
nematocyst

mouth

tentacle

gastrovascular
cavity

mesoglea

epidermis

gastrodermis

mouth

Medusa

Polyp

cnidocyte
with
nematocyst

epidermis

mesoglea

gastrodermis

gastrovascular
cavity

receptor

food
particle

Cnidarian Microscopic Anatomy

Body Forms of Cnidarians
Figure 30.6

180

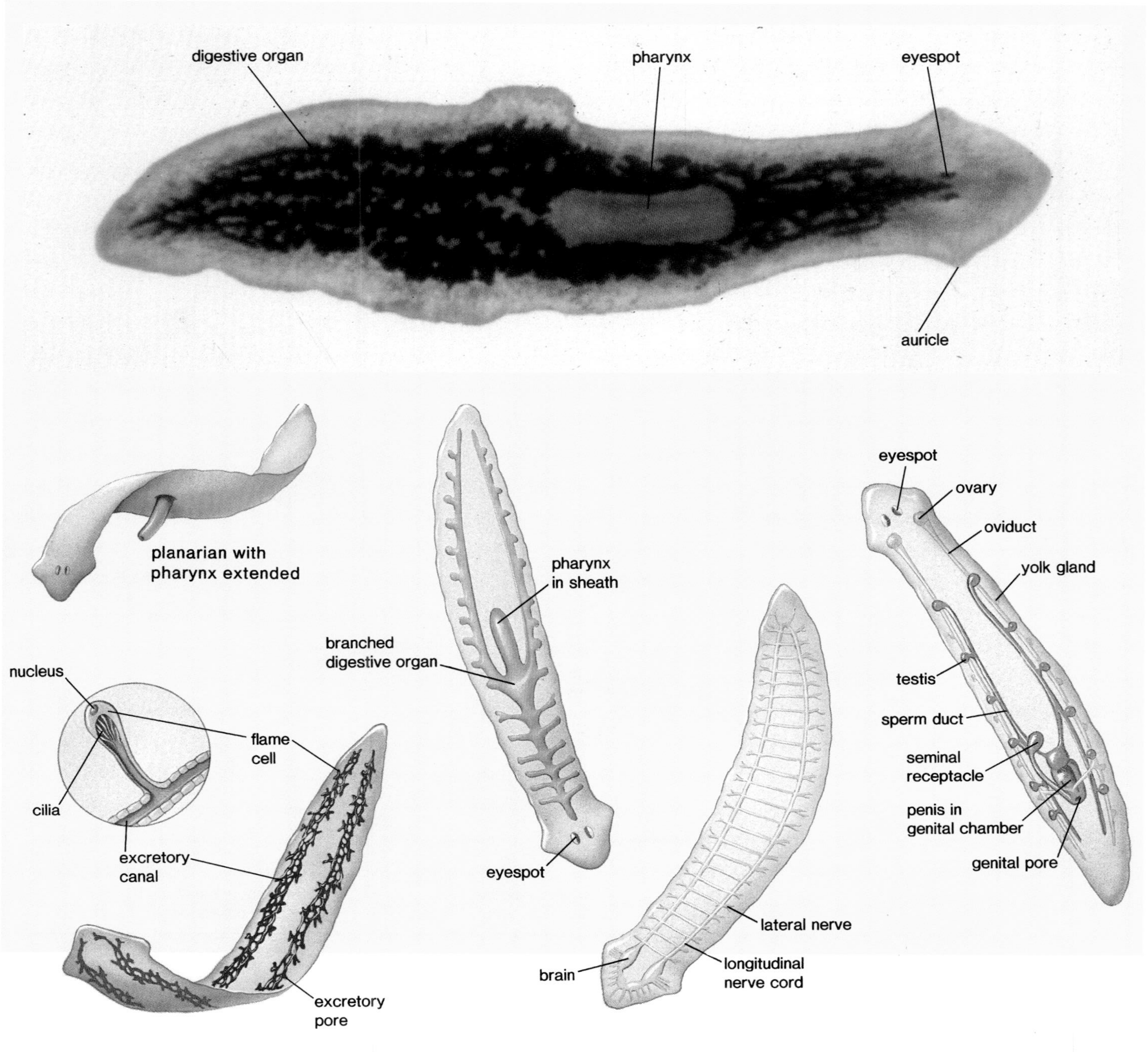

Flatworm Anatomy
Figure 30.7

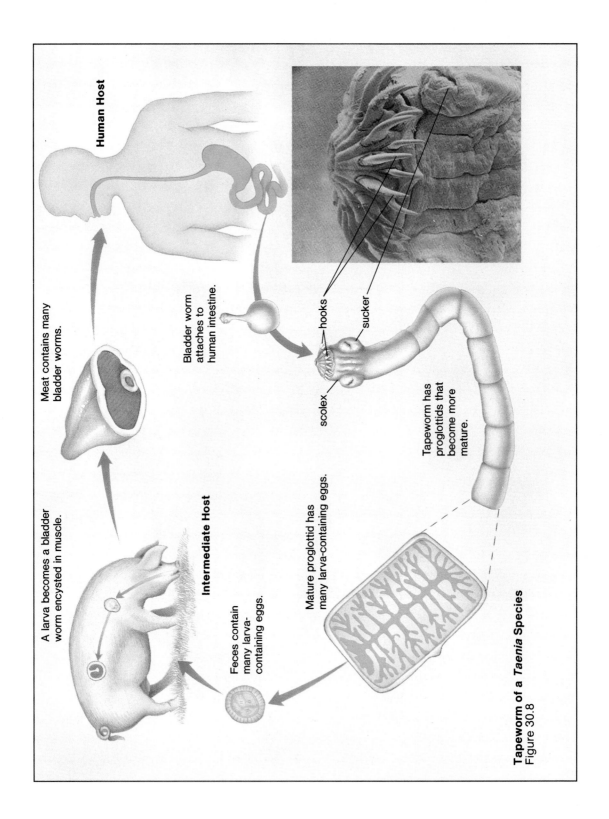

Human Host

Meat contains many bladder worms.

Bladder worm attaches to human intestine.

hooks

sucker

scolex

Tapeworm has proglottids that become more mature.

A larva becomes a bladder worm encysted in muscle.

Intermediate Host

Feces contain many larva-containing eggs.

Mature proglottid has many larva-containing eggs.

Tapeworm of a *Taenia* Species
Figure 30.8

Roundworm Anatomy
Figure 30.9

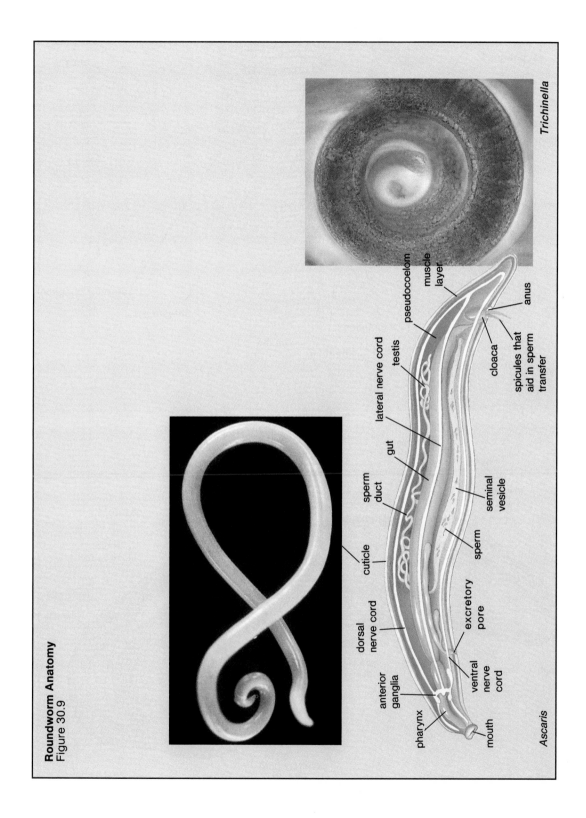

Trichinella

pseudocoelom

muscle layer

anus

testis

lateral nerve cord

cloaca

spicules that aid in sperm transfer

gut

seminal vesicle

sperm duct

sperm

cuticle

dorsal nerve cord

excretory pore

anterior ganglia

ventral nerve cord

pharynx

mouth

Ascaris

183

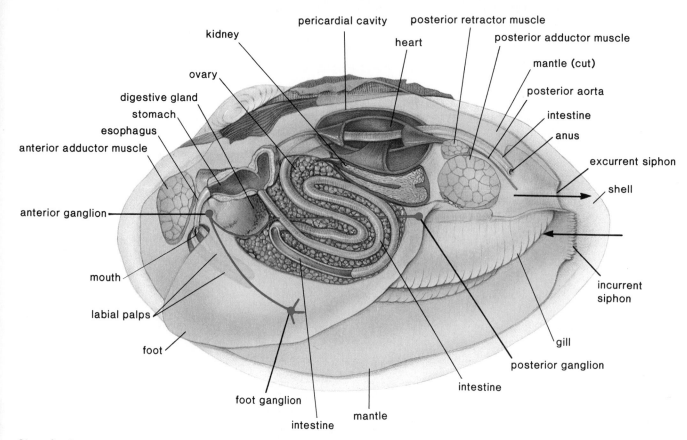

Clam Anatomy
Figure 30.12

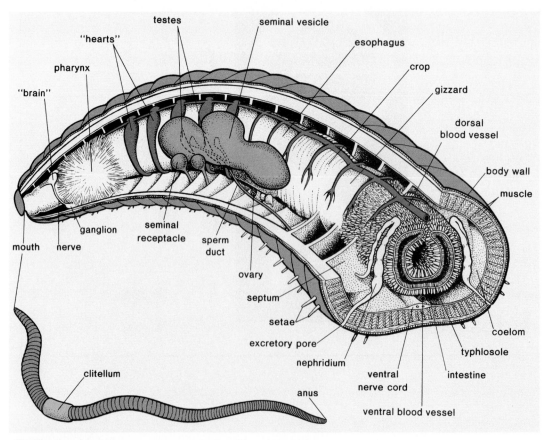

Earthworm Anatomy
Figure 30.14

184

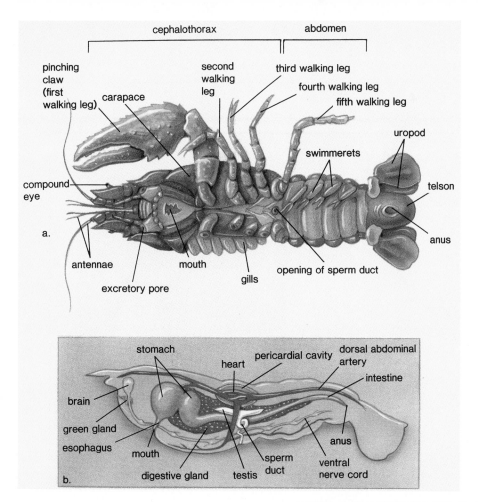

Crayfish Anatomy
Figure 30.16

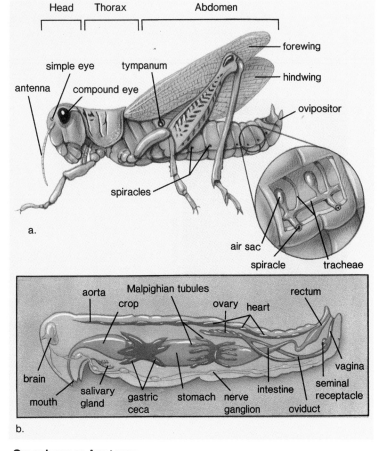

Grasshopper Anatomy
Figure 30.17

185

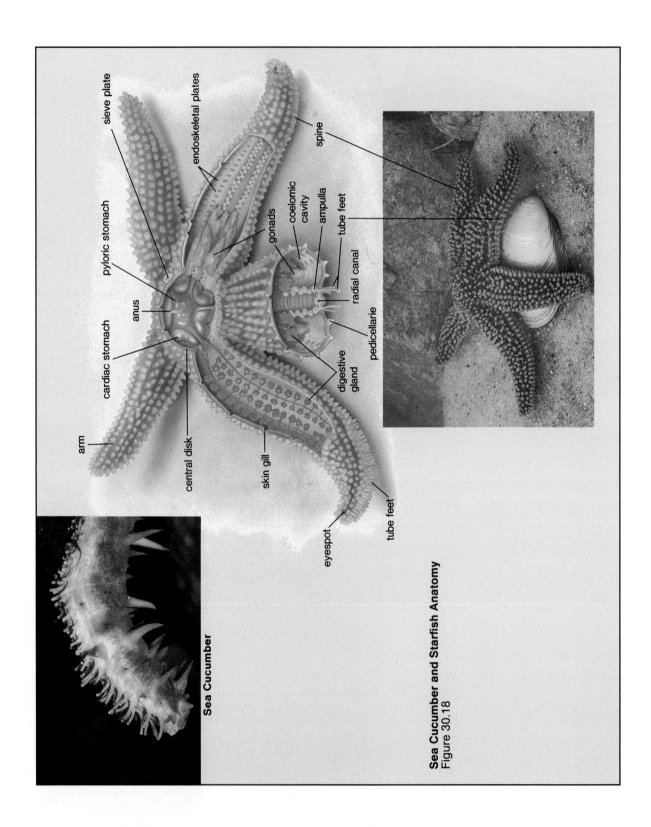

sieve plate

endoskeletal plates

spine

pyloric stomach

gonads

coelomic cavity

ampulla

tube feet

anus

radial canal

cardiac stomach

pedicellarie

arm

digestive gland

central disk

skin gill

tube feet

eyespot

Sea Cucumber

Sea Cucumber and Starfish Anatomy
Figure 30.18

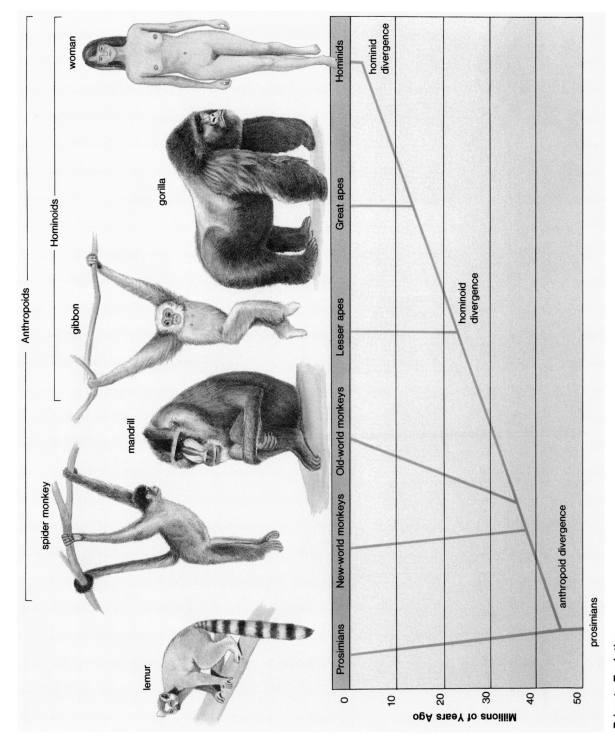

Primate Evolution
Figure 30.25

187

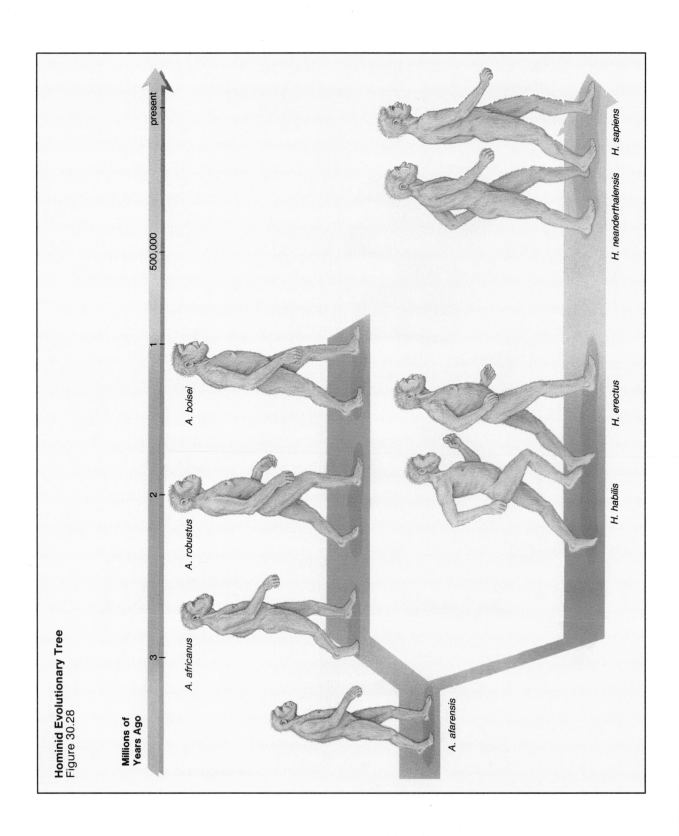

Hominid Evolutionary Tree
Figure 30.28

Millions of
Years Ago

present

500,000

1

2

3

A. boisei

A. robustus

A. africanus

A. afarensis

H. neanderthalensis   H. sapiens

H. erectus

H. habilis

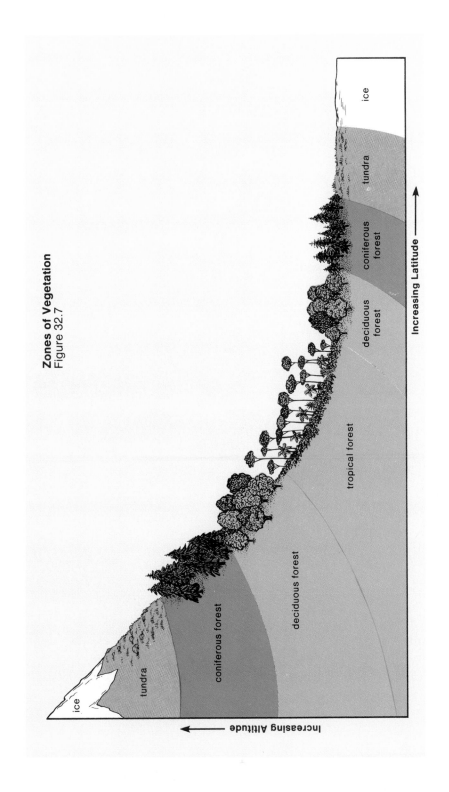

Zones of Vegetation
Figure 32.7

ice

tundra

coniferous forest

deciduous forest

tropical forest

deciduous forest

coniferous forest

tundra

ice

Increasing Altitude

Increasing Latitude

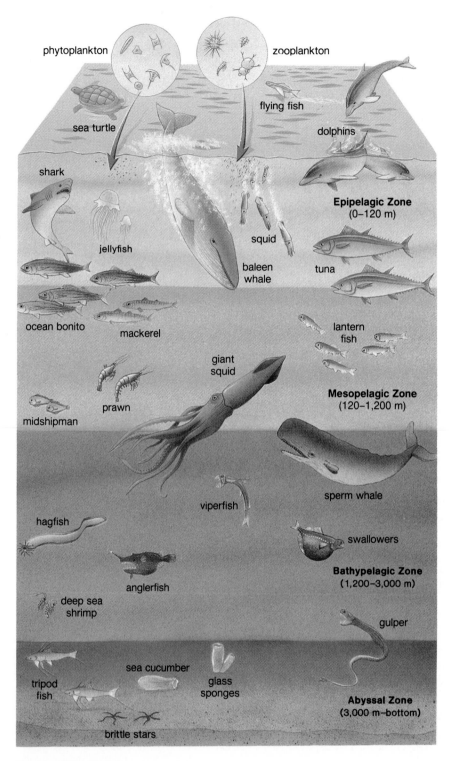

phytoplankton

zooplankton

flying fish

sea turtle

dolphins

shark

Epipelagic Zone
(0–120 m)

jellyfish

squid

baleen whale

tuna

ocean bonito

mackerel

lantern fish

giant squid

Mesopelagic Zone
(120–1,200 m)

prawn

midshipman

sperm whale

viperfish

hagfish

swallowers

anglerfish

Bathypelagic Zone
(1,200–3,000 m)

deep sea shrimp

gulper

tripod fish

sea cucumber

glass sponges

Abyssal Zone
(3,000 m–bottom)

brittle stars

Zones of the Ocean
Figure 32.8

Ecosystem Composition
Figure 33.2

Examples of Food Chains
Figure 33.3

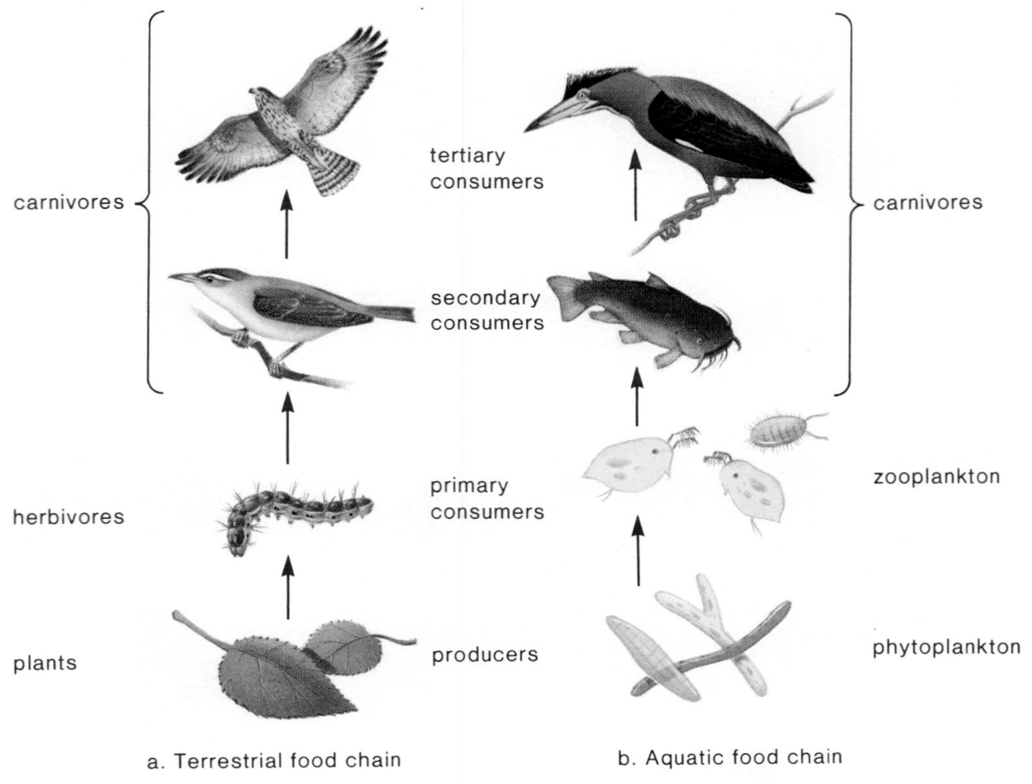

tertiary
consumers

secondary
consumers

primary
consumers

producers

carnivores

zooplankton

phytoplankton

b. Aquatic food chain

carnivores

herbivores

plants

a. Terrestrial food chain

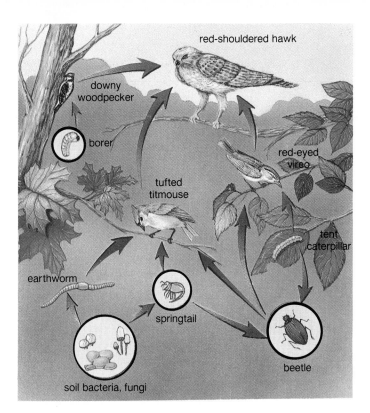

Deciduous Forest Ecosystem
Figure 33.4

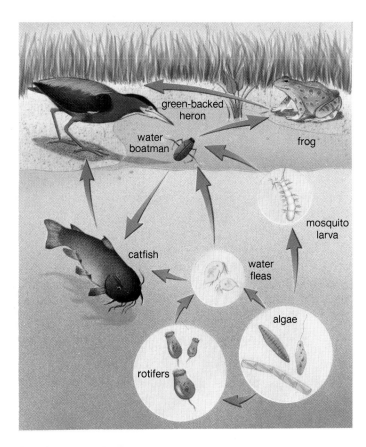

Freshwater Pond Ecosystem
Figure 33.5

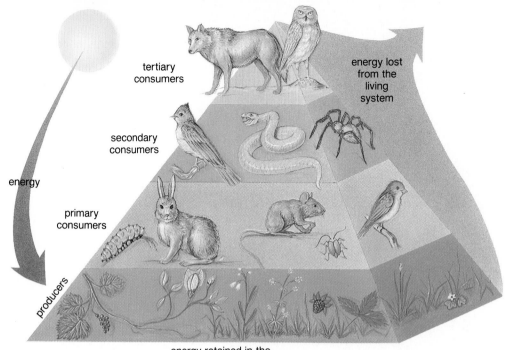

energy lost from the living system

tertiary consumers

secondary consumers

energy

primary consumers

producers

energy retained in the living system

Pyramid of Energy
Figure 33.6

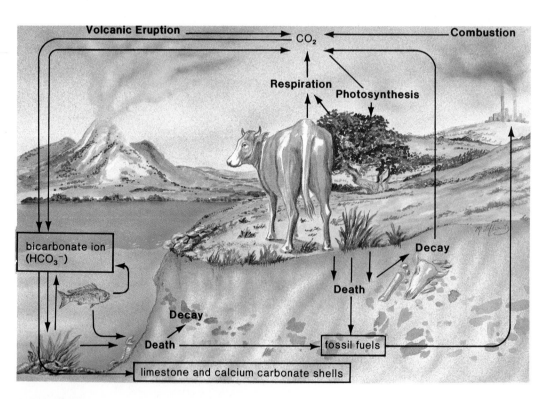

Volcanic Eruption → CO_2 ← Combustion

Respiration   Photosynthesis

bicarbonate ion (HCO_3^-)

Decay

Death

Decay

Death

Decay

Death → fossil fuels

limestone and calcium carbonate shells

Carbon Cycle
Figure 33.8

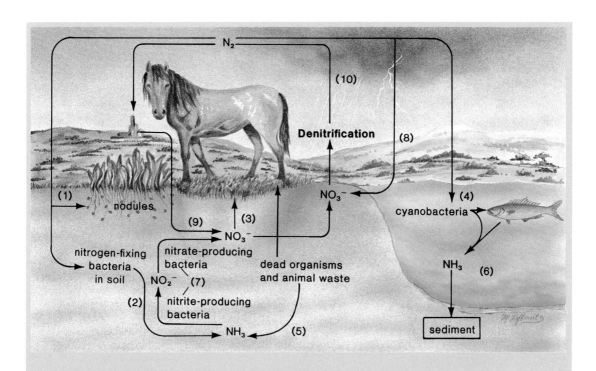

Nitrogen fixation: Reduction and incorporation of nitrogen into organic compounds.

*Nitrogen-fixing bacteria in nodules of legumes reduce nitrogen gas and produce organic compounds (1).

*Nitrogen-fixing bacteria in soil reduce nitrogen gas to ammonia (2).

*Plants reduce nitrates in soil and produce organic compounds (3).

*Cyanobacteria reduce nitrogen gas and produce organic compounds (4).

Decomposition: Decomposing bacteria break down dead organic remains and give off ammonia (5), (6).

Nitrification: Production of nitrates that can be used by plants.

*Nitrite-producing and nitrate-producing bacteria convert ammonia to nitrate (7).

*Lightning converts nitrogen gas to nitrate (8).

*Humans convert nitrogen gas to nitrate for use in fertilizers (9).

Denitrification: Denitrifying bacteria convert nitrate to nitrogen gas (10).

Nitrogen Cycle
Figure 33.10

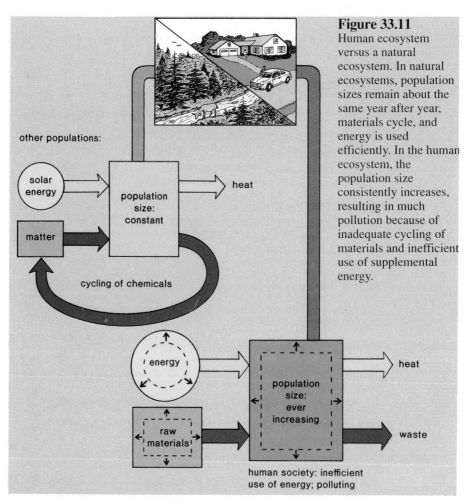

Figure 33.11
Human ecosystem versus a natural ecosystem. In natural ecosystems, population sizes remain about the same year after year, materials cycle, and energy is used efficiently. In the human ecosystem, the population size consistently increases, resulting in much pollution because of inadequate cycling of materials and inefficient use of supplemental energy.

other populations:

solar energy

matter

population size: constant

heat

cycling of chemicals

energy

raw materials

population size: ever increasing

heat

waste

human society: inefficient use of energy; polluting

Human Ecosystem vs. Natural Ecosystem
Figure 33.11

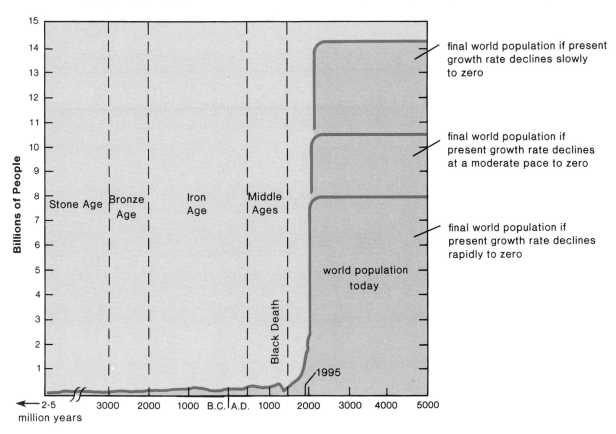

Growth Curve for Human Population
Figure 34.2

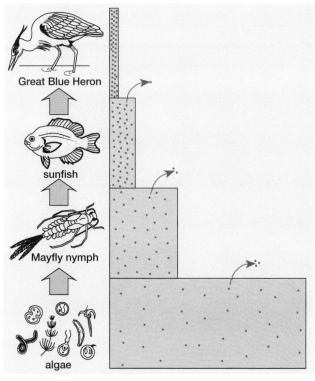

Biological Magnification
Figure 34.8

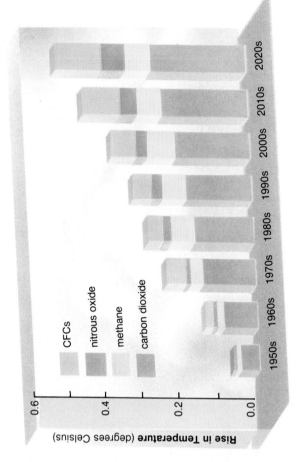

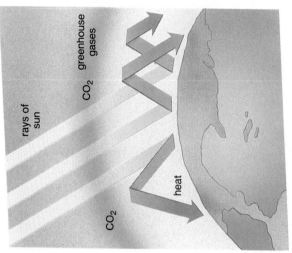

Global Warming
Figure 34.12

198

CREDITS

Line Art

Fig. 10.7: Wallace, Wallechinsky and Wallace. 1983. Significa. E. P. Dutton, Inc., NY.

Fig. 12.2: Copyright © Mark Lefkowitz.

Fig. 12.3a,b: Copyright © Mark Lefkowitz.

Fig. 14.10: From John W. Hole, Jr., *Human Anatomy and Physiology,* 5th ed. Copyright © 1990 Wm. C. Brown Communications, Inc., Dubuque, Iowa. All Rights Reserved. Reprinted by permission.

Fig. 15.5: From Kent M. Van De Graaff and Stuart Ira Fox, *Concepts of Human Anatomy and Physiology,* 3d ed. Copyright © 1992 Wm. C. Brown Communications, Inc., Dubuque, Iowa. All Rights Reserved. Reprinted by permission.

Fig. 15.8: From Kent M. Van De Graaff and Stuart Ira Fox, *Concepts of Human Anatomy and Physiology,* 3d ed. Copyright © 1992 Wm. C. Brown Communications, Inc., Dubuque, Iowa. All Rights Reserved. Reprinted by permission.

Fig. 16.10: Copyright © Mark Lefkowitz.

Fig. 16.13: Copyright © Mark Lefkowitz.

Fig. 17.12: (bottom) From John W. Hole, Jr., *Human Anatomy and Physiology,* 5th ed. Copyright © 1990 Wm. C. Brown Communications, Inc., Dubuque, Iowa. All Rights Reserved. Reprinted by permission.

Fig. 20.5: From John W. Hole, Jr., *Human Anatomy and Physiology,* 5th ed. Copyright © 1990 Wm. C. Brown Communications, Inc., Dubuque, Iowa. All Rights Reserved. Reprinted by permission.

Fig. 21.3: From John W. Hole, Jr., *Human Anatomy and Physiology,* 5th ed. Copyright © 1990 Wm. C. Brown Communications, Inc., Dubuque, Iowa. All Rights Reserved. Reprinted by permission.

Fig. 23.1: From Robert F. Weaver and Philip W. Hedrick, *Genetics,* 2d ed. Copyright © 1992 Wm. C. Brown Communications, Inc., Dubuque, Iowa. All Rights Reserved. Reprinted by permission.

Fig. 24.16: Copyright © Mark Lefkowitz.

Photographs

Fig. 2.21b: © Dr. Jeremy Burgess/Science Photo Library/Photo Researchers, Inc.

Fig. 2.22b: © Don Fawcett/Photo Researchers, Inc.

Fig. 2.23b: © Ulrike Welsch/Photo Researchers, Inc.

Fig. 3.4a: © Richard Rodewald/Biological Photo Service

Fig. 3.4b: © W. P. Werglin, University of Wisconsin, Courtesy of E. A. Newcomb, Biological Photo Service

Fig. 3.5a: © Warren Rosenberg, Iona College/Biological Photo Service

Fig. 3.6a: © David Phillips/Visuals Unlimited

Fig. 3.6c: © K. G. Murti/Visuals Unlimited

Fig. 3.7a: Courtesy of Dr. Keith Porter

Fig. 3.8a: Courtesy of Dr. Herbert Israel, Cornell University

Fig. 3.12a: © David Phillips/Visuals Unlimited

Fig. 3.12b: © Biophoto Associates/Photo Researchers, Inc.

Fig. 6.1a: Courtesy of Dr. Herbert Israel, Cornell University

Fig. 6.6a: Courtesy of Dr. Keith Porter

Fig. 7.5: © Michael Abbey/Photo Researchers, Inc.

Fig. 8.1a: © Philip Harris/Photo Researchers, Inc.

Fig. 8.1b: © John Cunningham/Visuals Unlimited

Fig. 8.3b: Carolina Biological Supply Company

Fig. 8.7a: Carolina Biological Supply Company

Fig. 8.8a: Carolina Biological Supply Company

Fig. 8.8b: © Runk/Schoenberger/Grant Heilman

Fig. 8.8c: © Runk/Schoenberger/Grant Heilman

Fig. 8.10: Carolina Biological Supply Company

Fig. 8.12b: © Dr. Jeremy Burgess/Science Photo Library/Photo Researchers, Inc.

Fig. 9.1b: © Biological Photo Service

Fig. 9.4a: © George Wilder/Visuals Unlimited

Fig. 10.2a: © David Phillips/Visuals Unlimited

Fig. 10.2c: © Don Fawcett/Visuals Unlimited

Fig. 10.2d: © D. Allbertini/D. Fawcett/Visuals Unlimited

Fig. 10.5a: © Edwin Reschke

Fig. 10.5b: © Edwin Reschke

Fig. 10.5c: © Michael Abbey/Science Source/Photo Researchers, Inc.

Fig. 11.7: © Manfred Kage/Peter Arnold, Inc.

Fig. 13.1b: © John Cunningham/Visuals Unlimited

Fig. 13.1c: © Astrid & Hans-Frieder Michler/Science Photo Library/Photo Researchers, Inc.

Fig. 13.12b: Courtesy of Schering-Plough Corp. Photo by Philip Harrington

Fig. 13.13a: Courtesy of Stuart I. Fox

Fig. 15.7b: © CNRI/Science Photo Library/Photo Researchers, Inc.

Fig. 16.4: © Linda Bartlett

Fig. 17.6c: © Robert Brons/Biological Photo Service

Fig. 17.8a: International Biomedical, Inc.

Fig. 17.10b: Courtesy of H. E. Huxley

Fig. 17.12a: © Eric Grave/Photo Researchers, Inc.

Fig. 17.12b: © Victor Eichler

Fig. 20.2b: © Biophoto Associates/Photo Researchers, Inc.

Fig. 20.6a: © Edwin Reschke/Peter Arnold, Inc.

Fig. 21.6a: © Lennart Nilsson

Fig. 24.16a: © A. L. Olins, University of Tennessee/Biological Photo Service

Fig. 27.10b: © Oxford Scientific Films/Animals Animals

Fig. 28.5a: © Francis Leroy

Fig. 28.5b: © D. M. Phillips/Visuals Unlimited

Fig. 28.5c: © John Cunningham/Visuals Unlimited

Fig. 28.6a–d: © Biological Photo Service

Fig. 28.16a: © R. Knauft/Biomedia/Photo Researchers, Inc.

Fig. 28.17b: © M. I. Walker/Science Source/Photo Researchers, Inc.

Fig. 28.18a: © John Cunningham/Visuals Unlimited

Fig. 28.21a: © David M. Phillips/Visuals Unlimited

Fig. 28.21b: © Biophoto Associates/Photo Researchers, Inc.

Fig. 28.24b: © W. J. Weber/Visuals Unlimited

Fig. 28.25b: © Gordon Leedale/Biophoto Associates